AF873222

Studying Law Tomorrow

The New Legal Way

Bookie Bander

ISBN: 978-1-77961-966-2
Imprint: No Matter Which Way You Go
Copyright © 2024 Bookie Bander.
All Rights Reserved.

Contents

Introduction to Legal Studies

The Importance of Legal Studies

The role of law in society

Law plays a fundamental role in shaping and regulating society. It provides the framework within which individuals, businesses, and institutions interact, ensuring order, justice, and stability. The role of law in society is multi-faceted and encompasses various functions, including the establishment of rights, the resolution of disputes, and the maintenance of social order.

1. **Establishment of rights:** One of the primary functions of law is to establish and protect individual rights. Laws define and guarantee rights and freedoms, such as the right to life, liberty, and property. These rights create a framework within which individuals can pursue their goals and aspirations without undue interference. For example, the United States Constitution and the Universal Declaration of Human Rights outline key rights and freedoms that individuals are entitled to, such as freedom of speech, equal protection under the law, and the right to a fair trial.

2. **Resolution of disputes:** Law provides a mechanism for the peaceful resolution of disputes. Disagreements and conflicts are inevitable in any society, and law provides a framework within which these conflicts can be addressed and resolved. The legal system provides a fair and impartial forum where parties can present their arguments and evidence, and a neutral judge or jury can make a decision based on the facts and applicable laws. Through the legal system, individuals are able to seek justice and resolve their disputes in a peaceful and orderly manner.

3. **Maintenance of social order:** Law plays a crucial role in maintaining social order and harmony. It sets clear boundaries and expectations for behavior, defining what is acceptable and what is not. By establishing rules and regulations,

law provides a framework for individuals and communities to coexist peacefully. It discourages harmful behavior and provides consequences for those who violate societal norms. For example, criminal laws deter individuals from committing offenses by outlining punishments for criminal conduct.

The legal system also ensures that power is properly distributed and balanced within society. It establishes and regulates governmental institutions, ensuring that they operate within defined boundaries and are accountable to the people. Laws create a system of checks and balances, preventing any individual or institution from abusing their power.

In addition to these primary functions, law also has secondary roles in society. It serves as a tool for social engineering, shaping behavior and promoting social goals. For example, laws promoting environmental protection or prohibiting discrimination aim to bring about social change and create a more equitable society. Law also plays a role in economic development and regulation, providing a framework for business transactions and protecting consumers.

However, it is important to note that the role of law in society is not without its challenges and limitations. Legal systems must constantly adapt to societal changes and evolving needs. They must address complex issues such as technological advancements, globalization, and cultural diversity. Furthermore, the effectiveness of law in achieving its objectives is influenced by various factors, including enforcement mechanisms, public perception, and access to justice.

To gain a deeper understanding of the role of law in society, readers are encouraged to explore additional resources such as legal journals, books, and websites. Engaging in discussions and debates on legal philosophy, social justice, and the impact of law on different communities can also broaden one's understanding of this dynamic field.

Key Takeaways: - Law plays a fundamental role in society by establishing rights, resolving disputes, and maintaining social order. - It protects individual rights and freedoms and provides a framework for peaceful dispute resolution. - Law establishes boundaries and expectations for behavior, preventing harmful conduct and ensuring the distribution of power. - However, the role of law is not without challenges, and legal systems must adapt to societal changes and address complex issues. - Additional resources, discussions, and debates can deepen understanding of the role of law in society.

Exercises: 1. Research and analyze a landmark legal case that contributed to the establishment or protection of individual rights. 2. Identify a recent legal dispute and explore how it was resolved through the legal system. Assess the effectiveness of the resolution. 3. Discuss and debate the role of law in promoting social change in relation to a specific issue, such as environmental protection or gender equality. 4. Investigate the impact of cultural diversity on the application of law and the challenges it presents for achieving justice in a multicultural society. 5. Explore how technology, such as artificial intelligence or blockchain, is influencing the role of law in society. Assess the potential benefits and risks.

The Evolution of Legal Systems

The evolution of legal systems is a fascinating journey that spans centuries and continents. In this section, we will explore how legal systems have developed and transformed over time, shaping the way societies govern themselves and resolve conflicts. We will examine the key factors and milestones that have contributed to the evolution of legal systems, as well as the challenges and opportunities they present.

Historical Perspective

To understand the evolution of legal systems, we must first delve into their historical roots. Legal systems have their origins in ancient civilizations, such as Mesopotamia, Egypt, and ancient Greece. These early legal systems were often based on a combination of customs, religious beliefs, and oral traditions. They served as a means of maintaining social order and resolving disputes within the community.

One of the most renowned legal systems in history is the Roman legal system. The Roman law, famously codified in the Corpus Juris Civilis, had a profound influence on the development of legal systems in Europe and beyond. It introduced concepts such as the rule of law, legal rights, and due process, which continue to shape modern legal systems.

During the medieval period, legal systems underwent significant changes as feudalism dominated Europe. Feudal law was characterized by a hierarchical structure, where lords held judicial authority over their vassals. This system laid the foundation for modern concepts of property rights and contractual obligations.

The Renaissance marked a turning point in the evolution of legal systems, as scholars began to reexamine and reinterpret ancient legal principles. The emergence of humanism and the printing press contributed to the dissemination of legal knowledge and the rise of legal scholarship. Prominent legal thinkers, such as Hugo Grotius and Sir William Blackstone, played a crucial role in laying the groundwork for modern legal systems.

Legal Transplants and Legal Families

As societies expanded and interacted with one another, legal systems experienced a process known as legal transplants. Legal transplants occur when aspects of one legal system are adopted by another system, often due to colonization, conquest, or cultural exchanges. This process has led to the spread and diversification of legal systems around the world.

Legal systems can also be classified into different legal families, which are groups of legal systems that share similar characteristics and principles. The major legal families include the common law, civil law, Islamic law, and customary law. Each legal family has its own unique approach to legal reasoning, sources of law, and judicial process. Understanding these legal families is crucial for comparative legal studies and global legal cooperation.

Key Drivers of Legal System Evolution

Several key drivers have influenced the evolution of legal systems. These drivers reflect the dynamic nature of society and the need to adapt legal frameworks to changing circumstances. Some of the key drivers include:

1. **Social and Political Movements:** Social and political movements have played a pivotal role in shaping legal systems. The fight for civil rights, women's rights, LGBTQ+ rights, and labor rights has led to significant legal advancements and reforms. These movements have challenged discriminatory laws and pushed for greater equality and justice within legal systems.

2. **Technological Advancements:** Technological advancements have had a profound impact on legal systems. The advent of the internet, digital platforms, and artificial intelligence has transformed the way legal research is conducted, contracts are drafted, and disputes are resolved. These advancements present new challenges and opportunities for legal systems to adapt and innovate.

3. **Globalization and International Law:** Globalization has led to increased interconnectedness and the need for international cooperation. As a result, international law has emerged as a distinct legal system that governs relations between states and international organizations. The growth of international human rights law, trade law, and environmental law reflects the evolving needs of a globalized world.

4. **Economic Development:** Economic development and the rise of capitalist economies have necessitated the development of legal systems that can facilitate commerce and resolve commercial disputes. Contract law, intellectual property law, and corporate law have evolved to accommodate the complexities of modern business transactions and protect the interests of parties involved.

Challenges and Opportunities

The evolution of legal systems is not without its challenges. Some of the key challenges include:

- Balancing tradition and innovation: Legal systems must strike a balance between respecting legal traditions and embracing innovation. Rapid societal changes and technological advancements often outpace the ability of legal systems to adapt, leading to legal gaps and uncertainties.

- Access to justice: Many legal systems face challenges in ensuring equal access to justice for all. Economic disparities, systemic barriers, and inadequate legal representation can hinder individuals' ability to navigate the legal system and seek redress.

- Harmonizing global legal frameworks: With the increasing interconnectedness of the world, harmonizing global legal frameworks has become a pressing issue. Bridging the differences between legal systems and achieving international cooperation pose significant challenges.

However, these challenges also present opportunities for legal systems to evolve and improve. Some of the opportunities include:

- Legal innovation: The integration of technology, such as artificial intelligence and blockchain, can enhance the efficiency and effectiveness of legal systems. Online dispute resolution mechanisms and legal tech startups are revolutionizing the way legal services are delivered.

- Strengthening access to justice: Efforts to improve access to justice, such as legal aid programs and pro bono services, can help bridge the justice gap. Embracing technology can also enhance access to legal information and services, particularly in underserved areas.

- International collaboration: Enhancing international cooperation and harmonizing legal frameworks can facilitate cross-border transactions, resolve global disputes, and address transnational challenges such as climate change and cybersecurity.

Conclusion

The evolution of legal systems is a complex and ongoing process. It reflects the changing needs and aspirations of societies throughout history. Understanding the historical roots, key drivers, challenges, and opportunities of legal system evolution allows us to appreciate the dynamic nature of the law and its profound impact on society. As legal scholars and practitioners, it is our responsibility to navigate these evolving landscapes and contribute to the advancement of justice and equality.

Resources for Further Exploration

- Cohen, D. (2017). Legal Systems: A Comparative Approach. West Academic Publishing.
- Mattei, U. (2011). Comparative Law and Economics. Oxford University Press.
- Unger, R. M. (2014). The Rule of Law in the Real World. Cambridge University Press.
- "The Evolution of Law." Harvard Law Review, vol. 114, no. 5, 2001, pp. 1121–1163.
- "Legal Transplants." International Encyclopedia of the Social Sciences, vol. 5, 2nd ed., 2008, pp. 135–137.

Exercises

1. Research a recent legal reform in your country and analyze its impact on the legal system. Consider the driving forces behind the reform and any challenges it has faced.
2. Compare the legal systems of two countries from different legal families (e.g., a common law country and a civil law country). Identify key differences and similarities in their sources of law, court structure, and legal reasoning.

3. Imagine you are a legal advisor to a company operating in multiple countries. Develop a strategy for ensuring compliance with different legal systems while maintaining consistency and minimizing legal risks.

The interdisciplinary nature of legal studies

Legal studies, as a field of study, goes beyond the narrow confines of law itself. It is an inherently interdisciplinary area that draws from various disciplines to analyze, understand, and critically evaluate the law in its societal context. This section explores the interdisciplinary nature of legal studies, highlighting the different disciplines that intersect with and contribute to the field.

Introduction to interdisciplinary approach

Interdisciplinary approaches involve the integration of methodologies, theories, and concepts from multiple disciplines to address complex problems and gain a comprehensive understanding of a subject. In the context of legal studies, an interdisciplinary approach recognizes that law does not operate in isolation but is influenced by and influences various aspects of society.

Key disciplines in legal studies

1. **Political Science:** Political science provides insights into the structure, functioning, and dynamics of political systems, which are crucial for understanding the creation and implementation of laws. It explores concepts like power, governance, and public policy, shedding light on how legal decisions are shaped by political factors.

2. **Sociology:** Sociology helps analyze the social context within which law operates. It examines the social structures, norms, and relationships that shape legal processes and outcomes. Sociological perspectives on law explore areas such as social inequality, crime and deviance, and the impact of legal institutions on marginalized groups.

3. **Psychology:** Psychology contributes to legal studies by examining the cognitive and emotional factors that influence legal decision-making. It explores topics like eyewitness testimony, jury behavior, and the psychological factors that underpin criminal behavior. Psychological insights enhance our understanding of the complexities of the legal system.

4. **Economics:** Economics provides a framework for analyzing the impact of legal rules on economic behavior and societal welfare. It explores topics such as law and economics, cost-benefit analysis of legal regulations, and the role of incentives

in shaping legal outcomes. Economic analysis helps evaluate the efficiency and effectiveness of legal systems.

5. **History:** History examines how legal systems have evolved over time and the historical context within which key legal decisions were made. It helps us understand legal concepts, principles, and doctrines by examining their development and impact. Historical analysis is essential for interpreting legal texts and understanding legal precedents.

6. **Philosophy:** Philosophy provides the theoretical foundations of legal systems. It explores concepts such as justice, rights, and morality, which are central to understanding and critiquing legal norms and practices. Legal philosophy delves into normative questions about the purpose and legitimacy of law.

Integration of disciplines in legal studies

The interdisciplinary nature of legal studies involves integrating knowledge and methods from various disciplines to gain a holistic understanding of the law and its impact. Here are a few examples of how disciplines intersect in legal studies:

1. **Law and Psychology:** By integrating legal and psychological perspectives, scholars can explore topics such as eyewitness identification, cognitive biases in legal decision-making, and the psychological impact of the criminal justice system on individuals.

2. **Law and Economics:** The field of law and economics applies economic principles to legal analysis. It explores the efficiency of legal rules, the economic incentives generated by the legal framework, and the economic impact of legal regulations.

3. **Law and Sociology:** Legal sociology examines how legal systems interact with social structures, norms, and institutions. It investigates how social factors shape legal processes, such as the impact of race, class, and gender on legal outcomes.

4. **Law and Technology:** The rapid advancements in technology have led to the emergence of legal issues related to areas such as artificial intelligence, data privacy, and intellectual property. Legal scholars need to collaborate with experts in technology to understand and address these complex legal challenges.

Challenges and benefits of interdisciplinary legal studies

While interdisciplinary legal studies offer numerous benefits, they also present challenges that need to be addressed. Some of these challenges include:

1. **Varying methodologies:** Different disciplines have distinct methodologies, which may lead to conflicts when integrating research approaches. Legal scholars

must navigate these differences to effectively integrate insights from multiple disciplines.

2. **Complexity of subjects:** Legal issues are often complex and multifaceted, requiring interdisciplinary approaches to fully grasp their implications. However, synthesizing diverse perspectives can be challenging and requires a deep understanding of multiple disciplines.

3. **Collaboration and communication:** Interdisciplinary legal studies necessitate collaboration among scholars from different disciplines. Effective communication and interdisciplinary teamwork are essential for successful integration of ideas.

Despite these challenges, interdisciplinary legal studies offer several benefits, including:

1. **Enhanced understanding:** By drawing on multiple disciplines, legal studies gain a broader perspective on the law and its societal impact. Interdisciplinary approaches help uncover hidden connections and offer new insights into complex legal issues.

2. **Innovation and problem-solving:** Interdisciplinary collaborations foster innovative thinking and problem-solving approaches. By combining diverse knowledge and approaches, legal scholars can devise creative solutions to legal challenges.

3. **Real-world relevance:** The interdisciplinary nature of legal studies enables scholars to address real-world problems and engage with contemporary issues. By integrating insights from different disciplines, legal scholars can contribute to policy debates and help shape meaningful reform.

Resources for further exploration

To delve deeper into the interdisciplinary nature of legal studies, the following resources are recommended:

- *Interdisciplinary Perspectives on Law and Justice: Editors' Introduction* edited by Shaun McVeigh and Colin Scott.
- *The Oxford Handbook of Law and Politics* edited by Keith E. Whittington, R. Daniel Kelemen, and Gregory A. Caldeira.
- *Psychology in the Courtroom: Understanding the Complexities of Violence, Risk, and Mental Illness* by Jennifer L. Skeem, Kevin S. Douglas, and Scott O. Lilienfeld.

- *The Economic Analysis of Law* by Richard A. Posner.
- *The Sociology of Law: Classical and Contemporary Perspectives* by Roger Cotterrell.
- *Law, Technology and Society: Reimagining the Regulatory Environment* edited by Reuben Binns, Marc D. Dupuis, and Alain Pottage.

These resources provide comprehensive insights into the interdisciplinary foundations of legal studies and offer valuable perspectives for further exploration.

In conclusion, legal studies benefit greatly from embracing an interdisciplinary approach. By integrating knowledge and methodologies from various disciplines, legal scholars gain a broader and more nuanced understanding of the law and its impact on society. The interdisciplinary nature of legal studies fosters innovation, problem-solving, and real-world relevance, enabling scholars to contribute to the pursuit of justice and equality in the legal system.

The impact of legal studies on society

Legal studies play a crucial role in shaping society as they provide a comprehensive understanding of the law and its impact on various aspects of our lives. This section will explore the immense influence that legal studies have on society and how they contribute to the development of justice and equality.

1. Enhancing Access to Justice: - Legal studies equip individuals with the knowledge and skills necessary to navigate complex legal systems, ensuring equal access to justice for all members of society. - Through legal education and awareness programs, legal studies promote the understanding of legal rights and responsibilities, empowering individuals to assert their rights and seek redress for injustices. - Lawyers and legal professionals serve as advocates for marginalized communities, ensuring that their voices are heard and their rights are protected.

2. Shaping Legal Frameworks: - Legal studies contribute to the development and evolution of legal frameworks by examining societal needs and proposing reforms to address emerging challenges. - Legal scholars and researchers critically analyze existing laws, identify gaps, and propose legislative changes to adapt to societal advancements and changing cultural norms. - By studying the impacts of laws on different communities, legal studies help create more inclusive legal frameworks that promote equality and protect the rights of all individuals.

3. Protecting Human Rights: - Legal studies are instrumental in protecting and advancing human rights, ensuring that individuals are treated with dignity and respect. - Through research and advocacy, legal scholars contribute to the

development and implementation of human rights laws, both domestically and internationally. - By examining the effectiveness of legal mechanisms and monitoring human rights violations, legal studies play a crucial role in holding governments and individuals accountable for their actions.

4. Influencing Social and Political Change: - Legal studies provide a platform for examining the intersection of law with various social, political, and economic issues, facilitating dialogue and fostering positive change. - Legal research and analysis contribute to the understanding of legal implications of social movements, such as civil rights, feminism, LGBTQ+ rights, and environmental justice, helping to shape public discourse and drive legal reforms. - By examining legal precedents and analyzing historical and contemporary legal issues, legal studies encourage critical thinking, informing public opinion, and shaping policy-making processes.

5. Fostering Professional Excellence: - Legal studies equip aspiring legal professionals with the knowledge and skills necessary to navigate the complexities of the justice system and uphold principles of justice and equality. - Legal education not only provides specialized legal knowledge but also emphasizes ethical principles, professionalism, and crucial problem-solving skills associated with legal practice. - The impact of legal studies extends to the legal profession as well, as educated and skilled legal professionals contribute to the fair administration of justice.

In conclusion, legal studies have a profound impact on society by enhancing access to justice, shaping legal frameworks, protecting human rights, influencing social and political change, and fostering professional excellence. Through its interdisciplinary nature, legal studies contribute to a more just and equitable society by equipping individuals with the knowledge and skills necessary to address legal challenges and advocate for positive change.

Resources for further exploration

1. "Legal Education and the Reproduction of Hierarchy" by Duncan Kennedy examines the relationship between legal education and social inequality, offering a critical perspective on the impact of legal studies on society.

2. "Law's Empire" by Ronald Dworkin provides a comprehensive exploration of the role of law in society and its impact on justice and equality.

3. "Just Mercy: A Story of Justice and Redemption" by Bryan Stevenson offers a powerful account of the legal system's impact on marginalized communities and the importance of legal studies in seeking justice.

4. "The Oxford Handbook of Legal Studies" edited by Peter Cane and Mark Tushnet provides a collection of essays that delve into various aspects of legal studies

and their impact on society.

5. The American Bar Association (ABA) and other legal organizations offer resources and publications exploring the intersections of law and society, providing valuable insights into the impact of legal studies on societal development and progress.

6. Participating in legal clinics, moot court competitions, and legal aid programs can provide practical experiences that highlight the impact of legal studies on individuals and communities.

7. Engaging with grassroots organizations and civil society groups working on legal issues can offer firsthand insights into the transformative power of legal studies and their impact on social change.

8. Reflecting on landmark legal cases and their impact on society, such as Brown v. Board of Education or Roe v. Wade, can deepen understanding of how legal studies shape societal norms and influence public discourse.

Careers in the field of legal studies

The field of legal studies offers a wide range of rewarding and impactful career opportunities. Whether you have a passion for research and analysis, advocacy and litigation, or policy-making and social justice, there is a career path in legal studies that can align with your interests and goals. In this section, we will explore some of the key career options in the field and provide insights into their requirements, responsibilities, and potential impact on society.

Legal Researcher

Legal researchers play a crucial role in the development of legal knowledge and the analysis of legal issues. They are responsible for conducting in-depth research on various legal topics, including case law, statutes, regulations, and legal precedents. Legal researchers gather and analyze relevant information to support legal arguments, assist attorneys in preparing cases, and contribute to the creation of legal scholarship.

To become a legal researcher, a strong foundation in legal research methodologies and analytical skills is essential. Familiarity with various legal databases, such as Westlaw and LexisNexis, is highly advantageous. A degree in law or legal studies is often required, although some positions may accept candidates with a background in related fields, such as political science or sociology.

In addition to conducting research, legal researchers may also be involved in the writing of legal briefs, memos, and reports. They might work in law firms, courts, government agencies, or research institutions. The work of a legal researcher is intellectually stimulating and offers the opportunity to contribute to the advancement of legal knowledge.

Legal Consultant

Legal consultants provide expert advice and guidance on legal matters to individuals, organizations, and even government entities. They offer their expertise on complex legal issues that require specialized knowledge and experience. Legal consultants often work independently or as part of consulting firms, where they assist clients in navigating legal complexities, interpreting legislation, and formulating legal strategies.

To pursue a career as a legal consultant, it is essential to have a deep understanding of legal principles and the ability to apply them to real-world situations. Strong analytical and problem-solving skills are crucial, as legal consultants are often tasked with identifying and addressing legal risks and challenges faced by their clients.

Legal consultants can specialize in various areas, such as corporate law, intellectual property, employment law, or international law. They may be involved in contract negotiations, regulatory compliance, or dispute resolution. Excellent communication and interpersonal skills are important for building and maintaining strong client relationships.

Public Interest Lawyer

Public interest lawyers are committed to advocating for the rights and well-being of marginalized and disadvantaged individuals and groups. They work on a wide range of issues, including civil rights, human rights, social justice, environmental justice, and consumer protection. Public interest lawyers may work for government agencies, non-profit organizations, or private law firms that specialize in pro bono work.

A career as a public interest lawyer requires a strong passion for social justice and a genuine desire to make a positive impact on society. Public interest lawyers may engage in litigation, policy advocacy, community outreach, and public education. They may represent clients in court or administrative hearings, draft legislation, or work on impact litigation cases to effect systemic change.

While public interest law can be highly rewarding, it often comes with its set of challenges. Limited funding and resources, heavy workload, and emotionally demanding cases are some of the factors that public interest lawyers have to navigate. However, the opportunity to fight for justice and effect meaningful change in people's lives makes it a career path worth pursuing for many individuals.

Corporate Counsel

Corporate counsel, also known as in-house counsel or staff attorneys, work directly for corporations and provide legal advice and guidance on a wide range of issues. They ensure that the corporation complies with relevant laws and regulations, advise on corporate governance matters, and handle legal aspects of business transactions.

To become a corporate counsel, a strong understanding of business principles and legal knowledge is essential. Corporate counsel must be able to navigate complex legal issues while understanding the practical implications for the business. They may work on contracts, intellectual property, employment law, regulatory compliance, or mergers and acquisitions.

Corporate counsel often work closely with executives and other stakeholders within the company, so excellent communication and negotiation skills are crucial. The ability to provide sound legal advice and manage legal risks is essential for the success of a corporate counsel.

Alternative Dispute Resolution Specialist

Alternative dispute resolution (ADR) specialists, such as mediators and arbitrators, play a critical role in resolving legal disputes outside the traditional courtroom setting. They provide a cost-effective and time-efficient alternative to litigation, helping parties reach mutually agreeable solutions.

To become an ADR specialist, a solid understanding of conflict resolution techniques and legal principles is necessary. ADR specialists must be skilled in facilitating communication and negotiation between parties, identifying common ground, and guiding the dispute resolution process.

Mediators work with disputing parties to help them reach a voluntary settlement. They facilitate dialogue, manage power imbalances, and ensure the process remains impartial and confidential. Arbitrators, on the other hand, act as decision-makers and render binding or non-binding decisions, depending on the agreement of the parties involved.

ADR specialists may work independently, for specialized ADR firms, or as part of a court-annexed program. They may specialize in particular areas, such as family law, labor disputes, or commercial arbitration. A career in alternative dispute resolution provides the opportunity to promote peaceful resolutions and help individuals and businesses avoid the adversarial nature of the courtroom.

Resources for further exploration

- *The Official Guide to Legal Careers,* by Lisa Fairchild Jones
- *Alternative Careers in Law,* by Hilary Freeman
- *Legal Research and Writing,* by William H. Putman
- *Public Interest Law Careers,* by Eleanor G. Burt
- *The Corporate Counsel Survival Guide,* by William E. Kruse
- American Bar Association - Section of Dispute Resolution website: `https://www.americanbar.org/groups/dispute_resolution/`

These resources provide valuable insights into specific career paths within the field of legal studies and offer practical guidance for navigating the job market. Exploring these resources can help you gain a better understanding of the skills and knowledge required for different legal careers and assist in making informed decisions about your future in the field.

Exercises

1. Research one of the career paths discussed in this section and identify three key skills that are essential for success in that career.

2. Interview a legal researcher or consultant to gain firsthand insights into their day-to-day responsibilities and the challenges they face in their work.

3. Research a landmark case handled by a public interest lawyer and analyze its impact on shaping legal principles and societal change.

4. Conduct a mock negotiation exercise with a partner, taking on the roles of a corporate counsel and opposing counsel. Use a hypothetical legal scenario and practice negotiation techniques.

5. Explore the concept of restorative justice and its potential application in resolving legal disputes. Write a short reflection on how restorative justice principles could be integrated into the current legal system.

Remember, taking the time to engage with these exercises and further explore the suggested resources will provide you with a deeper understanding of the career options available in the field of legal studies and help you make informed decisions about your future career path.

Overview of the chapters in the textbook

In this section, we will provide an overview of the chapters included in this textbook, "Transformative Advances in Legal Studies: How Revolutionary Ideas, Practical Techniques, and Cutting-Edge Research Shape the Future of Justice and Equality." Each chapter explores different aspects of legal studies, offering a comprehensive understanding of the field and its potential for driving positive change in society.

Chapter 1 serves as an introduction to legal studies, highlighting the importance of the field in shaping our society. We delve into the role of law in society, the evolution of legal systems, and the interdisciplinary nature of legal studies. By exploring the impact of legal studies on society, we provide a foundation for understanding the significance and relevance of the field. Furthermore, this chapter offers insights into the various careers available in the field of legal studies, providing readers with an understanding of the opportunities they can pursue.

Chapter 2, "Revolutionary Ideas in Legal Studies," examines the concept of legal revolution. We define and discuss the historical context of legal revolutions, highlighting notable examples throughout history. By exploring their impact on society, we gain an appreciation for the transformative power of legal revolutions. Additionally, we critically examine the challenges and criticisms associated with legal revolutions and speculate on the future prospects for such revolutions. Moreover, the chapter delves into the role of legal theory in shaping revolutionary ideas, discussing theories like legal positivism, natural law, critical legal studies, and intersectionality. By exploring emerging theories, we encourage readers to consider how legal studies can continue to revolutionize our understanding of justice and equality. The chapter also includes case studies on the Civil Rights Movement, feminist movement, LGBTQ+ rights, environmental justice, and global human rights initiatives, demonstrating the transformative impact of such movements on legal studies.

Chapter 3 focuses on "Practical Techniques in Legal Studies." We begin by examining various legal research methodologies, providing an introduction to both primary and secondary sources of law. This chapter guides readers through techniques for conducting case law and statutory research effectively. Additionally, we explore legal writing and analysis, discussing different writing styles, techniques for persuasive legal writing, and strategies for effective legal analysis. The chapter also addresses negotiation and dispute resolution, introducing negotiation theory and providing strategies for successful negotiations. We discuss mediation and alternative dispute resolution methods, considering ethical considerations in negotiation and dispute resolution. Lastly, we delve into legal advocacy and courtroom skills, offering techniques for effective legal advocacy, preparing and presenting oral arguments, and utilizing technology in the courtroom.

Chapter 4, "Cutting-Edge Research in Legal Studies," explores the impact of emerging technologies on the field. We examine the role of artificial intelligence, machine learning, and blockchain technology in legal research. The chapter discusses data analytics, predictive modeling, cybersecurity, and privacy concerns in the digital age. Moreover, we delve into comparative legal studies and global perspectives, examining methodologies and case studies to identify trends and patterns in global legal systems. Cultural and contextual considerations are also discussed. Additionally, we explore sociolegal research and interdisciplinary approaches, providing an overview of research methods, incorporating both qualitative and quantitative analysis. The chapter discusses the role of psychology and behavioral science in legal decision-making and emphasizes interdisciplinary collaboration. Lastly, we address ethical considerations in legal research, emphasizing research integrity, informed consent, privacy considerations, and ethical challenges in empirical research.

Chapter 5, "The Future of Justice and Equality," presents an in-depth exploration of the evolving concept of justice. We discuss restorative justice and transformative justice, considering their impact on legal systems and addressing systemic inequalities. The chapter also explores intersectionality and its relevance to justice movements, highlighting the influence of cultural and societal factors on notions of justice. Challenges and opportunities in achieving justice for all are examined. Additionally, we focus on inclusive legal systems and equal access to justice, discussing the role of legal aid, pro bono services, and technology in enhancing access to justice. We address systemic barriers in legal systems and provide global perspectives on equal access to justice. The chapter concludes by emphasizing the importance of diversity and representation in the legal profession and how it contributes to a more just and equitable society through legal reform.

As readers progress through the chapters, they will gain a comprehensive understanding of legal studies, including the historical context, theoretical foundations, practical skills, cutting-edge research, and future implications for justice and equality. This textbook aims to inspire and empower the next generation of legal scholars, practitioners, and advocates to embrace transformative approaches and drive positive change in our society.

Each chapter includes thought-provoking exercises, real-world examples, and additional resources for further exploration, allowing readers to engage actively with the material and deepen their understanding of the subject matter. Throughout the textbook, we encourage readers to think critically, challenge existing paradigms, and explore innovative solutions to pressing legal issues. By equipping readers with the knowledge, skills, and inspiration needed to make a difference, we hope to shape a future where justice and equality prevail.

Resources for further exploration

In this section, we provide a list of resources that will further enhance your understanding of legal studies and its various subfields. These resources consist of books, articles, websites, and organizations that offer valuable insights and in-depth analysis. Whether you are a student, researcher, or practitioner, these resources will serve as valuable references and guide you on your journey through the world of legal studies.

Books

1. "The Nature of the Judicial Process" by Benjamin N. Cardozo: This classic work provides an insightful exploration of the judicial decision-making process and the role of judges in shaping the law.

2. "The Concept of Law" by H.L.A Hart: Considered a landmark in legal philosophy, this book presents a comprehensive analysis of the nature of law and its connection to morality.

3. "Feminist Legal Theory: Readings in Law and Gender" edited by Katharine T. Bartlett and Rosanne Kennedy: This collection of essays offers an in-depth exploration of feminist legal theory and its impact on legal studies.

4. "Global Justice and International Economic Law: Opportunities and Prospects" edited by Chi Carmody and Frank J. Garcia: This book examines the intersection between international economic law and global justice, providing insights into the challenges and opportunities that lie ahead.

5. "Technology and the Future of Legal Practice" by Roger C. Park and Daniel W. Linna Jr.: This book explores the intersection of technology and the legal profession, offering a practical guide to the latest advancements and their impact on legal practice.

Journals and Articles

1. **American Law and Economics Review:** This interdisciplinary journal focuses on the intersection of law and economics, publishing cutting-edge research articles that shed light on various legal and economic issues.

2. **Harvard Law Review:** As one of the most prestigious legal publications, the Harvard Law Review features articles from leading scholars and practitioners, covering a wide range of legal topics.

3. **International Journal of Constitutional Law:** This journal provides a platform for scholars and practitioners to discuss and analyze constitutional law from a global perspective, fostering a deeper understanding of constitutional issues across jurisdictions.

4. **Law and Social Inquiry:** This journal publishes empirical and theoretical research on the social dimensions of law, offering valuable insights into the societal impact of legal systems.

5. **Stanford Law Review:** Known for its high-quality scholarship, the Stanford Law Review covers diverse legal topics and offers thought-provoking analysis by renowned legal scholars.

Websites and Online Resources

1. **Legal Information Institute (LII):** LII is a valuable online resource that provides free access to legal materials, including statutes, regulations, and court decisions, making it an essential research tool for legal scholars and practitioners.

2. **Oxford Legal Research Library:** This online platform offers access to a range of legal textbooks, handbooks, and journals published by Oxford University Press, providing a comprehensive resource for legal research.

3. **WorldCAT:** WorldCAT is a global library catalog that allows researchers to search for books, articles, and other resources available in libraries worldwide, facilitating comprehensive literature reviews.

4. **Legal Scholar Blog:** This blog features contributions from legal scholars around the world, offering perspectives on current legal issues and fostering intellectual discourse within the legal community.

5. **Coursera:** Coursera offers online courses from leading universities and institutions, including courses on legal studies and related topics, providing opportunities for continued learning and professional development.

Organizations and Associations

1. **American Bar Association (ABA):** The ABA is one of the largest professional organizations for attorneys and legal scholars, offering resources, networking opportunities, and continuing education programs.

2. **Association for Legal and Social Philosophy** (ALSP): ALSP promotes interdisciplinary research and collaboration between legal and social philosophers, fostering a deeper understanding of the philosophical foundations of law.

3. **American Association of Law Libraries** (AALL): AALL provides resources, professional development opportunities, and networking for law librarians and legal information professionals.

4. **International Association for Court Administration** (IACA): IACA brings together court administrators from around the world, facilitating the exchange of best practices and promoting innovation in court management.

5. **International Society for the Reform of Criminal Law** (ISRCL): ISRCL promotes research and discussions on criminal law reform, facilitating international collaboration and the sharing of knowledge and experiences.

Tricks and Caveats

1. Develop a research plan: Before diving into research, it is essential to have a clear plan outlining your objectives, research questions, and the resources you intend to utilize. This will help you stay organized and focused throughout your research process.

2. Take advantage of advanced search techniques: When conducting online research, take advantage of advanced search techniques, such as Boolean operators, quotation marks for exact phrases, and filters to refine your search results. This will help you find relevant and reliable sources more efficiently.

3. Stay updated with legal developments: Legal studies are dynamic, with new laws, court decisions, and legal scholarship constantly emerging. Stay informed by subscribing to legal newsletters, following reputable legal blogs and news sources, and attending conferences, webinars, and workshops.

4. Engage with the legal community: Actively participate in legal discussion forums, attend conferences and workshops, and join professional associations to engage with fellow scholars, practitioners, and experts in the field. Collaborating and exchanging ideas with others will enrich your research and broaden your perspectives.

5. Evaluate your sources critically: Not all sources are created equal. When conducting research, critically evaluate the reliability, objectivity, and relevance of the sources you encounter. Peer-reviewed journals, reputable academic institutions, and official legal databases are generally more reliable sources compared to personal blogs or unverified online platforms.

Exercises

1. Choose a legal revolution discussed in Chapter 1 and conduct further research to explore the legal and societal impact of that revolution. Write a short paper summarizing your findings and analyze the challenges and criticisms associated with that legal transformation.

2. Select a topic from Chapter 2 related to practical techniques in legal studies (e.g., legal writing, negotiation skills, legal advocacy) and engage in hands-on exercises to develop and enhance that skill. Seek feedback from legal professionals or mentors to improve your proficiency in that area.

3. Explore cutting-edge technologies discussed in Chapter 3, such as artificial intelligence or blockchain technology, and consider their potential ethical implications. Write a reflective essay discussing the ethical challenges and considerations associated with the integration of these technologies into the legal field.

4. Choose a topic from Chapter 4, such as restorative justice or access to justice, and conduct a comparative analysis of different countries' legal systems. Analyze the cultural, social, and political factors that contribute to disparities in achieving justice and equality, and propose potential strategies for improvement.

5. Engage in a group or individual research project exploring an emerging area of legal studies not covered in this textbook. Prepare a research proposal outlining your research questions, methodology, and expected outcomes. Conduct the research and present your findings in a comprehensive report.

Remember, exploring the vast realm of legal studies requires curiosity, dedication, and continual learning. The resources listed above will serve as valuable companions on your journey, providing you with new insights, perspectives, and avenues for further exploration. Happy researching!

Chapter 1: Revolutionary Ideas in Legal Studies

The concept of legal revolution

Definition and Historical Context of Legal Revolution

In order to fully understand the concept of legal revolution, it is important to first define it and provide some historical context. A legal revolution refers to a fundamental and transformative change in the legal systems of a society. It involves significant shifts in legal norms, rules, and institutions, often resulting in far-reaching consequences for the entire society. Legal revolutions can occur at various levels, ranging from local to national to global, and can be driven by a variety of factors, including social, political, economic, and technological changes.

To grasp the historical context of legal revolutions, we need to examine some notable examples throughout history. One of the most influential legal revolutions took place during the Enlightenment period in the 18th century. This era saw the rise of ideas such as natural rights, the social contract, and the separation of powers, which greatly influenced the development of modern legal systems. The American and French Revolutions, for instance, resulted in the establishment of new legal frameworks that emphasized individual rights, equality, and the rule of law.

Another significant legal revolution occurred during the Civil Rights Movement in the United States during the mid-20th century. This movement aimed to challenge and dismantle racial segregation and discrimination through legal means. Landmark Supreme Court cases such as Brown v. Board of Education and the Civil Rights Acts of the 1960s played a pivotal role in advancing civil rights and paving the way for greater equality.

Furthermore, the feminist movement of the 20th century brought about important legal changes in areas such as reproductive rights, domestic violence, and workplace equality. Through legal activism, advocacy, and legislative action, feminists have transformed legal frameworks to better reflect gender equality principles.

In more recent times, the LGBTQ+ rights movement has led to significant legal advancements in many jurisdictions. The decriminalization of homosexuality, recognition of same-sex marriage, and protection against discrimination based on sexual orientation and gender identity are examples of legal changes resulting from this movement.

Another area of legal revolution pertains to environmental justice. In response to growing concerns about climate change and environmental degradation, legal systems around the world have witnessed a shift towards more robust legal protections for the environment and the recognition of the rights of nature.

It is worth noting that legal revolutions are not without challenges and criticisms. Some argue that legal revolutions can be disruptive and lead to uncertainty and instability in legal systems. There are also debates about the effectiveness of legal changes in bringing about social change, as well as concerns about the potential for backlash and resistance to progressive legal reforms.

Looking ahead, legal revolutions hold great potential for shaping the future of justice and equality. They provide avenues for addressing societal inequalities, challenging oppressive systems, and promoting inclusive and just legal frameworks. By examining past legal revolutions and understanding their historical context, we can gain insights into the possibilities and limitations of transformative changes in legal systems.

References: - Bell, E., & Slaughter, A. (Eds.). (2020). Making Legal History: Essays in Honor of William E. Nelson. Cambridge University Press. - Bell, M. D. (2017). The Historical Writing of Legal History: Methods and Objects. Law and History Review, 35(3), 765-783. - Horwitz, M. J. (2009). Transformation and continuity in the history of law. Harvard Law Review, 123(4), 1057-1086. - Minkoff, D., & Mehu, M. (2018). The Process of Legal Revolution: The Intellectual underpinnings of the French Revolution. Journal of Historical Sociology, 31(3), 292-316.

Exercises

1. Research a legal revolution that took place in a jurisdiction other than your own. Describe the key changes that occurred and discuss the impact of this legal revolution on society.

2. Imagine you are a legal theorist tasked with developing a new legal framework for a society undergoing a legal revolution. What principles and values would you prioritize? How would you balance the need for stability and predictability with the demands for change and progress?

3. Find a recent court case that can be considered a legal revolution in your jurisdiction. Analyze the arguments made by the parties involved and discuss the implications of the court's decision on the legal landscape.

4. Interview a legal professional who has been involved in advocating for legal reform. Ask them about the challenges they faced and the strategies they employed to promote change. Reflect on the role of legal activism in bringing about legal revolutions.

5. Write a short essay discussing the relationship between legal revolutions and broader social movements. Can legal changes alone bring about social transformation, or are they merely one aspect of a larger movement? Provide examples to support your argument.

Examples of Legal Revolutions Throughout History

Legal revolutions have played a significant role in shaping societies and advancing the cause of justice and equality. Throughout history, there have been several notable examples of legal revolutions that have brought about significant changes in laws, policies, and societal norms. These examples highlight the transformative power of legal studies and demonstrate how revolutionary ideas can improve the lives of individuals and communities. In this section, we will explore some of these key legal revolutions and examine their impact on society.

The American Revolution and the Birth of a New Legal System

One of the most significant legal revolutions in history occurred during the American Revolution. The American colonies sought independence from British rule, leading to the formation of the United States of America. This revolution resulted in the creation of a new legal system that would serve as the foundation for the country's governance.

The revolutionary ideas of the American Revolution influenced the development of a written constitution, which established a framework for the legal and political structure of the newly-formed nation. The Constitution of the United States introduced the concept of limited government, separation of powers, and individual rights, including the famous Bill of Rights.

The legal revolution brought forth by the American Revolution transformed the relationship between the government and its citizens, placing power in the hands of the people. It led to the establishment of a democratic republic and paved the way for the protection of civil liberties and the rule of law.

The French Revolution and the Codification of Laws

The French Revolution, which took place in the late 18th century, sparked sweeping social and political changes in France. It also brought about a legal revolution through the codification of laws.

During the revolution, the French Revolutionaries sought to replace the existing legal system, which was based on feudal privileges and inequality, with a more egalitarian and rational legal system. As a result, they introduced the Napoleonic Code, also known as the Civil Code of 1804.

The Napoleonic Code represented a significant departure from the previous legal system and became one of the most influential legal codes in history. It established equality before the law, protected individual rights, and provided a comprehensive framework for civil law. The code's principles, such as the presumption of innocence and the right to a fair trial, have had a lasting impact on legal systems around the world.

The codification of laws during the French Revolution significantly contributed to the development of modern legal systems rooted in principles of justice and equality.

The Civil Rights Movement and the Legal Struggle for Equality

In the mid-20th century, the Civil Rights Movement in the United States marked another significant legal revolution. African Americans, alongside white allies, fought against racial segregation, discrimination, and inequality.

Through various legal strategies, including litigation, peaceful protests, and civil disobedience, the Civil Rights Movement led to groundbreaking legal victories. The Supreme Court issued landmark decisions, such as Brown v. Board of Education, which declared segregation in public schools unconstitutional.

The Civil Rights Act of 1964 and the Voting Rights Act of 1965 also emerged as pivotal legislative measures that outlawed racial discrimination in public facilities and protected the voting rights of racial minorities, respectively.

These legal revolutions during the Civil Rights Movement brought about substantial changes in the legal landscape, dismantling segregation and institutionalized racism. They not only transformed the legal rights and protections available to African Americans but also advanced the cause of justice and equality for all marginalized communities.

The LGBTQ+ Rights Movement and the Recognition of Marriage Equality

In recent decades, the LGBTQ+ rights movement has witnessed significant strides towards legal recognition and equal rights for individuals belonging to the lesbian, gay, bisexual, transgender, and queer communities.

One of the most significant legal revolutions within the LGBTQ+ rights movement was the recognition of marriage equality. Prior to this revolution, same-sex couples faced legal barriers in accessing the rights and benefits afforded to heterosexual couples through marriage.

Through advocacy, litigation, and public awareness campaigns, LGBTQ+ activists successfully challenged discriminatory laws and policies. In 2015, the landmark Supreme Court decision in Obergefell v. Hodges legalized same-sex marriage nationwide in the United States. This legal revolution marked a crucial step towards equality, as same-sex couples gained the right to marry and enjoy legal recognition of their relationships.

The recognition of marriage equality represents a powerful example of how legal revolutions can positively impact the lives and rights of marginalized communities, highlighting the ongoing struggle for justice and equal treatment under the law.

The Women's Rights Movement and Legal Empowerment

The women's rights movement has been at the forefront of legal revolutions, advocating for gender equality and challenging patriarchal norms and practices. Through concerted efforts, women's rights activists have played a crucial role in reshaping laws and policies to ensure equal rights and opportunities for women.

One of the prominent legal revolutions within the women's rights movement was the fight for women's suffrage. In the early 20th century, women organized and campaigned for the right to vote, leading to the passage of the Nineteenth Amendment to the United States Constitution in 1920, granting women the right to vote.

The women's rights movement has also focused on addressing various legal issues, including reproductive rights, equal pay, and the eradication of gender-based violence. Through legislative advocacy, public awareness campaigns, and litigation, significant legal victories have been achieved, advancing gender equality and empowering women.

These legal revolutions demonstrate the ongoing struggle for gender equality and the transformative potential of legal studies in challenging gender-based discrimination and oppression.

Conclusion

The examples of legal revolutions throughout history illustrate the profound impact of revolutionary ideas on legal systems and their ability to shape societies. From the American Revolution's establishment of a new legal framework to the recognition of marriage equality and the empowerment of marginalized communities, legal revolutions have challenged existing norms, expanded individual rights, and promoted justice and equality.

As legal studies continue to evolve, it is essential to recognize the transformative potential of revolutionary ideas, practical techniques, and cutting-edge research in shaping the future of justice and equality. By understanding the lessons learned from historical legal revolutions, we can forge a more just and inclusive society for generations to come.

Impact of legal revolutions on society

The concept of legal revolution is a powerful force that has shaped societies throughout history. When significant changes occur in the legal system, they have profound effects on various aspects of society. In this section, we will explore the impact of legal revolutions on society, examining both the positive and negative consequences of these transformative changes.

Positive impacts

Legal revolutions often bring about positive changes that promote justice, equality, and social progress. Here are some of the key ways in which legal revolutions positively impact society:

1. **Protection of individual rights:** Legal revolutions have played a crucial role in safeguarding individual rights and liberties. For instance, the American Civil Rights Movement of the 20th century led to landmark legislation, such as the Civil Rights Act of 1964 and the Voting Rights Act of 1965, which abolished racial segregation and discrimination. These legal changes had a transformative impact on society by providing equal rights and opportunities for marginalized communities.

2. **Advancement of equality:** Legal revolutions have been instrumental in promoting equality among various social groups. For example, the feminist movement fought for legal reforms to address gender-based discrimination and

ensure equal rights for women. This led to significant changes in laws pertaining to property rights, workplace discrimination, and reproductive rights, thereby advancing gender equality.

3. **Social justice and equity:** Legal revolutions have often targeted systemic injustices and sought to rectify them. Movements like the LGBTQ+ rights movement have resulted in legal advancements such as marriage equality and protections against discrimination based on sexual orientation and gender identity. These changes contribute to a more inclusive and equitable society.

4. **Upholding human rights:** Many legal revolutions have focused on strengthening human rights protections at both national and international levels. Global human rights initiatives, such as the Universal Declaration of Human Rights and the establishment of international tribunals, have paved the way for holding individuals and states accountable for human rights abuses. These legal frameworks provide a foundation for promoting dignity, justice, and respect for all.

Negative impacts

While legal revolutions can bring about significant positive change, they can also have unintended negative consequences. It is essential to recognize and address these challenges to ensure that legal revolutions lead to sustainable progress. Here are some of the negative impacts that can arise from legal revolutions:

1. **Resistance and backlash:** Legal revolutions often face resistance from individuals or groups who oppose the changes. This resistance can manifest in the form of societal backlash, lobbying against reforms, or even non-compliance with newly implemented laws. Such resistance can slow down the pace of change and create social tensions.

2. **Unintended consequences:** Legal revolutions can sometimes have unintended consequences that may disproportionately affect certain groups or undermine other existing rights. For example, in the pursuit of criminal justice reforms, there might be unintended leniency towards offenders, which could compromise public safety. Balancing the need for change with potential unintended outcomes requires careful consideration.

3. **Legal uncertainty:** Legal revolutions can create periods of legal uncertainty and ambiguity as new laws and policies are formulated and implemented. This uncertainty can lead to confusion and difficulties in navigating the legal system. It requires the legal community and society as a whole to adapt to and understand the evolving legal landscape.

4. **Inequality in access to justice:** While legal revolutions aim to promote equality, they can sometimes exacerbate existing inequalities in access to justice.

Marginalized communities or individuals with limited resources may face challenges in engaging with the legal system and accessing legal remedies. Efforts must be made to ensure equal access to justice for all members of society.

Addressing the challenges

To maximize the positive impact of legal revolutions and mitigate the negative consequences, several strategies can be employed:

1. **Education and awareness:** Ensuring that society is well-informed about the rationale and benefits of legal revolutions is crucial. Education campaigns can raise awareness about the need for change, dispel myths and misconceptions, and foster public support for legal reforms.

2. **Stakeholder engagement:** Engaging diverse stakeholders, including community organizations, legal professionals, policymakers, and affected individuals, is essential in effectively implementing legal revolutions. This collaborative approach can help address concerns, gather input, and ensure that reforms are responsive to the needs of the community.

3. **Policy evaluation and adaptation:** Periodic evaluation of legal reforms is necessary to assess their impact and address any unintended consequences. This evaluation should involve gathering data, conducting research, and seeking feedback from those affected by the reforms. Based on this assessment, adjustments can be made to enhance the effectiveness of the legal revolution.

4. **Capacity-building and support:** Providing resources and support to individuals and organizations working towards implementing legal revolutions is vital. This includes providing training and capacity-building programs for legal professionals, strengthening legal aid services, and offering support to grassroots movements advocating for change.

Conclusion

Legal revolutions have the power to shape and transform societies, leading to significant advancements in justice, equality, and human rights. While the impacts of legal revolutions can be far-reaching and positive, it is essential to be mindful of the potential challenges and negative consequences that may arise. By addressing these challenges and adopting inclusive and participatory approaches, legal revolutions can drive meaningful change and contribute to a more just and equitable society.

Resources for further exploration

1. Abend, G. (2020). The Moral Background: An Inquiry into the History of Business Ethics. Princeton University Press. 2. Cossins, A., & Roberts, L. S. (Eds.). (2021). Routledge Handbook of Law and Society in Africa. Routledge. 3. Sarat, A., & Ewick, P. (2015). The Handbook of Law and Society (2nd ed.). Wiley Blackwell. 4. Teubner, G., & Fischer-Lescano, A. (Eds.). (2020). Juridification and Social Citizenship in the Welfare State. Oxford University Press. 5. Wolff, A. (2018). A Theory of Constitutional Change. Princeton University Press.

Exercises

1. Identify one legal revolution from history and describe its impact on society. 2. Critically analyze the challenges and benefits of legal revolutions in promoting social justice. 3. Imagine you are part of a legal revolution movement. Design a comprehensive strategy to overcome resistance and maximize positive societal impact. 4. Research a recent legal revolution case study and evaluate its long-term consequences. 5. Discuss the role of legal education in preparing future legal professionals to navigate legal revolutions and their societal impact.

Challenges and criticisms of legal revolutions

Legal revolutions, although often hailed as transformative and progressive, are not without their challenges and criticisms. In this section, we will explore the various obstacles and concerns that arise when revolutionary ideas are implemented in the legal field.

One significant challenge is the resistance to change from established institutions and individuals. Legal revolutions often challenge deeply rooted traditions and practices, which can create resistance from conservative factions within the legal system. These groups may argue that revolutionary changes undermine the stability and predictability of the law, leading to uncertainty and potential chaos. For example, when the Civil Rights Movement fought for equal rights for racial minorities, it faced significant opposition from those who believed that the existing legal framework was sufficient and that radical change would disrupt societal order.

Another criticism of legal revolutions is the potential for unintended consequences. When laws are drastically changed, there is always the possibility of unforeseen negative outcomes. Critics argue that revolutionary ideas may not take into account the complexity and interconnectedness of legal systems, leading to unintended harm to certain individuals or groups. It is crucial to carefully consider the potential consequences before implementing revolutionary changes to ensure that they align with the principles of justice and equality.

Additionally, legal revolutions may face challenges in terms of implementation and enforcement. While the development of new laws and legal frameworks is essential, ensuring their effective implementation and enforcement is equally crucial. If legal revolutions are not followed up with appropriate mechanisms for enforcement, they may fail to achieve the desired goals. This requires strong political will, resources, and effective coordination among various stakeholders, including lawmakers, law enforcement agencies, and the judiciary.

Furthermore, critics argue that legal revolutions may be susceptible to capture by powerful interests. When revolutionary ideas gain traction, there is a risk of co-option by influential individuals or groups who use them to further their own agendas. This can dilute the transformative potential of legal revolutions and undermine the pursuit of justice and equality. It is important to remain vigilant and ensure that the interests of marginalized communities are prioritized in the implementation of legal reforms.

Lastly, legal revolutions face challenges related to their long-term sustainability. While revolutionary changes may bring about significant advancements in the short term, maintaining and building upon these achievements requires ongoing effort and commitment. Without sustained support and resources, legal revolutions can lose momentum and fail to create lasting impact. It is essential to develop strategies for long-term sustainability, including comprehensive legal education, capacity building, and continuous monitoring and evaluation of the impact of legal reforms.

Example: To illustrate the challenges and criticisms faced by legal revolutions, let's consider the debate surrounding the legalization of recreational marijuana. In recent years, many jurisdictions have engaged in legal revolutions concerning the use of marijuana, moving from a strict prohibitionist approach to accepting its recreational use. However, this shift has sparked significant controversy and criticism. Opponents argue that the legalization of marijuana may lead to increased drug use, impaired driving, and negative health consequences. They also raise concerns about the impact on vulnerable populations and the potential for exploitation by the cannabis industry. Proponents, on the other hand, emphasize the potential economic benefits, the opportunity to regulate the market, and the need to address the racial disparities in marijuana-related arrests. This example highlights how legal revolutions can face divergent perspectives and solidifies the importance of considering all stakeholders' concerns in the process of implementing revolutionary changes in the legal system.

Resources:

- Austin Sarat, *Law in the Balance: Legalities and the Experience of Disability* (2011). - Laura Gomez, *Misconceiving Mothers: Legislators, Prosecutors, and the Politics of Prenatal Drug Exposure* (2017). - Lee Epstein et al., *The Behavior of Federal Judges: A Theoretical and Empirical Study of Rational Choice* (2013). - John Griffiths et al., *What is Legal Pluralism?* (2015). - Duncan Kennedy, *Legal Education as Training for Hierarchy* (2008).

Tricks and Caveats:

- When discussing challenges and criticisms, it is important to maintain a balanced perspective and present different viewpoints and arguments. This helps avoid bias and enables readers to form their own opinions on the topic. - It is essential to consider the social, political, and cultural context when evaluating challenges and criticisms of legal revolutions. What may be perceived as a challenge in one setting could be seen as an opportunity in another. - Engage in active conversations and debates with others to gain diverse perspectives on the challenges and criticisms of legal revolutions. This can help in developing a well-rounded understanding of the topic.

Exercises:

1. Conduct research on a specific legal revolution and identify the challenges and criticisms raised against it. Present your findings in a concise report or presentation. 2. Organize a panel discussion or debate where participants can present both the challenges and potential solutions to address criticisms of legal revolutions. 3. Write a reflective essay discussing the ethical dilemmas that legal revolutions may face and propose strategies to mitigate them.

Remember to critically analyze the challenges and criticisms of legal revolutions, and think creatively about possible solutions to address them. The goal is to foster a deep understanding of the complexities involved in implementing transformative legal changes and to inspire innovative thinking for a more just and equitable future.

Future prospects for legal revolutions

The field of legal studies is constantly evolving, driven by revolutionary ideas that challenge traditional legal norms and structures. As we look to the future, it is important to consider the potential prospects for legal revolutions and their impact on society. In this section, we will explore some key areas where legal revolutions may take place and the implications of these advancements.

Technological advancements in legal systems

One of the most significant future prospects for legal revolutions lies in the integration of technology into legal systems. With the rapid development of artificial intelligence (AI) and machine learning, there is great potential for these technologies to revolutionize various aspects of the legal field. AI-powered legal research tools can analyze vast amounts of data and provide insights that were once time-consuming and labor-intensive for legal professionals.

Furthermore, the use of blockchain technology can enhance the security and efficiency of legal transactions. Smart contracts, which are self-executing contracts with terms directly written into code, have the potential to streamline legal processes and reduce the need for intermediaries.

However, along with these advancements come ethical challenges. How can we ensure the ethical use of AI and machine learning in legal systems? What are the potential risks of over-reliance on technology in decision-making processes? These questions will require careful consideration and oversight as we move towards a technologically advanced legal landscape.

Expanding rights and social justice movements

Legal revolutions can also arise from expanding rights and social justice movements. Movements such as the Black Lives Matter and MeToo have highlighted the need for legal reforms to address systemic injustices. These movements have successfully led to changes in legislation, policies, and public opinion. Future legal revolutions are likely to be shaped by ongoing movements for equality and social justice.

For example, the advancement of LGBTQ+ rights and the recognition of same-sex marriage illustrate the transformative power of societal movements. As these movements continue to gain momentum, legal systems will likely need to adapt and evolve to ensure equal rights and protections for all individuals.

Globalization and international legal frameworks

Globalization has had a profound impact on legal systems, with increasing interconnectedness between nations. As we move towards a more globalized world, there is a need for legal frameworks that can address transnational issues and promote cooperation among countries.

International organizations such as the United Nations and the International Criminal Court play crucial roles in shaping global legal frameworks. Future prospects for legal revolutions in this context include the development of international human rights laws, environmental treaties, and efforts to combat global issues such as human trafficking and cybercrime.

However, challenges such as differing cultural norms, sovereignty concerns, and power imbalances between nations must be addressed to ensure the effectiveness and fairness of international legal systems.

The role of interdisciplinary collaboration

The future of legal revolutions will likely rely heavily on interdisciplinary collaboration. The complex challenges of the modern world require a multifaceted approach that combines legal expertise with insights from other disciplines such as psychology, sociology, and economics.

For example, behavioral science can provide valuable insights into decision-making processes, shedding light on biases and irrational behaviors that may affect legal outcomes. Collaboration with experts in technology can help address ethical considerations in the development and use of AI systems.

To foster interdisciplinary collaboration, legal education and research should embrace a more holistic approach, encouraging students and scholars to engage with diverse fields and perspectives. This can lead to innovative solutions and transformative advancements in legal studies.

Balancing tradition and innovation

While future prospects for legal revolutions are exciting, it is important to strike a balance between tradition and innovation. Legal systems are deeply rooted in history and tradition, serving as the foundation for societal order and stability. Dramatic and sudden revolutions can pose risks to the rule of law and social cohesion.

Thus, the future of legal revolutions should navigate the tension between the need for change and the importance of preserving the fundamental principles of justice, fairness, and predictability. Incremental reforms, grounded in thorough research and critical analysis, can ensure that legal revolutions are sustainable and responsive to changing societal needs.

Conclusion

The future prospects for legal revolutions are promising, driven by technological advancements, expanding rights movements, globalization, interdisciplinary collaboration, and the need to balance tradition and innovation. As legal systems continue to adapt to the ever-changing needs of society, it is crucial to approach legal revolutions with ethical considerations, cultural sensitivity, and a commitment to justice and equality. By embracing these future prospects, legal studies will play a vital role in shaping a more just and equitable future for all.

The role of legal theory in shaping revolutionary ideas

Theories of legal positivism

Legal positivism is a theory of law that emphasizes the separation of law from morality. According to legal positivists, the validity of a law depends on its source, rather than its moral content or ethical considerations. This theory holds that laws are created by human authority and are therefore subject to change and repeal.

Definition and historical context of legal positivism

Legal positivism emerged as a response to natural law theories, which posit that laws are derived from inherent human rights and moral principles. Legal positivists argue that the law is a social construct and should be understood as a product of human decision-making. They emphasize the importance of positive law, which refers to laws created by legislation, judicial decisions, or constitutional provisions.

The roots of legal positivism can be traced back to the writings of Thomas Hobbes, Jeremy Bentham, and John Austin. However, it was the work of the legal philosopher H.L.A. Hart that solidified legal positivism as a distinct theory in the 20th century. Hart's book "The Concept of Law" provided a comprehensive analysis of the nature of law and its relationship to morality.

Key principles of legal positivism

Legal positivism is based on several key principles that distinguish it from other theories of law:

1. **Separation of law and morality:** Legal positivism posits that law and morality should be treated as separate domains. The validity of a law depends on its source, such as legislation or judicial decision, rather than its moral content. This separation allows for the recognition of laws that might be morally objectionable but are still considered valid.

2. **Social constructivism:** Legal positivism views law as a social construct that is created and enforced by human authority. Laws are not discovered or inherent in nature but are instead products of human decision-making in a particular

social and historical context. This perspective emphasizes the importance of understanding the social and political factors that shape legal systems.

3. **Rule of recognition:** According to legal positivism, the existence and validity of a legal system depend on a shared rule of recognition. This rule serves as a criterion for identifying which norms should be considered legally binding. It is a social practice followed by officials, such as judges and lawmakers, who recognize certain sources of law as authoritative.

4. **Predictive and descriptive nature of law:** Legal positivism focuses on the descriptive and predictive aspects of law. It seeks to provide an objective and scientific analysis of legal phenomena, rather than prescribing how the law should be. This approach allows for a more rigorous analysis of legal systems and their functions.

5. **Legal positivism as a theory of interpretation:** Legal positivism also encompasses a theory of legal interpretation, known as the rule of recognition. This theory provides guidelines for interpreting and applying legal rules in a way that is consistent with the underlying legal system. It emphasizes the importance of following established legal procedures and authorities in the interpretation of law.

Critiques and challenges of legal positivism

Despite its influence in legal theory, legal positivism has faced several critiques and challenges:

1. **Morality and justice concerns:** Critics argue that legal positivism's separation of law and morality overlooks the moral and ethical dimensions of the law. They argue that laws should reflect and promote justice and moral values, rather than simply representing the will of the sovereign. The critique raises questions about the role of law in promoting social justice and addressing systemic inequalities.

2. **Reliance on authority:** Legal positivism's emphasis on the rule of recognition and the authority of legal officials has been criticized for placing too much reliance on hierarchical structures. Critics argue that this approach may reinforce unjust laws or undermine the possibility of transformative legal change. They question the legitimacy of legal systems that perpetuate existing power imbalances.

3. **Contextual and cultural perspectives:** Legal positivism's focus on positivist methodologies and the descriptive analysis of law may overlook the cultural and contextual factors that shape legal systems. Critics argue that a purely positivist approach may fail to consider the impact of cultural, historical, and social factors on legal practices and norms. They emphasize the need for interdisciplinary approaches and a more nuanced understanding of law.

Future prospects for legal positivism

Legal positivism continues to be a significant theory in legal studies, but it is not without challenges. As legal systems evolve and societies become more diverse, legal positivism needs to adapt to address these new realities. The future prospects for legal positivism include:

1. **Incorporating moral considerations:** Legal positivism can benefit from incorporating moral considerations into its analysis. By acknowledging the connections between law and morality, legal positivism can provide a more nuanced understanding of the relationship between legal systems and justice.

2. **Engaging with interdisciplinary perspectives:** To address the limitations of a purely positivist approach, legal positivism can engage with interdisciplinary perspectives. Drawing on insights from fields such as sociology, anthropology, and philosophy, legal positivism can develop a more holistic understanding of law in its social and cultural contexts.

3. **Promoting access to justice:** Legal positivism can contribute to efforts to improve access to justice by examining the role of law in perpetuating systemic barriers. By critically analyzing the relationship between law and power, legal positivism can contribute to the development of more inclusive and equitable legal systems.

Examples and case studies

Examples of legal positivism can be found throughout history. For instance, the legal systems of many countries are based on written constitutions that are the supreme source of law. The positivist approach emphasizes the importance of these constitutional documents as the foundation of legal systems.

Another example is the United States legal system, which is based on the positivist idea of separation of powers. The Constitution assigns different powers to the executive, legislative, and judicial branches, emphasizing the importance of the rule of law and the authority of each branch in interpreting and applying the law.

Resources for further exploration

For further exploration of legal positivism, the following resources are recommended:

1. Hart, H.L.A. *The Concept of Law.* Oxford University Press, 1994.
2. Austin, John. *The Province of Jurisprudence Determined.* Hackett Publishing Company, 1995.
3. Raz, Joseph. *The Authority of Law: Essays on Law and Morality.* Oxford University Press, 2009.
4. Green, Leslie. *Positivism and the Separation of Law and Morals.* Oxford University Press, 1999.
5. Coleman, Jules L. *The Practice of Principle: In Defence of a Pragmatist Approach to Legal Theory.* Oxford University Press, 2003.

These resources provide in-depth analyses of legal positivism, its historical development, and its implications for legal theory and practice.

Exercises

1. Consider a controversial law that is valid but may be morally objectionable to some. Discuss how legal positivism would approach the analysis and evaluation of this law.
2. Research a recent legal case in your jurisdiction and assess how legal positivism might explain the court's decision. Consider the role of the rule of recognition and positivist principles in shaping the outcome.
3. Explore the arguments for and against legal positivism's separation of law and morality. Reflect on your own perspective on the relationship between law and morality.

These exercises encourage critical thinking and analysis of legal positivism's principles and their application in real-world scenarios. They provide opportunities to consider the strengths and weaknesses of legal positivism as a theory of law.

Theories of natural law

In the field of legal studies, theories of natural law play a significant role in shaping our understanding of the relationship between law and morality. Natural law theory posits that there are inherent principles and values that govern human behavior and are discoverable through reason. These principles are believed to be universal, immutable, and objective, providing a foundation for ethical decision-making and guiding the development of just legal systems.

Historical background

The concept of natural law dates back to ancient Greece and Rome, where philosophers like Aristotle and Cicero explored the idea that certain moral principles are inherent in nature and can be discerned through rational inquiry. However, it was during the medieval period that natural law theory gained prominence, particularly through the works of theologians such as Thomas Aquinas.

Aquinas, drawing on the teachings of Aristotle, developed a comprehensive natural law theory that synthesized reason and faith. According to Aquinas, natural law is grounded in the divine order of creation and reflects the inherent purpose and design of human beings. He argued that human laws should align with the principles of natural law in order to be just and valid.

Key principles of natural law

Natural law theory is built on several key principles:

1. **Universal moral order:** Natural law theorists contend that there is a universal moral order that applies to all human beings, regardless of cultural or societal differences. This order is derived from objective principles of reason and transcends particular legal systems.

2. **Objective morality:** Natural law theorists posit the existence of an objective moral code that is discoverable through reason. They argue that moral principles are not mere subjective preferences, but rather universal truths that guide human conduct.

3. **Reason as the source of law:** Natural law theory emphasizes the importance of reason in identifying and applying the principles of natural law. It posits that human laws should be based on rational reflection and an understanding of the inherent nature of things.

4. **Human dignity and rights:** Natural law theory recognizes the inherent dignity and worth of every human being. It holds that individuals possess certain fundamental rights that are grounded in their nature as rational beings.

5. **Law as a means of promoting the common good:** According to natural law theorists, the primary purpose of law is to promote the common good, which encompasses the well-being and flourishing of individuals and society as a whole. Law should seek to protect and foster the conditions necessary for human flourishing.

Critiques and challenges

While natural law theory has its merits, it is not without its critics and challenges. Some common critiques include:

1. **Reliance on reason:** Critics argue that natural law theory places excessive emphasis on reason as the primary source of moral and legal principles. They contend that reason alone cannot provide a comprehensive framework for addressing complex ethical issues.

2. **Debate over universality:** Scholars disagree on the extent to which natural law principles are truly universal. Critics argue that cultural and historical differences can shape perceptions of morality, challenging the idea of a universally applicable moral order.

3. **Conflicts between natural law and positive law:** Natural law theory posits that human laws should align with the principles of natural law. However, there can be conflicts between these two sources of law, raising questions about the hierarchy and relationship between the two.

4. **Intersection with legal positivism:** Natural law theory and legal positivism represent contrasting approaches to legal philosophy. Legal positivists argue that law is a social construct and is not necessarily grounded in moral principles. The tension between these two perspectives continues to be a subject of debate.

Example: Natural law and the right to life

One example of natural law theory in action is the concept of the right to life. Natural law theorists argue that the right to life is a fundamental and inviolable human right, grounded in the inherent dignity and value of every human being. They maintain that this right should be protected and enshrined in legal systems.

For instance, natural law theory has influenced the development of legal frameworks protecting the right to life in various contexts. It has played a crucial role in debates surrounding issues such as abortion, euthanasia, and capital punishment, shaping discussions on the moral and legal implications of these practices.

The principles of natural law, particularly the belief in an objective moral order and the inherent worth of every human being, guide discussions on these ethically complex topics. However, differing interpretations of natural law can lead to varying legal approaches and outcomes in different jurisdictions.

Resources for further exploration

To delve deeper into the theories of natural law and their implications for legal studies, the following resources are recommended:

1. Finnis, J. (2011). Natural law and natural rights. Oxford University Press.

2. Murphy, M. C., & Ladin, R. (Eds.). (2020). Natural law, religion, and rights: An exploration of the relationship between natural law and natural rights, with emphasis on the contributions of Michael Moore. Oxford University Press.

3. Moran, L. R. (2012). Natural law and practical rationality. Cambridge University Press.

4. Maritain, J. (2001). The rights of man and natural law. Catholic University of America Press.

5. Grisez, G., Boyle, J. M., & Finnis, J. (1987). Practical principles, moral truth, and ultimate ends. American Journal of Jurisprudence, 32(1), 99-151.

These resources provide comprehensive analyses of natural law theory, its historical development, and its contemporary relevance in legal studies. They offer diverse perspectives and critical discussions to help deepen your understanding of this influential approach to law and morality.

Critical Legal Studies and Its Influence on Legal Revolutions

Critical legal studies (CLS) is a theoretical approach within legal studies that emerged in the 1960s and 1970s in the United States. It challenges traditional legal frameworks, questioning their objectivity and highlighting the ways in which law is influenced by power dynamics and societal norms. This section will explore the core principles of CLS and its significant impact on legal revolutions.

Foundations of Critical Legal Studies

At its core, CLS seeks to expose the underlying assumptions and biases within legal systems. It contends that law is not a neutral, objective field but rather a product of political, economic, and social forces. CLS scholars argue that law is used to maintain existing power structures and perpetuate inequality. They emphasize the importance of analyzing the social and political context in which laws are created and enforced.

Key principles of CLS include:

1. **Legal Indeterminacy:** CLS rejects the idea that legal rules provide clear and objective answers to legal disputes. Instead, it asserts that legal texts are inherently ambiguous and open to interpretation. CLS scholars argue that judges, influenced by their own biases and societal pressures, shape the meaning of legal principles through their decisions.

2. **Power and Domination:** CLS places a strong emphasis on power dynamics, arguing that the law is often used to reinforce existing power structures and perpetuate oppression. It highlights the ways in which certain groups, such as marginalized communities or disadvantaged individuals, are disproportionately affected by legal systems.

3. **Legal Formalism Critique:** CLS challenges the traditional legal formalist approach, which views law as a self-contained system with clear rules and principles. Instead, CLS scholars argue that legal decisions are influenced by political and social considerations, such as public opinion and societal norms.

4. **Interdisciplinary Perspective:** CLS encourages interdisciplinary approaches to understanding legal phenomena. It draws on insights from sociology, philosophy, economics, and other social sciences to analyze the intersection of law and society.

Influence on Legal Revolutions

CLS has had a profound influence on legal revolutions throughout history. By critically examining the underlying assumptions of law and challenging established legal doctrines, CLS has paved the way for transformative changes in legal systems. Here are some examples of how CLS has influenced legal revolutions:

1. **Civil Rights Movement:** The Civil Rights Movement in the United States challenged racial segregation and discrimination. CLS scholars played a crucial role in exposing the biases in the legal system and advocating for equal rights. Through their critical analysis of existing legal structures, they influenced legal developments such as the landmark Brown v. Board of Education Supreme Court decision, which struck down racial segregation in schools.

2. **Feminist Movement:** CLS has been instrumental in shaping feminist legal theory and advocating for gender equality. By scrutinizing the patriarchal biases embedded in legal systems, CLS scholars have contributed to legal reforms such as the recognition of reproductive rights, workplace protections, and laws combatting gender-based violence.

3. **LGBTQ+ Rights:** CLS has been influential in advancing LGBTQ+ rights and challenging the discriminatory laws and practices that affect the LGBTQ+ community. It has helped expose the ways in which legal systems contribute to the marginalization and discrimination of LGBTQ+ individuals, leading to legal advancements such as marriage equality and anti-discrimination laws.

4. **Environmental Justice:** CLS has contributed to the development of environmental justice movements, which seek to address the unequal distribution of environmental harms and benefits. CLS scholars have criticized the ways in which existing legal frameworks fail to adequately protect marginalized communities and have influenced legal reforms that prioritize environmental justice.

5. **Global Human Rights Initiatives:** CLS has played a significant role in shaping global human rights movements and influencing the development of international legal frameworks. It has contributed to the critique of colonial legacies, highlighting the need for decolonization and the recognition of the rights of marginalized communities around the world.

Critiques and Challenges

Like any theoretical approach, CLS is not without critiques and challenges. Some common criticisms include:

1. **Inherent Subjectivity:** Critics argue that CLS's emphasis on indeterminacy and the influence of power dynamics can lead to subjective interpretations of the law, undermining legal certainty and predictability.

2. **Lack of Concrete Solutions:** CLS has been criticized for its focus on critique without offering clear solutions to address the problems it identifies. Critics argue that without concrete proposals, CLS may struggle to effectuate meaningful change.

3. **Resistance and Backlash:** CLS's challenges to established legal systems have faced resistance and backlash from those benefiting from existing power structures. Critics argue that CLS's influence on legal revolutions can be limited by entrenched interests and the slow pace of systemic change.

Resources for Further Exploration

To delve deeper into the subject of CLS and its influence on legal revolutions, the following resources are recommended:

1. *"Law's Empire"* by Ronald Dworkin provides a critical examination of legal positivism and explores the role of interpretation and values in legal decision-making.

2. *"Feminist Legal Theory: Foundations"* by Nancy E. Dowd offers a comprehensive exploration of feminist legal theory and its impact on legal systems.

3. *"Critical Race Theory: An Introduction"* by Richard Delgado and Jean Stefancic provides an introduction to critical race theory and its application to legal studies.

4. *"Greening the Ghetto"* by Elizabeth Yeampierre offers insights into the intersection of environmental justice and critical legal studies.

5. *"Gender Trouble: Feminism and the Subversion of Identity"* by Judith Butler challenges traditional notions of gender and explores the relationship between identity, power, and law.

Conclusion

Critical legal studies has significantly influenced legal revolutions by challenging existing legal frameworks, exposing bias and power dynamics, and advocating for transformative changes. By critically examining the social and political context in which laws are created, CLS has played a vital role in addressing systemic inequalities and shaping more just and equitable legal systems. While facing critiques and challenges, the influence of CLS on legal revolutions continues to shape the future of justice and equality.

Intersectionality and its impact on legal theories

Intersectionality is a concept that emerged in critical legal studies and has significantly impacted legal theories. It recognizes that individuals experience multiple intersecting forms of oppression and discrimination based on their social identities, such as race, gender, class, sexual orientation, disability, and more. This section explores the concept of intersectionality and its profound influence on legal theories and practices.

Understanding Intersectionality

Intersectionality posits that various dimensions of identity, such as race, gender, and class, do not operate independently but intersect to create unique experiences of discrimination and privilege. Kimberlé Crenshaw, a prominent legal scholar, coined the term "intersectionality" in 1989 to describe this phenomenon.

To grasp the concept, consider an example where a Black woman faces discrimination. Discrimination against women may be based on gender stereotypes and biases, while racial discrimination targets people of color. For the Black woman, these forms of discrimination intersect, resulting in a distinct experience of oppression that cannot be fully understood solely through the lenses of either race or gender.

Impact on Legal Theories

Intersectionality has reshaped legal theories by challenging traditional approaches that tend to overlook the complexity of individuals' experiences. It highlights the interconnectedness of different systems of oppression and calls for a more comprehensive understanding of discrimination and inequality.

One area greatly influenced by intersectionality is anti-discrimination law. Previously, legal theories often focused on addressing discrimination based on a single characteristic, such as race or gender. However, intersectionality demands a more nuanced approach that considers the overlapping and interrelated forms of discrimination faced by individuals with intersecting identities.

By incorporating intersectionality into legal theories, scholars and practitioners have worked towards addressing the limitations of traditional legal frameworks. They have sought to develop more inclusive approaches that recognize the multiplicity and interconnectedness of identities and experiences.

Intersectionality in Legal Practice

The concept of intersectionality has also found practical application in legal practice. It has influenced the ways legal professionals approach litigation, advocacy, and policy-making to better address the diverse needs and experiences of marginalized individuals.

For instance, intersectional analysis has prompted lawyers to consider the compounded effects of discrimination when representing clients. Understanding the interactions between various forms of disadvantage allows for a more comprehensive legal strategy that accounts for the unique challenges faced by individuals with intersecting identities.

Moreover, intersectionality has informed legal advocacy by promoting collaborations and coalitions across different social justice movements. Recognizing the interconnected struggles of various marginalized groups has facilitated collective action and solidarity, leading to more effective advocacy efforts.

Critiques and Challenges

While intersectionality has been instrumental in advancing legal theories and practices, it is not without its critiques and challenges. Some argue that intersectionality can be overly complex and difficult to implement effectively in legal contexts. Critics also highlight the potential for the concept to be co-opted and diluted in ways that obscure the underlying power dynamics and structural inequalities it seeks to address.

Additionally, the application of intersectionality in legal settings may encounter resistance from entrenched legal norms and structures. Successfully integrating intersectionality into legal theories and practices requires ongoing efforts to challenge existing power dynamics, biases, and discriminatory practices.

Conclusion and Further Exploration

Intersectionality has significantly impacted legal theories, bringing attention to the complex and interconnected nature of discrimination and oppression. By recognizing the intersecting dimensions of identity, legal frameworks can better address the unique experiences of individuals with intersecting identities.

Further exploration of intersectionality in legal studies involves delving into specific legal disciplines, such as constitutional law, criminal law, or family law. It also includes examining the impact of intersectionality on policy-making, court decisions, and social justice movements. As legal scholars and practitioners continue to explore intersectionality, it promises to remain a vital tool for challenging systemic inequalities and promoting justice for all.

Resources for further exploration: - Crenshaw, Kimberlé. "Mapping the Margins: Intersectionality, Identity Politics, and Violence against Women of Color." Stanford Law Review 43, no. 6 (1991): 1241-1299. - Cho, Sumi, Kimberlé Crenshaw, and Leslie McCall, eds. "Toward a Field of Intersectionality Studies: Theory, Applications, and Praxis." Signs: Journal of Women in Culture and Society 38, no. 4 (2013): 785-810. - Harris, Angela P., ed. "The Intersectionality Controversy." In Sisterhood, Interrupted: From Radical Women to Girls Gone Wild, 103-119. New York: Palgrave Macmillan, 2007. - Tomlinson, Barbara. "Intersectionality as Buzzword: A Sociology of Science Perspective on What Makes a Feminist Theory Successful." Feminist Theory 18, no. 1 (2017): 67-85.

Emerging theories and their potential for revolutionizing legal studies

The field of legal studies is constantly evolving, and new theories are emerging that have the potential to revolutionize the way we understand and approach the law. In this section, we will explore some of these emerging theories and discuss their implications for legal studies.

Emancipatory Legal Theory

Emancipatory legal theory is a concept grounded in the belief that the law can be used as a tool to challenge and dismantle existing power structures and systems of oppression. It focuses on the empowerment of marginalized groups and seeks to bring about social justice and equality through legal means.

One prominent example of emancipatory legal theory is critical race theory, which examines how race intersects with law and shapes societal power dynamics.

This theory highlights the ways in which the legal system can perpetuate racial inequalities and provides a framework for addressing these injustices.

Another emerging theory is feminist legal theory, which explores how gender intersects with the law and aims to challenge gender-based discrimination. It examines the ways in which legal systems have historically reinforced patriarchal norms and advocates for legal reforms to promote gender equality.

Emancipatory legal theories have the potential to revolutionize legal studies by shifting the focus from traditional legal analysis to a more critical examination of the law's impact on marginalized communities. By centering the experiences of those who have been historically disadvantaged, these theories provide alternative perspectives that can lead to more just and equitable legal systems.

Law and Economics

Law and economics is an interdisciplinary field that applies economic principles to analyze legal issues. It seeks to understand how laws and legal structures impact economic behavior and outcomes. By examining the incentives created by legal rules and regulations, law and economics theorists propose efficient solutions to legal problems.

One influential theory in this field is the economic analysis of law, which posits that individuals act rationally and seek to maximize their own self-interest. This theory suggests that legal rules should be designed to align individual incentives with societal goals, leading to more efficient outcomes.

Another emerging theory in law and economics is behavioral economics, which takes into account the effects of cognitive biases and psychological factors on decision-making. This theory challenges the assumption of perfect rationality and suggests that legal rules should be designed to account for these cognitive limitations.

Law and economics theories have the potential to revolutionize legal studies by providing a framework for analyzing the economic impact of legal rules and policies. By incorporating economic insights into legal analysis, these theories can help policymakers make more informed decisions and promote economic efficiency in the legal system.

Law and Society

Law and society is an interdisciplinary field that examines the interaction between legal systems and broader social, cultural, and political contexts. It seeks to understand how legal rules and institutions are influenced by societal factors and, in turn, shape social behavior and norms.

One emerging theory in this field is the social construction of law, which posits that legal rules are not fixed or absolute but are socially constructed through ongoing processes of interpretation and negotiation. This theory challenges the notion of law as a fixed and objective entity and highlights the ways in which legal meanings and interpretations are shaped by social actors.

Another important theory in law and society is the new legal realism, which seeks to bridge the gap between legal theory and empirical research. It emphasizes the importance of studying law in action and examines how legal rules are applied and interpreted by judges, lawyers, and other legal actors.

Law and society theories have the potential to revolutionize legal studies by providing a more nuanced understanding of how legal rules operate in real-world contexts. By studying the social, cultural, and political factors that influence the law, these theories can help uncover hidden biases and power dynamics and promote more just and equitable legal systems.

Conclusion

The emerging theories discussed in this section have the potential to revolutionize legal studies by challenging traditional approaches and providing alternative perspectives. Emancipatory legal theories can help uncover and address systemic inequalities, while law and economics theories offer insights into the economic impact of legal rules. Law and society theories shed light on the social dynamics that shape and are shaped by legal systems.

As legal scholars and practitioners, it is crucial to engage with these emerging theories and incorporate their insights into our research and practice. By broadening our understanding of the law and its impact on society, we can contribute to the advancement of justice and equality.

Further exploration of these emerging theories can be done through extensive reading and research. Some recommended resources include:

- "Critical Race Theory: An Introduction" by Richard Delgado and Jean Stefancic
- "Feminist Legal Theory: Foundations" edited by Nancy Levit and Robert R.M. Verchick
- "An Introduction to Law and Economics" by A. Mitchell Polinsky and Steven Shavell

- "Law and Society" by Matthew Lippman
- "Legal Realism: Regaining a Naturalistic Science of Law" by Brian Leiter and Michael Sevel

Engaging with these theories and building upon them can contribute to the ongoing evolution of legal studies and help shape a more just and equitable future.

Case studies in legal revolution

The Civil Rights Movement and its Legal Impact

The Civil Rights Movement, which took place primarily in the United States during the 1950s and 1960s, was a significant social and political movement aimed at ensuring equal rights and eliminating racial segregation and discrimination. This movement had a profound impact on legal studies, leading to important legal advancements that continue to shape our understanding of justice and equality today.

Historical context of the Civil Rights Movement

To understand the legal impact of the Civil Rights Movement, it is essential to examine its historical context. During this period, racial segregation was deeply entrenched in American society, particularly in the Southern states, where Black individuals faced significant institutionalized discrimination and limited opportunities for advancement. Public facilities, such as schools, restaurants, and transportation, were strictly segregated, denying Black individuals access to the same resources and services enjoyed by white individuals.

Legal foundations of the Civil Rights Movement

The legal foundations of the Civil Rights Movement can be traced back to the Reconstruction Era Amendments to the United States Constitution, particularly the Thirteenth, Fourteenth, and Fifteenth Amendments. The Thirteenth Amendment abolished slavery, the Fourteenth Amendment granted equal protection under the law, and the Fifteenth Amendment prohibited racial discrimination in voting rights.

Despite these constitutional protections, racial segregation persisted through the Jim Crow laws enacted in many Southern states. These laws enforced racial segregation in public facilities and denied African Americans their basic civil rights.

It was in this context that the Civil Rights Movement emerged, seeking to challenge and overturn these discriminatory laws.

Key legal achievements of the Civil Rights Movement

The Civil Rights Movement utilized various legal strategies and advocacy efforts to combat racial discrimination and secure equal rights. Some of the key legal achievements of the movement include:

- **Brown v. Board of Education (1954):** This landmark Supreme Court case declared racial segregation in public schools unconstitutional, overturning the doctrine of "separate but equal" established by the earlier Plessy v. Ferguson case. The Court's ruling in Brown v. Board of Education marked a significant victory for the Civil Rights Movement and set a precedent for desegregating public facilities.

- **Civil Rights Act of 1964:** This sweeping federal legislation, signed into law by President Lyndon B. Johnson, outlawed racial segregation in public accommodations, prohibited discrimination in employment based on race, color, religion, sex, or national origin, and established the Equal Employment Opportunity Commission (EEOC) to enforce these provisions. The Civil Rights Act of 1964 was a major milestone in the fight against racial discrimination.

- **Voting Rights Act of 1965:** This legislation aimed to overcome barriers that prevented African Americans from exercising their right to vote. It banned racial discrimination in voting practices, such as literacy tests and poll taxes, and provided federal oversight of elections in jurisdictions with a history of discriminatory voting practices. The Voting Rights Act of 1965 played a pivotal role in promoting equal access to the ballot box.

These legal victories marked significant milestones in the Civil Rights Movement and led to tangible improvements in the lives of African Americans. They demonstrated the power of using legal avenues to challenge systemic injustice and served as catalysts for subsequent civil rights advancements.

Challenges and limitations

While the legal victories of the Civil Rights Movement were undeniably transformative, it is important to recognize the ongoing challenges and limitations in achieving full equality and justice. Despite legal victories, racial disparities persist in various aspects of society, including education, employment, criminal justice, and housing. Systemic racism continues to be a pervasive issue, demanding continued efforts to address structural inequalities.

Furthermore, legal change alone cannot eradicate deeply ingrained prejudices and discriminatory attitudes. Social and cultural changes are necessary to complement legal advancements and promote true equality. The Civil Rights Movement provides important lessons on the complementarity of legal reform and social activism in achieving lasting change.

Resources for further exploration

To delve deeper into the legal impact of the Civil Rights Movement, the following resources provide valuable insights:

- *The Civil Rights Movement: A Legal History* by Michael J. Klarman offers a comprehensive analysis of the legal strategies and key court cases that shaped the movement.

- *From Jim Crow to Civil Rights: The Supreme Court and the Struggle for Racial Equality* by Michael J. Klarman explores the role of the Supreme Court in advancing civil rights and dismantling racial segregation.

- The National Museum of African American History and Culture in Washington, D.C., provides exhibits and archives highlighting the legal aspects of the Civil Rights Movement.

These resources offer valuable perspectives on the legal, social, and political dimensions of the Civil Rights Movement, promoting a deeper understanding of the efforts and impact of this transformative period in history.

Conclusion

The Civil Rights Movement was a pivotal moment in legal studies, inspiring significant legal advancements in the fight against racial discrimination and for equal rights. Through landmark court cases and legislative achievements, the movement laid the groundwork for dismantling racial segregation and affirming the principle of equality under the law. However, the struggle for justice and equality continues, calling for ongoing efforts to address systemic racism and build a more just and equitable society. The legal impact of the Civil Rights Movement serves as a powerful reminder of the potential for transformative change through advocacy, litigation, and social activism.

The feminist movement and its influence on legal studies

The feminist movement has had a profound influence on legal studies, challenging long-held assumptions and advocating for gender equality within the legal system. This section explores the key contributions of the feminist movement to legal studies, including its impact on legal theory, case law, and legislative reforms.

Feminist legal theory

Feminist legal theory emerged as a response to the gender biases inherent in traditional legal concepts and frameworks. It seeks to analyze and critique the ways in which the law reinforces and perpetuates gender-based inequalities. Two prominent strands of feminist legal theory are liberal feminism and radical feminism.

Liberal feminism emphasizes equal treatment under the law and the removal of legal barriers that limit women's opportunities. It argues for the inclusion of women's perspectives in legal decision-making processes and the recognition of gender-based discrimination as a violation of constitutional rights. For example, through liberal feminism, the concept of "equal pay for equal work" gained legal traction, leading to laws and policies aimed at addressing the gender pay gap.

Radical feminism, on the other hand, challenges the foundations of legal systems by interrogating the power structures that underpin them. Radical feminists argue that the law serves to perpetuate patriarchy and gender inequality. They advocate for transformative changes in legal systems, such as reimagining the concept of consent in sexual assault laws and highlighting the systemic discrimination faced by marginalized groups of women.

Intersectionality, a concept developed within feminist legal theory, recognizes that gender intersects with other axes of oppression such as race, class, and sexuality. It underscores the importance of addressing the unique challenges faced by women who experience multiple forms of discrimination. Intersectional feminism has influenced legal studies by bringing attention to the ways in which gender intersects with other social identities and shaping legal analysis accordingly.

Feminist legal activism and case law

The feminist movement has been instrumental in driving legal activism and shaping landmark case law. By strategically using the legal system, feminists have challenged discriminatory laws, policies, and practices.

One significant example is the case of Roe v. Wade, which recognized a woman's constitutional right to have access to safe and legal abortion. This case marked a turning point in the feminist movement and established a legal precedent for reproductive rights. Feminist legal activism also played a crucial role in securing legal protections against workplace sexual harassment, as seen in cases like Meritor Savings Bank v. Vinson.

Furthermore, feminist legal scholars and activists have advocated for changes in family law, aiming to address gender disparities and promote gender equality within family structures. The feminist-inspired no-fault divorce laws, for instance, have played a pivotal role in allowing women to leave abusive marriages and gain financial independence.

Legislative reforms and policy changes

The feminist movement's influence extends beyond case law to legislative reforms and policy changes. Feminist activists and scholars have successfully pushed for the creation and amendment of laws that promote gender equality and protect women's rights.

For example, the Violence Against Women Act (VAWA) in the United States, passed in 1994, provides federal funding for programs that assist victims of domestic violence, sexual assault, and stalking. This legislation was a direct response to feminist advocacy, highlighting the need for comprehensive legal protections for survivors of gender-based violence.

Feminist activists have also campaigned for the adoption of affirmative action policies to address historic gender disparities. These policies seek to promote equal opportunities for women in education, employment, and public life. While affirmative action remains a contentious issue, it reflects feminist efforts to challenge structural barriers that impede women's progress.

Challenges and ongoing work

Despite the significant achievements of the feminist movement in legal studies, challenges persist. Gender bias and patriarchal norms continue to influence legal decision-making, and gaps in legal protections for marginalized women remain.

Feminist legal scholars and activists continue to work towards addressing these challenges. They advocate for the incorporation of gender perspectives in legal education, the diversification of the judiciary, and the establishment of specialized courts to deal with gender-based violence cases. Additionally, they call for greater sensitivity to intersectionality and the experiences of women from different backgrounds within legal scholarship and practice.

Conclusion

The feminist movement has had a transformative impact on legal studies, challenging traditional legal frameworks and advocating for gender equality. Feminist legal theory has provided new insights and critiques, while feminist legal activism has led to significant changes in case law and legislative reforms. Despite ongoing challenges, the feminist movement continues to shape legal studies by promoting inclusive and equitable approaches to justice. It invites students and scholars alike to critically examine the law through a lens of gender equality and justice.

For further exploration of this topic, the following resources are recommended: - MacKinnon, C. A. (1989). Toward a Feminist Theory of State. Harvard University Press. - Crenshaw, K. W. (1989). Demarginalizing the Intersection of Race and Sex: A Black Feminist Critique of Antidiscrimination Doctrine, Feminist Theory and Antiracist Politics. University of Chicago Legal Forum, 1989(1), 139–167. - Smart, C. (1989). Feminism and the Power of Law. Routledge.

LGBTQ+ rights and legal advancements

In recent years, there have been significant advancements in the legal recognition and protections of LGBTQ+ rights. This section explores the progress that has been made, the challenges that remain, and the potential future directions for LGBTQ+ legal studies.

Historical context of LGBTQ+ rights

The struggle for LGBTQ+ rights has a long and complex history. Throughout much of history, individuals who identified as lesbian, gay, bisexual, transgender, or queer faced widespread discrimination and persecution. Laws criminalizing same-sex relationships were common, and societal attitudes towards gender and sexuality were often oppressive.

However, over the past few decades, there has been a remarkable change in the legal landscape. The LGBTQ+ rights movement has gained momentum, leading to significant legal advancements that have transformed the lives of many.

Legal advancements in LGBTQ+ rights

There have been several key legal advancements in the recognition and protection of LGBTQ+ rights:

1. Decriminalization: Many countries have repealed laws that criminalized consensual same-sex relationships. This has been a crucial step towards ending legal discrimination against LGBTQ+ individuals.

2. Anti-discrimination laws: Numerous countries and jurisdictions have implemented legislation that prohibits discrimination based on sexual orientation and gender identity. These laws aim to ensure equal rights and opportunities for LGBTQ+ individuals in various areas, including employment, housing, and public accommodations.

3. Same-sex marriage: The legalization of same-sex marriage has been a significant milestone in the LGBTQ+ rights movement. Countries like the Netherlands, Canada, and the United States have recognized the right of same-sex couples to marry, granting them legal recognition and the associated rights and benefits.

4. Adoption and parenting rights: LGBTQ+ individuals and couples have fought for and secured the right to adopt and raise children. Laws have been enacted to ensure that sexual orientation or gender identity cannot be used as a basis for denying individuals the opportunity to become parents.

5. Transgender rights: Legal advancements have been made to protect the rights of transgender individuals. This includes legislation allowing for gender recognition and the ability to change legal documents, as well as protections against discrimination in healthcare, education, and employment.

Challenges and ongoing issues

While significant progress has been made, challenges and ongoing issues persist in relation to LGBTQ+ rights. Some of these challenges include:

1. Legal gaps and inconsistencies: Despite advancements, legal protections for LGBTQ+ individuals vary greatly between countries and jurisdictions. In some places, there is still a lack of comprehensive anti-discrimination legislation or legal recognition of same-sex relationships.

2. Violence and hate crimes: LGBTQ+ individuals continue to face violence and hate crimes based on their sexual orientation or gender identity. Addressing this issue requires strengthening legal frameworks and ensuring effective enforcement to protect the safety and well-being of LGBTQ+ individuals.

3. Transgender rights: While progress has been made in transgender rights, there are still significant challenges. Access to gender-affirming healthcare, legal recognition of non-binary and gender-diverse identities, and protection against discrimination in various areas of life remain ongoing issues.

4. Intersectionality: LGBTQ+ individuals may face multiple forms of discrimination and marginalization based on intersecting identities such as race, gender, and socioeconomic status. Legal studies need to adopt an intersectional lens to understand the unique challenges faced by individuals within the LGBTQ+ community and develop inclusive legal frameworks.

Future directions and emerging issues

As LGBTQ+ rights continue to evolve, new challenges and emerging issues require attention and research within legal studies. Some of these future directions include:

1. Global perspectives: There is a need for comparative legal studies to examine LGBTQ+ rights on a global scale. Understanding the legal frameworks and cultural contexts across different countries can inform strategies for advancing LGBTQ+ rights worldwide.

2. Transnational advocacy: Collaboration between LGBTQ+ activists, organizations, and legal scholars across borders can amplify the impact of advocacy efforts. Transnational advocacy can address issues such as criminalization of same-sex relationships, discrimination, and the protection of LGBTQ+ refugees and asylum seekers.

3. Non-discrimination protection for gender identity and expression: Many legal systems lack explicit protections specifically addressing discrimination based on gender identity or gender expression. Expanding legal frameworks to include these protections is crucial to ensure equal rights and opportunities for transgender and gender-diverse individuals.

4. Rights of LGBTQ+ youth: Focus on the rights of LGBTQ+ youth is essential, as they may face unique challenges related to education,

homelessness, and family acceptance. Exploring legal strategies to protect and empower LGBTQ+ youth is an important area for future research.

Resources and further exploration

The field of LGBTQ+ legal studies is rich with resources and avenues for further exploration. Some recommended resources include:

- Organizations: LGBTQ+ rights organizations such as Human Rights Campaign, Lambda Legal, and the International Lesbian, Gay, Bisexual, Trans, and Intersex Association (ILGA) provide valuable information and resources on legal issues and advocacy.
- Scholarly journals: Academic journals like the *Journal of Homosexuality*, *Law and Sexuality*, and the *Yale Journal of Law and Feminism* publish scholarly articles on LGBTQ+ legal studies and related topics.
- Legal cases: Examining landmark legal cases that have shaped LGBTQ+ rights, such as Obergefell v. Hodges in the United States or Goodridge v. Department of Public Health in Massachusetts, can deepen understanding of the legal issues involved.

Exploring the intersection of law, LGBTQ+ rights, and social change provides a unique opportunity to contribute to a more inclusive and equitable society. By addressing ongoing challenges and embracing emerging issues, legal studies can continue to play a crucial role in advancing LGBTQ+ rights and promoting justice for all.

Environmental justice and its legal implications

Environmental justice is a critical issue in today's society, as the impact of human activities on the environment becomes increasingly evident. It raises concerns about the fair distribution of environmental benefits and burdens within communities, with particular attention to the marginalized and vulnerable populations who often bear the brunt of environmental degradation.

Defining environmental justice

Environmental justice refers to the fair treatment and meaningful involvement of all people, regardless of their race, color, national origin, or income, in the development, implementation, and enforcement of environmental laws, regulations, and policies. It recognizes the importance of addressing the unequal distribution of environmental risks and benefits, especially in low-income communities and communities of color.

Legal frameworks for environmental justice

Various legal frameworks have been established to address environmental justice concerns. One key piece of legislation in the United States is the Civil Rights Act of 1964, which prohibits discrimination based on race, color, national origin, and gender. This legislation has been instrumental in addressing the disproportionate environmental burdens faced by minority communities.

Additionally, the National Environmental Policy Act (NEPA) requires federal agencies to consider the environmental impacts of their actions and ensure the involvement of affected communities in the decision-making process. It has been a powerful tool in promoting environmental justice by providing opportunities for public participation and inclusion.

Furthermore, the Environmental Protection Agency (EPA) has developed guidelines and policies to assist in addressing environmental justice concerns. For example, the EPA's Environmental Justice Small Grants Program aims to empower communities to address local environmental and public health concerns through community-based projects.

Challenges and obstacles to environmental justice

Despite the progress made in recognizing and addressing environmental justice issues, significant challenges remain. One key challenge is the lack of access to legal resources and information for affected communities, especially those with limited financial resources. This often hinders their ability to effectively engage in legal processes and advocate for their rights.

Another challenge is the burden of proof often placed on communities to demonstrate that they have been disproportionately impacted by environmental harms. This can be a daunting task, requiring extensive scientific evidence and resources that communities may not have access to.

Additionally, the complexity of environmental laws and regulations can make it difficult for communities to navigate the legal system and seek justice. Legal processes can be time-consuming and expensive, creating barriers for impacted communities to seek remedies for environmental injustices.

Case studies on environmental justice

To better understand the legal implications of environmental justice, let us explore two case studies:

Case Study 1: Flint Water Crisis

The Flint water crisis serves as a prominent example of environmental injustice. In 2014, the city of Flint, Michigan, switched its water source to the Flint River, resulting in high levels of lead contamination in the water supply. This crisis disproportionately impacted the predominantly African American population, highlighting the intersection of race and environmental harms.

Legal action was taken to address this environmental injustice. Lawsuits were filed against state and local officials, alleging negligence and violations of the Safe Drinking Water Act. These legal actions aimed to hold accountable those responsible for the crisis and seek compensation for the affected community.

Case Study 2: Standing Rock and the Dakota Access Pipeline

The Dakota Access Pipeline protests at the Standing Rock Indian Reservation in North Dakota brought attention to the environmental justice concerns faced by Indigenous communities. The pipeline threatened the reservation's water supply and sacred sites, raising concerns about tribal sovereignty and treaty rights.

Legal strategies were employed to challenge the construction of the pipeline. Litigation centered on violations of the National Historic Preservation Act, the National Environmental Policy Act, and the Clean Water Act. The legal battle drew national attention to the issue of environmental justice for Indigenous communities and highlighted the need for meaningful consultation and participation in decision-making processes.

Resources and further exploration

- Environmental Protection Agency (EPA) Office of Environmental Justice: provides information on environmental justice initiatives, resources, and grants.

- Center for International Environmental Law: offers research and publications on environmental justice and international environmental law.

- Environmental Justice Atlas: an interactive online database that maps and documents environmental justice struggles worldwide.

- "Dumping in Dixie: Race, Class, and Environmental Quality" by Robert D. Bullard: a book exploring the intersection of race, class, and environmental justice.

- "Environmental Justice: Law, Policy, and Regulation" by Clifford Rechtschaffen and Eileen Gauna: a comprehensive resource on environmental justice law and policy.

Exercises

1. Research a local environmental justice issue in your community and identify any legal actions or policies that have been implemented to address it. Discuss the effectiveness of these measures.

2. Debate the pros and cons of using litigation as a strategy to address environmental justice concerns. Consider the potential benefits and drawbacks of legal action in promoting environmental justice.

3. Design a community-based project aimed at addressing an environmental justice issue. Outline the steps you would take to engage the community, identify legal strategies, and seek appropriate resources.

By understanding the legal implications of environmental justice, we can work towards creating a more equitable and sustainable future. It requires the collaboration of legal scholars, policymakers, communities, and activists to ensure that environmental justice is a fundamental aspect of our legal systems. Together, we can strive for a world where all individuals have equal rights and access to a clean and healthy environment.

Global human rights initiatives and their legal significance

The protection and promotion of human rights have become crucial issues on the global stage. As societies have become more interconnected and interdependent, ensuring that individuals are afforded basic rights and liberties has emerged as a priority for nations worldwide. In this section, we will explore various global human rights initiatives and their legal significance, looking at the frameworks and mechanisms put in place to safeguard individual rights and hold violators accountable.

The Universal Declaration of Human Rights

One of the most significant global human rights initiatives is the Universal Declaration of Human Rights (UDHR). Adopted by the United Nations General Assembly in 1948, the UDHR sets out a comprehensive framework of fundamental human rights that should be universally protected. It encompasses civil, political, economic, social, and cultural rights, and provides a basis for international human rights law.

The UDHR has had a profound legal significance, serving as a foundation for subsequent human rights treaties, conventions, and national legislations. It has inspired and guided the development of international human rights norms, ensuring that governments uphold their obligations to respect, protect, and fulfill human rights for all individuals.

International Human Rights Treaties and Conventions

Building on the UDHR, several international treaties and conventions have been adopted to strengthen the legal protection of human rights. These binding agreements cover a wide range of human rights issues, such as racial discrimination, torture, women's rights, child rights, and the right to self-determination.

For example, the International Covenant on Civil and Political Rights (ICCPR) guarantees civil and political rights, including the right to life, freedom of speech, and the right to a fair trial. The International Covenant on Economic, Social and Cultural Rights (ICESCR) protects economic, social, and cultural rights, such as the right to work, education, and an adequate standard of living.

By ratifying these treaties, states commit themselves to upholding and implementing the rights enshrined in these instruments. Individuals can also invoke these treaties domestically, providing a legal framework for seeking redress when their rights are violated.

Regional Human Rights Systems

In addition to global initiatives, regional human rights systems play a crucial role in protecting and promoting human rights at the regional level. Regional organizations have established legal frameworks and institutions to address human rights violations within their respective jurisdictions.

For example, the European Convention on Human Rights (ECHR) establishes a regional human rights system for Europe. The Inter-American Court of Human Rights (IACHR) and the African Commission on Human and Peoples' Rights (ACHPR) oversee human rights protection in the Americas and Africa, respectively.

These regional systems complement global human rights initiatives by addressing region-specific challenges and facilitating accountability for human rights violations. They provide avenues for individuals to file complaints and seek remedies at the regional level when domestic legal remedies are exhausted.

Non-governmental Organizations (NGOs) and Human Rights Advocacy

Non-governmental organizations (NGOs) play a vital role in advancing human rights globally. These organizations monitor human rights situations, conduct research, provide legal assistance, and advocate for the protection of human rights.

Human rights NGOs work alongside states and international bodies to shed light on human rights abuses, push for legal reforms, and hold governments accountable. They serve as a voice for marginalized communities and provide support to individuals who have suffered human rights violations.

Prominent human rights NGOs include Amnesty International, Human Rights Watch, and the International Federation for Human Rights (FIDH). These organizations, among others, initiate campaigns, carry out fact-finding missions, and mobilize public support to address human rights challenges worldwide.

Challenges and Future Directions

Despite the progress made in global human rights initiatives, significant challenges remain. Some states fail to uphold their human rights obligations, leading to ongoing violations and abuses. The enforcement mechanisms of international and regional human rights systems can also be limited by political considerations or lack of resources.

Moreover, emerging global issues, such as climate change and technological advancements, pose new challenges to human rights protection. Ensuring that human rights frameworks adapt to these evolving challenges and remain relevant is crucial.

In the future, there is a need for continued efforts to strengthen the implementation of human rights standards at all levels. This includes raising awareness, promoting education on human rights, fostering cooperation between states and NGOs, and enhancing accountability mechanisms.

By actively participating in global human rights initiatives, individuals can contribute to shaping a future where the dignity and rights of all people are respected, protected, and fulfilled. It is through collective action and legal advocacy that the vision of a just and equitable global society can be realized.

Further Resources

- United Nations Human Rights: `https://www.ohchr.org/EN/Pages/Home.aspx`
- Human Rights Watch: `https://www.hrw.org/`

- Amnesty International: `https://www.amnesty.org/`
- International Federation for Human Rights (FIDH): `https://www.fidh.org/`
- European Court of Human Rights: `https://www.echr.coe.int/`
- Inter-American Court of Human Rights: `https://www.corteidh.or.cr/`
- African Commission on Human and Peoples' Rights: `https://www.achpr.org/`

Discussion Questions

1. Choose a specific human rights treaty or convention and explain its significance in addressing a particular human rights issue.

2. How do regional human rights systems complement global initiatives? Provide examples of regional human rights bodies and the impact they have had in their respective regions.

3. Investigate the work of a human rights NGO and discuss their approach to promoting and protecting human rights. Analyze the challenges they face in their advocacy efforts.

4. What are the major obstacles to the effective implementation of human rights standards globally? Suggest strategies to address these obstacles and enhance compliance with human rights obligations.

5. Explore a contemporary human rights issue and discuss how advancements in technology and communication can be utilized to address the issue effectively. Consider ethical implications and potential challenges.

Exploration Exercise

Select a specific human rights issue (e.g., refugee rights, freedom of expression, gender equality) and research recent cases or developments related to this issue. Examine the legal significance of these cases and their impact on human rights protection. Identify any gaps or challenges that still need to be addressed. Present your findings in the form of a short report or presentation, highlighting the practical implications for individuals and communities affected by the issue.

Chapter 2: Practical Techniques in Legal Studies

Legal research methodologies

Introduction to Legal Research

In the field of legal studies, the ability to conduct thorough and effective legal research is of utmost importance. Legal research involves the process of finding and analyzing legal sources in order to address specific legal issues and answer legal questions. Whether you are a law student, a legal professional, or simply interested in understanding the law, developing strong legal research skills is essential for success. In this section, we will explore the fundamentals of legal research, including its importance, primary sources of law, secondary sources of law, case law research techniques, and statutory research techniques.

The Importance of Legal Research

Legal research serves as the foundation for legal analysis and decision-making. It enables individuals to understand and apply the law in various contexts, such as drafting legal documents, providing legal advice, preparing for litigation, or advocating for legal reform. Without proper legal research, legal professionals would struggle to effectively represent their clients and uphold justice. Additionally, legal research plays a crucial role in shaping legal scholarship, influencing legal theories, and promoting the development of the law itself.

Primary Sources of Law

Primary sources of law are the official documents and materials that establish the law. They include constitutions, statutes, regulations, and case law. Understanding how to navigate and use primary sources of law is essential to conduct comprehensive legal research.

Constitutions: A constitution is the supreme law of a country or a state. It provides the framework for the government and outlines the fundamental rights and duties of citizens. Legal researchers analyze constitutional provisions to interpret and apply the law.

Statutes: Statutes, also known as legislation or acts of law, are laws enacted by legislative bodies such as Congress or state legislatures. Statutes cover a wide range of legal issues and are the primary source of law in many jurisdictions. Researchers must know how to locate and interpret statutes relevant to their research questions.

Regulations: Regulations are rules and standards created by administrative agencies to implement and enforce statutes. Researchers should be aware of the specific regulations that apply to their legal issues, as these regulations often provide additional details and guidance.

Case Law: Case law consists of judicial decisions issued by courts. It interprets and applies statutes, constitutions, and regulations to specific fact patterns. Researchers must understand how to find and analyze relevant case law to support their legal arguments or understand legal precedents.

Secondary Sources of Law

Secondary sources of law are resources that summarize, explain, analyze, or interpret primary sources of law. These sources help legal researchers gain a deeper understanding of legal principles, find additional authorities, and identify relevant legal arguments. Some common secondary sources of law include:

Legal Treatises: Legal treatises are in-depth scholarly works that analyze and explain a specific area of law. They provide comprehensive coverage of legal principles, theories, and case law in a particular field.

Legal Journals: Legal journals publish articles written by legal scholars, practitioners, and judges. These articles offer insights, analysis, and critical discussions on current legal issues.

Legal Databases: Legal databases, such as Westlaw and LexisNexis, provide access to a vast collection of legal materials, including case law, statutes, regulations, and secondary sources. Researchers can use sophisticated search tools to find relevant legal information efficiently.

Legal Encyclopedias: Legal encyclopedias provide broad summaries of legal topics, offering explanations, definitions, and references to primary sources. They serve as a useful starting point for legal research and provide references for further exploration.

Case Law Research Techniques

When conducting case law research, researchers need to follow specific techniques to find relevant cases and extract meaningful information from them. Here are some key steps involved in case law research:

Identification of Relevant Jurisdiction: Determine the jurisdiction(s) relevant to your research question. Different jurisdictions have different legal principles and case law, so you need to narrow down your search accordingly.

Keyword Search: Identify the keywords or key phrases that are relevant to your research question. Using these keywords, search in legal databases or search engines to find relevant cases. Be creative in choosing your keywords to yield more accurate results.

Shepardize or KeyCite: After identifying a relevant case, Shepardize it (using Shepard's Citations) or KeyCite it (using Westlaw's KeyCite feature). These tools allow you to check if the case has been subsequently overturned, overruled, or questioned in other cases.

Analyze the Case: Read the selected case thoroughly and identify its key elements, such as the facts, legal issues, reasoning, and holding. Look for relevant legal principles, arguments, or interpretations that support your research question.

Find Similar Cases: Use the identified case as a starting point to find similar cases. Legal databases often provide options to find related cases based on key factors such as legal issues, jurisdiction, or procedural posture.

Statutory Research Techniques

Statutory research involves finding and interpreting statutes relevant to a legal issue. To effectively conduct statutory research, consider the following techniques:

Identify the Applicable Jurisdiction: Determine which jurisdiction's statutes are applicable to your research question. It could be federal, state, or local statutes, depending on the scope and context of the issue.

Key Sections and Definitions: Identify the key sections or provisions of the statute that address your research question. Pay attention to how the statute defines relevant terms or phrases, as these definitions may impact its interpretation.

Legislative History: If necessary, review the legislative history of the statute. Legislative history includes committee reports, floor debates, and other documents that provide insight into the lawmakers' intent behind the statute.

Consider Amendments and Modifications: Check if the statute has been amended, modified, or repealed by subsequent legislation. Also, consider any relevant court decisions that have interpreted or applied the statute.

Cross-Reference Other Statutes: Some statutes may cross-reference or refer to other statutes. Make sure to follow these references and consider the interplay between related statutes.

Tips and Tricks

- Take advantage of advanced search features provided by legal research databases to effectively filter and narrow down your search results. - Keep track of your research process by maintaining a research log or using citation management software. - Use legal research guides and tutorials provided by libraries, legal associations, or online resources to enhance your research skills. - When analyzing statutes or case law, always consider alternative interpretations and conflicting authorities to develop a well-rounded understanding of the legal issue. - Engage in discussions with colleagues, professors, or legal professionals to gain different perspectives and insights into your research.

Resources for Further Exploration

To deepen your understanding of legal research, consider exploring the following resources:

- "Legal Research in a Nutshell" by Kent C. Olson - "Legal Research, Analysis, and Writing" by William H. Putman - "Fundamentals of Legal Research" by Steven M. Barkan, Roy M. Mersky, and Donald J. Dunn - Online legal research databases such as Westlaw, LexisNexis, and Bloomberg Law, which offer research guides, tutorials, and webinars.

Remember, effective legal research skills are acquired through practice and exposure to real-world legal issues. Embrace the research process, be persistent, and continuously improve your research techniques to become a proficient legal researcher.

Primary Sources of Law

In understanding the field of legal studies, it is important to have a firm grasp of the primary sources of law. These are the fundamental documents and instruments that establish, interpret, and enforce the laws of a given jurisdiction. Primary sources of law serve as the foundation upon which legal principles and rules are built, and they provide the authoritative basis for legal decision-making.

Constitutions

Constitutions are arguably the most significant primary sources of law. They represent the supreme law of a nation or state and outline the fundamental principles and rights upon which the legal system is built. Constitutions establish the structure of the government, delineate the powers and limitations of each branch, and provide a framework for the protection of individual rights.

For example, the United States Constitution is the bedrock of the American legal system. It outlines the organization and powers of the federal government, protects the fundamental rights of individuals, and sets the parameters within which all other laws must operate. Constitutional law plays a crucial role in shaping legal systems and often serves as a benchmark for evaluating the constitutionality of other laws.

Statutes and Legislation

Statutes, also known as legislation or acts, are laws enacted by the legislative branch of government. They are a primary source of law that covers a wide range of issues and governs various aspects of society. Statutory law originates from the legislative process, where proposals are introduced, debated, and voted upon by elected representatives.

Statutes can be enacted at the federal, state, or local level, depending on the jurisdiction. They can address issues such as criminal offenses, contract law, property rights, taxation, and many others. Once a statute is enacted, it becomes binding and enforceable.

For instance, the Civil Rights Act of 1964 in the United States is a federal statute that prohibits discrimination based on race, color, religion, sex, and national origin. This landmark legislation has had a profound impact on promoting equality and combating lawful discrimination in various areas of public life, including employment, education, and public accommodations.

Case Law

Case law, also referred to as common law or judicial precedent, comprises the decisions and rulings of courts. It is an essential primary source of law, particularly in jurisdictions that follow the common law legal tradition. Case law is based on the principle of stare decisis, which means that courts are bound by the precedents set by higher courts and must apply similar reasoning to cases with similar facts.

When courts decide cases, they interpret and apply statutory law, constitutional provisions, and other legal principles to the specific circumstances of the case. These decisions become part of the body of case law, which forms a binding authority for future cases. Case law allows for the evolution of legal principles and the adaptation of the law to changing societal norms and circumstances.

For example, the landmark case of Brown v. Board of Education (1954) in the United States Supreme Court declared racial segregation in public schools unconstitutional. This decision overturned the "separate but equal" doctrine established in the case of Plessy v. Ferguson (1896) and marked a significant milestone in the civil rights movement.

Administrative Regulations

Administrative regulations are another important primary source of law, particularly in the realm of administrative law. Administrative agencies, empowered by legislative bodies, promulgate regulations to implement and enforce laws within their area of expertise. These regulations have the force of law and provide guidance and specific requirements within the context of a particular industry or sector.

Regulations are typically formulated through a process that involves public notice, comment, and review. They address various issues such as public health, safety standards, environmental protection, employment regulations, and more. Violation of administrative regulations may result in penalties, fines, or other legal consequences.

An example of administrative regulation is the Occupational Safety and Health Administration (OSHA) regulations in the United States. These regulations establish safety standards and guidelines to protect the health and well-being of workers in various industries. Employers are legally obligated to comply with these regulations to ensure a safe working environment.

Treaties and International Agreements

Treaties and international agreements are primary sources of law in the realm of international law. They are formal agreements between nations or international organizations that establish rights, obligations, and principles governing their relations. Treaties can cover a wide range of issues, including human rights, trade, environmental protection, and diplomatic relations.

Once ratified or acceded to by the participating parties, treaties become legally binding and enforceable. They are often incorporated into domestic legal systems through legislation or other means, allowing individuals, businesses, and governments to rely on them in legal disputes or actions.

An illustrative example is the United Nations Convention on the Rights of the Child (UNCRC), which sets out the civil, political, economic, social, and cultural rights of children. By ratifying the UNCRC, nations commit to ensuring the protection, development, and well-being of children within their jurisdiction.

Conclusion

Understanding the primary sources of law is crucial to comprehending the legal landscape and functioning effectively within it. Constitutions, statutes, case law, administrative regulations, and treaties form the backbone of legal systems, providing guidance, interpretation, and enforcement of laws. Each source of law plays a distinct role in shaping legal principles, establishing rights, and ensuring justice and fairness in society.

To deepen your understanding of primary sources of law, it is valuable to consult legal databases, legal scholars, and authoritative legal texts. Additionally, analyzing landmark cases, studying historical legal documents, and engaging in legal research methodologies can help sharpen your skills in navigating primary sources of law. Remember, a robust understanding of primary sources lays the groundwork for a successful career in legal studies.

Secondary sources of law

In legal studies, secondary sources of law play a crucial role in providing interpretive and explanatory material that helps to understand and apply the law. While primary sources of law, such as statutes and case law, represent the actual law itself, secondary sources offer analysis, commentary, and scholarly perspectives on the law. These sources are created by legal scholars, practitioners, and experts in specific fields and are essential tools for legal research and writing.

Definition and purpose of secondary sources

Secondary sources of law encompass a wide range of materials that provide legal analysis and commentary. These sources include legal treatises, law review articles, legal encyclopedias, annotated codes, and legal dictionaries. Their main purpose is to assist legal professionals and scholars in interpreting and understanding the law, as well as to provide guidance on how to apply it in real-world situations.

Unlike primary sources, secondary sources are not binding authority in a legal sense. However, they are highly influential and can greatly influence legal arguments and decision-making. They often provide historical context, theoretical frameworks, and practical guidance that can inform legal analysis and reasoning.

Types of secondary sources

There are several types of secondary sources that legal researchers commonly rely on. Let's explore some of the most significant ones:

1. **Legal treatises:** These are comprehensive scholarly books that delve into specific areas of law. Treatises provide in-depth analysis, explanations of legal principles, and practical guidance. They are often written by recognized experts in their respective fields and are considered authoritative sources.

2. **Law review articles:** Published in specialized legal journals, law review articles offer critical analysis and commentary on legal topics. These articles are typically written by legal scholars, practitioners, and students. They provide a platform for exploring emerging legal issues, debating legal theories, and discussing recent developments in the law.

3. **Legal encyclopedias:** Legal encyclopedias provide comprehensive overviews of legal topics, covering a wide range of legal principles and concepts. They offer concise explanations, definitions, and cross-references to relevant primary sources. Legal encyclopedias are valuable resources for gaining a general understanding of a specific area of law.

4. **Annotated codes:** Annotated codes are compilations of statutory law that include additional commentary and references to case law and secondary sources. They provide valuable insights into legislative intent, historical development, and judicial interpretation of statutes. Annotated codes are particularly useful when conducting statutory research.

5. **Legal dictionaries:** Legal dictionaries provide definitions and explanations of legal terms and phrases. They help clarify legal terminology and promote consistent understanding and usage of legal language. Legal dictionaries are indispensable tools for legal research and writing.

Using secondary sources in legal research

When conducting legal research, it is essential to use secondary sources effectively. Here are some tips for using secondary sources:

- **Understanding the hierarchy of sources:** Knowing the hierarchy of sources is crucial for legal research. Primary sources, such as statutes and case law, hold more weight than secondary sources. While secondary sources are not binding authority, they can provide valuable insights and persuasive arguments.

- **Identifying authoritative sources:** Look for secondary sources that are authored by recognized experts or institutions with credibility in the legal field. Peer-reviewed articles, well-regarded treatises, and publications from reputable publishers are typically considered authoritative sources.
- **Checking for currency and relevance:** Ensure that the secondary sources you rely on are up-to-date and address the specific legal issue you are researching. The law is constantly evolving, so it is critical to consult recent publications that accurately reflect the current state of the law.
- **Using secondary sources for context and analysis:** Secondary sources provide valuable context, analysis, and explanations that can aid in understanding complex legal issues. They can offer alternative viewpoints, highlight emerging trends, and provide historical perspectives that can strengthen legal arguments.
- **Citing secondary sources appropriately:** When referencing secondary sources in legal writing, proper citation is essential. Follow the citation guidelines specified by legal authorities, such as The Bluebook or the relevant citation style guide. Accurate citation ensures credibility and allows readers to locate and verify your sources.

Example: Using secondary sources in a legal research project

To illustrate the importance of secondary sources in legal research, let's consider a hypothetical scenario. Imagine you are conducting research on the constitutionality of a recently passed law related to freedom of speech in a democratic country.

In this research project, you might start by consulting legal encyclopedias to gain a general understanding of constitutional law principles and freedom of speech jurisprudence. The encyclopedia entries can provide key definitions, historical context, and summaries of relevant Supreme Court decisions.

Next, you could refer to legal treatises written by renowned constitutional law experts. These treatises would offer more in-depth analysis of freedom of speech issues, exploring various theories, approaches, and interpretive methods. They may also discuss the impact of recent legal developments or emerging technologies on freedom of speech rights.

You might then turn to law review articles to explore recent scholarly debates on freedom of speech and its limits. These articles can help you understand different perspectives, arguments, and legal theories related to the constitutionality of the law in question. They may also provide insights into the social and political implications of restricting or expanding freedom of speech rights.

Finally, you might consult annotated codes to analyze relevant constitutional provisions and statutes related to freedom of speech. The annotations, which include references to case law and secondary sources, can help you understand how courts have interpreted and applied these provisions in previous cases.

By utilizing a combination of these secondary sources, you would be able to gather a comprehensive understanding of the legal principles and scholarly debates surrounding freedom of speech. This knowledge would form the foundation for your legal analysis, enabling you to present a well-rounded argument in your research project.

Further resources for secondary source research

- *Legal Research in a Nutshell* by Morris L. Cohen and Kent C. Olson: This book provides a comprehensive guide to legal research techniques, including the effective use of secondary sources.

- *The Bluebook: A Uniform System of Citation* by the Harvard Law Review Association: The Bluebook is the accepted authority for legal citation in the United States. It provides detailed guidelines for properly citing secondary sources.

- Legal databases and online libraries: Platforms such as Westlaw, LexisNexis, and HeinOnline offer extensive collections of legal treatises, law review articles, and other secondary sources. These databases can be invaluable resources for legal research.

- Legal research guides and tutorials: Many universities and law schools provide online research guides and tutorials that explain the use of secondary sources in legal research. These resources offer step-by-step instructions and tips for utilizing secondary sources effectively.

Remember to always critically evaluate your sources and consult multiple secondary sources to ensure a comprehensive and well-informed understanding of the law. Secondary sources are powerful tools that can enrich your legal research, deepen your knowledge, and enhance your ability to analyze complex legal issues.

Exercises

1. Identify a legal treatise or law review article that analyzes a recent Supreme Court decision. Summarize the main arguments and conclusions of the author and critically evaluate the analysis presented.

2. Choose a specific area of law (e.g., intellectual property, criminal law, environmental law) and locate a comprehensive legal encyclopedia entry that provides an overview of that area. Note the key concepts, historical developments, and significant cases discussed in the entry.

3. Locate an annotated code relevant to your jurisdiction. Identify a specific statute and review its annotations, including references to case law and secondary sources. Determine how these annotations can help in interpreting and applying the statute.

4. Select a legal term or concept related to your area of interest. Consult a legal dictionary to find its definition and any additional explanations or notes provided. Use the definition to create a concise explanation of the term in your own words.

These exercises are designed to strengthen your research skills and deepen your understanding of secondary sources in legal studies.

Case law research techniques

In legal studies, case law research is a critical component of understanding the development, interpretation, and application of laws. Case law refers to the body of legal decisions made by judges in various courts, which establishes legal principles and precedents. This section will discuss the techniques and methods involved in conducting effective case law research.

Understanding the hierarchy of courts

One of the first steps in case law research is understanding the hierarchy of courts within a legal system. Different jurisdictions may have varying court structures, but generally, there are trial courts, appellate courts, and supreme courts. It is essential to identify the relevant court(s) for the legal issue under investigation to ensure accurate and comprehensive research.

Identifying authoritative sources

Once the relevant court(s) have been determined, the next step is to identify authoritative sources of case law. These sources typically include official court reports, which contain written judgments and decisions of judges. It is crucial to consult the most current and up-to-date versions of these sources to ensure accuracy.

In addition to official court reports, there are also commercially published law reports that compile and analyze selected cases from different jurisdictions. These publications often provide additional commentary, annotations, and cross-references, making them valuable resources for case law research.

Using legal databases and online resources

With the advancement of technology, legal databases and online resources have become indispensable tools for case law research. These platforms provide easy access to a vast collection of court judgments and decisions. Some popular legal databases include LexisNexis, Westlaw, and HeinOnline.

When utilizing legal databases, it is essential to use effective search techniques to retrieve relevant cases. Boolean operators (e.g., AND, OR, NOT) can be used to refine search queries, while advanced search features like proximity searching and field-specific searching can help narrow down results.

It is also worth noting that online resources, such as official court websites, might provide free access to selected case law. These resources can be helpful when cross-referencing or verifying information found in other sources.

Reading and analyzing cases

Once relevant cases have been identified, the next step is to thoroughly read and analyze them. This process involves understanding the facts, issues, reasoning, and legal principles outlined in the judgment. It is crucial to pay attention to the ratio decidendi (the legal principle on which the decision is based) and obiter dicta (other statements by the judge that are not essential to the decision).

To facilitate analysis, it can be helpful to create case summaries or briefs that capture the essential elements of each case. These summaries should include relevant facts, issues, holdings, and any significant dissenting opinions. The use of annotation techniques, such as highlighting, underlining, or margin notes, can aid in organizing and retrieving information during further research.

Identifying and applying legal precedents

A key aspect of case law research is the identification and application of legal precedents. Precedents refer to previous court decisions that establish binding principles applicable to similar or related legal issues. By examining precedents, legal researchers can understand how courts have interpreted and applied the law in specific contexts.

When identifying legal precedents, it is crucial to consider the hierarchy of courts. Generally, decisions from higher courts have more persuasive authority than those from lower courts. However, it is essential to evaluate the jurisdictional relevance and the persuasive value of each precedent, as legal systems may vary in their treatment of precedents.

When applying legal precedents to a current case, it is necessary to analyze the facts and legal principles involved and consider any distinguishing factors that may affect the applicability of the precedent. Legal researchers must also be aware of any subsequent overruling or distinguishing of a precedent, as the law is not static, and court decisions may evolve over time.

Keeping up with updates and developments

Case law is constantly evolving, and it is crucial for legal researchers to keep up with updates and developments. Courts may issue new judgments that modify or clarify existing legal principles, and these developments can significantly impact the interpretation and application of the law.

Legal researchers must stay abreast of new case law through various means, including subscribing to legal newsletters, following legal blogs, attending conferences or seminars, and monitoring updates from legal databases or online resources. These measures ensure that the research remains current, accurate, and reflective of the most recent legal interpretations.

Ethical considerations

Lastly, it is essential to highlight the ethical considerations involved in case law research. Legal researchers have a responsibility to cite and reference cases accurately and honestly, giving credit to the original authors and acknowledging the legal authorities correctly. Plagiarism and misrepresentation of case law are serious ethical infractions that can undermine the integrity of legal research and potentially lead to legal consequences.

Additionally, legal researchers must be mindful of ethical guidelines regarding the use of personal information present in judgments. Privacy considerations and confidentiality rules apply to both the parties involved in a case and any individuals referenced in the judgment. Researchers must handle and cite such information responsibly, ensuring that privacy rights are respected.

Resources for further exploration

Case law research is a vast and intricate process, and this section only scratches the surface. For further exploration, the following resources can provide more in-depth knowledge and guidance:

- *Legal Research and Writing* by William H. Putman
- *Case Analysis and Fundamentals of Legal Writing* by William P. Statsky
- *Legal Research in a Nutshell* by Morris L. Cohen, Kent C. Olson, and Robert C. Berring
- Law journals and legal articles focusing on case law research techniques
- Online tutorials and webinars offered by legal research platforms
- Research guides and materials provided by law schools and libraries

By exploring these resources, legal researchers can enhance their understanding of case law research techniques and improve their ability to navigate the complex world of legal precedents.

Statutory Research Techniques

In legal studies, statutory research refers to the process of examining and analyzing statutes or enactments passed by legislative bodies, such as national or state governments. Statutory law is a vital source of legal authority and plays a significant role in shaping the legal landscape. This section will provide an overview of statutory research techniques, including the steps involved, the resources available, and the strategies employed to effectively navigate through statutory law.

Understanding Statutory Law

Before diving into the research process, it is essential to grasp the fundamentals of statutory law. Statutory law consists of written laws enacted by a legislative body. These laws are often organized into codes or statutes, which can vary depending on the jurisdiction. Understanding the structure and format of statutory codes is crucial for efficient research.

Statutes can be broadly categorized into public and private laws. Public laws pertain to matters of public concern, such as criminal offenses, taxation, or constitutional rights. Private laws, on the other hand, deal with individual or private interests, such as contracts or property rights. Familiarizing yourself with the different types of statutes will help you narrow down your search when conducting statutory research.

Steps in Statutory Research

Effective statutory research involves a systematic approach to ensure thoroughness and accuracy. By following these steps, you can streamline your research process and retrieve the most relevant and up-to-date information:

Step 1: Identify the Jurisdiction Statutory law varies across jurisdictions, so the first step is to determine the relevant jurisdiction or jurisdictions for your research. Depending on the issue at hand, you may need to examine statutes at the federal, state, or municipal level.

Step 2: Locate the Applicable Statute Once you have identified the jurisdiction, locate the specific statute or code relevant to your research topic. Statutory codes are typically organized by subject matter and sequentially numbered. Utilize online legal databases, law libraries, or official government websites to access the statutes.

Step 3: Analyze the Statutory Language Carefully examine the language used in the statute. Pay attention to definitions, key provisions, exceptions, and any cross-references to other statutes. Understanding the precise wording of the law is crucial for accurate interpretation and application.

Step 4: Determine the Legislative Intent To gain deeper insights into the intended scope and purpose of the statute, review any accompanying legislative history. Legislative history includes records of legislative debates, committee reports, and other documents related to the statute's enactment. This helps interpret the law in light of the legislature's intent.

Step 5: Research Case Law and Secondary Sources To fully comprehend the application and interpretation of the statute, consult relevant case law and secondary sources. Case law refers to court decisions that have interpreted and applied the statute, providing valuable insights into its meaning and scope. Secondary sources, such as legal treatises, law journals, or annotations, offer analysis and commentary on the statute.

Step 6: Update and Verify the Statute Statutory law may undergo changes over time due to subsequent amendments, legislative repeals, or judicial decisions.

It is crucial to ensure that the statute you are relying on is current and has not been modified or invalidated. Check for updates and verify its validity through reliable legal databases or official government sources.

Resources for Statutory Research

Numerous resources are available to aid in statutory research, both in print and online. Here are some key resources to consider:

1. **Legal Databases and Online Platforms:** Online legal databases such as Westlaw, LexisNexis, or Bloomberg Law provide comprehensive collections of statutes from various jurisdictions. These databases offer advanced search capabilities, annotations, and links to related cases, enabling efficient research.
2. **Official Government Websites:** Government websites, such as the U.S. Government Publishing Office or official state legislative websites, provide free access to statutory codes and related legislative materials. These websites can be a valuable resource for accessing current and authoritative statutes.
3. **Law Libraries:** Law libraries house extensive collections of legal materials, including statutory codes, case reporters, and legal treatises. Librarians can provide guidance and assistance in navigating through these resources effectively.

Tricks and Caveats

1. **Use Boolean Operators and Keyword Searching:** When conducting online statutory research, utilize advanced search functions by employing Boolean operators (AND, OR, NOT) and utilizing keyword searching techniques. This allows for more precise and targeted search results.
2. **Check for Annotations and Cross-References:** Statutory codes often include annotations or references to other statutes or secondary sources. These annotations can provide additional context, interpretations, or explanations that may impact your research. Always review the annotations and cross-references to gain a comprehensive understanding of the law.

Example Scenario

To illustrate the application of statutory research techniques, let's consider a scenario. Suppose you are researching the legality of online gambling in a specific U.S. state.

Step 1: Identify the Jurisdiction: Determine the relevant state jurisdiction where the online gambling issue arises.

Step 2: Locate the Applicable Statute: Access the state's statutory code related to gambling or gaming regulation.

Step 3: Analyze the Statutory Language: Examine the specific provisions within the gambling statute to determine if the law explicitly addresses online gambling.

Step 4: Determine the Legislative Intent: Refer to the legislative history associated with the gambling statute to understand the lawmakers' intent behind the law's creation.

Step 5: Research Case Law and Secondary Sources: Investigate any relevant court decisions or secondary sources that interpret and apply the gambling statute in the context of online gambling.

Step 6: Update and Verify the Statute: Check for any recent amendments or judicial decisions that may impact the current validity and interpretation of the gambling law.

Conclusion

Statutory research techniques are crucial in legal studies to understand and apply the laws enacted by legislative bodies. Following a systematic approach, utilizing relevant resources, and staying updated on changes and interpretations are key to effective statutory research. By mastering these techniques, legal professionals are better equipped to navigate through statutory law and contribute valuable insights to the field.

Legal writing and analysis

Overview of legal writing styles and formats

Legal writing is a specialized form of communication that requires clarity, precision, and adherence to specific conventions. In this section, we will explore the various styles and formats commonly used in legal writing. Understanding these styles and formats is essential for effectively conveying legal concepts and arguments.

Formal language and tone

Legal writing is characterized by its use of formal language and a professional tone. The use of precise and unambiguous terminology is crucial to ensure clarity and minimize misinterpretation. Legal documents should avoid colloquialisms, slang, and informal expressions.

Organization and structure

Legal writing typically follows a structured format to facilitate understanding and logical flow. The most common organizational structures include:

1. **IRAC (Issue, Rule, Application, Conclusion)**: This format is widely used in legal analysis. It involves identifying the legal issue, stating the applicable rule, applying the rule to the facts, and concluding with a reasoned decision.

2. **CREAC (Conclusion, Rule, Explanation, Application, Conclusion)**: This format is similar to IRAC but includes an additional explanation section. It is commonly used in persuasive legal writing, such as briefs and motions.

3. **Chronological order:** In some legal documents, such as contracts, a chronological order may be more appropriate. This format presents the information in the order events occurred or the contract provisions are arranged.

Citations and references

Legal writing heavily relies on citations to support arguments and demonstrate the legal basis for a claim. The Bluebook, a widely recognized citation style guide, provides rules for citing legal authorities accurately. Proper citation includes referencing the specific case, statute, regulation, or secondary sources relied upon in the legal document.

Plain language principles

In recent years, there has been a movement towards using plain language in legal writing to improve accessibility and comprehension. Plain language aims to simplify legal terminology, sentence structure, and overall readability without sacrificing accuracy or precision. It helps ensure that legal documents can be understood by a diverse audience, including non-lawyers.

Formatting and grammar

Consistency in formatting and grammar is critical in legal writing. Documents should be organized using headings, subheadings, and numbered paragraphs for ease of reference. Additionally, punctuation, grammar, and spelling should adhere to established rules of English composition.

Clarity and conciseness

Legal writing values clarity and conciseness. It is essential to express complex legal concepts in a straightforward and succinct manner. Long, convoluted sentences should be avoided, and unnecessary jargon or legalese should be eliminated whenever possible.

Avoiding bias and prejudice

Legal writing should be free from bias, prejudice, or discriminatory language. It is important to use inclusive language that respects all individuals and maintains professional and ethical standards.

Resources and tools

There are several resources and tools available to assist legal writers in improving their writing skills and adhering to established conventions. These include:

- **Style guides:** The Bluebook, the Chicago Manual of Style, and the APA Publication Manual provide comprehensive guidance on legal citation and writing styles.
- **Writing courses and workshops:** Many law schools and professional organizations offer writing courses and workshops specifically tailored to legal writing.
- **Online writing resources:** Websites and online platforms, such as Legal Writing Pro and the Legal Writing Institute, provide a wealth of information, tips, and exercises to enhance legal writing skills.
- **Writing software:** Writing software tools like Grammarly and ProWritingAid can assist in grammar and style checking, improving the overall quality of legal writing.

Tricks and caveats

Developing effective legal writing skills takes time and practice. Here are a few tricks and caveats to keep in mind:

- Be concise: Eliminate unnecessary words and phrases to improve readability and clarity.

- Use headings and subheadings: Utilize headings and subheadings to guide the reader and create a logical structure within the document.

- Proofread carefully: Thoroughly proofread your writing to catch any typographical errors, grammatical mistakes, or inconsistencies.

- Seek feedback: Share your writing with peers, professors, or colleagues to receive constructive feedback and improve your writing skills.

- Keep learning: Stay updated on current legal writing trends and best practices by regularly reading articles, attending workshops, and engaging in professional development opportunities.

Exercises

To enhance your understanding of legal writing styles and formats, consider the following exercises:

1. Rewrite a paragraph from a legal document using plain language principles to improve its accessibility and comprehension.

2. Identify a legal document (e.g., a court opinion, a statute) and analyze its organizational structure using the IRAC or CREAC format.

3. Practice proper citation by referencing a recent legal case or statute using the appropriate citation style (e.g., Bluebook).

By mastering the various styles and formats of legal writing, you will be able to effectively communicate legal concepts, persuade others, and contribute to the advancement of justice and equality.

Techniques for Effective Legal Analysis

In the field of legal studies, effective legal analysis plays a crucial role in understanding and interpreting the law. It encompasses the exploration and evaluation of legal principles, statutes, regulations, precedents, and other legal sources to derive meaningful conclusions and arguments. This section will provide an overview of key techniques for conducting effective legal analysis.

The IRAC Method

One widely used technique for legal analysis is the IRAC (Issue, Rule, Application, Conclusion) method. This structured approach helps legal professionals and students organize their thoughts and present their analysis in a clear and logical manner.

The IRAC method involves the following steps:

Issue: Identify the legal issue or problem at hand. This step requires a careful examination of the facts and understanding of the relevant legal concepts. Clearly articulating the issue ensures that the subsequent analysis remains focused.

Rule: State the relevant legal rules or principles that apply to the issue. This could include statutes, regulations, case law, or other legal authorities. It is crucial to accurately identify and comprehend the rules applicable to the given situation.

Application: Apply the identified legal rules to the specific facts of the case. This step involves a careful analysis and interpretation of the rules, considering how they interact with the given facts. It is important to explain the reasoning behind applying each rule and how it supports or undermines the argument.

Conclusion: Summarize the analysis and draw a well-reasoned conclusion based on the application of the rules to the facts. The conclusion should directly address the legal issue identified in the beginning and provide a clear resolution or recommendation.

By following the IRAC method, legal professionals can present their analysis in a logical and organized manner, enhancing the clarity and persuasiveness of their arguments.

Case Briefing

Another important technique for effective legal analysis is case briefing. Case briefing involves summarizing and analyzing court decisions to distill the key legal principles and reasoning behind the judgment. It is commonly used in legal education and professional practice as a means to extract important information from legal cases for future reference and analysis.

When briefing a case, it is essential to include the following components:

Name and Citation: Provide the full name of the case, including the parties involved, and cite the appropriate legal citation.

Facts: Summarize the relevant facts of the case, including those essential to understand the legal issue and decision.

Issue: Identify the legal issue or question the court had to address.

Decision: Summarize the court's holding or decision regarding the legal issue.

Reasoning: Analyze the court's reasoning and the legal principles the court relied upon in reaching its decision. This includes identifying any precedents cited and the court's interpretation and application of the law.

Rationale: Discuss the underlying policy considerations or public interests that influenced the court's decision.

Disposition: Note any additional orders or instructions provided by the court beyond the decision itself.

Case briefing helps legal professionals develop a deeper understanding of legal reasoning, interpret judicial decisions, and apply relevant legal principles to new situations.

Legal Research Tools

Conducting effective legal analysis requires access to reliable and comprehensive legal research tools. Legal professionals rely on various resources to find relevant legal authorities, including:

Primary Sources: These include statutes, regulations, constitutions, and court decisions. Accessing primary sources directly ensures the most accurate and up-to-date information.

Secondary Sources: These include legal treatises, law review articles, and textbooks that provide commentary and analysis on legal issues. Secondary sources can offer valuable insights and guidance on interpreting and applying the law.

Online Databases: Legal research platforms such as Westlaw, LexisNexis, and HeinOnline provide access to a vast collection of legal materials, including case law, statutes, regulations, and secondary sources. These platforms offer robust search capabilities, citation analysis tools, and annotations to aid legal analysis.

Legal Encyclopedias: Legal encyclopedias, such as Corpus Juris Secundum and American Jurisprudence, provide comprehensive summaries of legal topics and can be helpful in gaining a general understanding of a particular area of law.

Legal Citators: Citators, such as Shepard's Citations or KeyCite, assist in verifying the current status and validity of legal authorities, identifying subsequent appellate decisions, and analyzing the treatment of a particular case or statute.

Legal research tools empower legal professionals to conduct thorough and efficient legal analysis, ensuring that their conclusions are based on accurate and authoritative legal sources.

Ethical Considerations

Ethics play a vital role in legal analysis. Legal professionals must adhere to ethical guidelines when conducting analysis, including:

Honesty and Integrity: Legal analysts should approach their work with honesty, ensuring that their analysis accurately reflects the law and the facts of the case. Plagiarism, misrepresentation, and dishonesty in legal analysis are serious ethical breaches.

Confidentiality and Privacy: Legal analysts must respect confidentiality obligations and privacy rights when conducting research and analyzing legal issues. They should handle sensitive information appropriately and protect client or personal data from unauthorized disclosure.

Independence and Objectivity: Legal analysts should strive to maintain their independence and objectivity, avoiding any conflicts of interest that may compromise their analysis. Their analysis should be impartial and free from personal bias or undue external influence.

Professional Competence: Legal analysts should possess the necessary knowledge and skills to conduct effective legal analysis. They have a professional responsibility to maintain and enhance their competence through continuous learning and staying updated on legal developments.

Accountability: Legal analysts should be accountable for the accuracy and integrity of their analysis. They should acknowledge and correct any errors or omissions promptly.

By adhering to these ethical considerations, legal professionals can ensure the integrity and reliability of their legal analysis while upholding the values and standards of the legal profession.

Practical Exercise

To apply the techniques discussed, let's consider a hypothetical case:

Case Scenario: A tenant, Alice, believes that her landlord, Bob, is unjustly withholding a significant portion of her security deposit when she moved out of her apartment. Alice wants to analyze her legal rights and options in this situation.

Using the IRAC method, Alice would begin by identifying the legal issue. Let's assume the issue is whether Bob is legally entitled to withhold a portion of Alice's security deposit.

Next, Alice would identify the relevant legal rules governing security deposits, such as state landlord-tenant laws. She would research and analyze these laws to understand the rights and responsibilities of both the landlord and tenant concerning security deposits.

Applying the identified legal rules to the specific facts of the case, Alice would consider factors such as the condition of the apartment at the end of the tenancy, any documented damages, and the terms outlined in the rental agreement.

Finally, Alice would draw her conclusion based on her analysis of the facts and legal rules. If she determines that Bob is unlawfully withholding a portion of her security deposit, she may decide to pursue legal remedies such as filing a lawsuit, engaging in negotiation or mediation, or seeking assistance from a local housing agency.

By following the IRAC method and conducting thorough legal research, Alice can make an informed decision based on a well-reasoned analysis of her rights and potential legal recourse.

Additional Resources

For further exploration of the techniques for effective legal analysis, consider the following resources:

- *Legal Research and Writing for Paralegals* by Deborah E. Bouchoux provides comprehensive guidance on legal research methodologies and techniques for effective legal writing and analysis.
- *How to Brief a Case* by William P. Statsky offers practical guidance on case briefing techniques and strategies.
- Online legal research platforms such as Westlaw, LexisNexis, and HeinOnline offer extensive resources, tutorials, and guides on legal research techniques and effective legal analysis.

Remember, mastering the techniques for effective legal analysis requires practice and continuous learning. Engage in exercises, engage with legal professionals, and seek feedback to enhance your skills in this essential aspect of legal studies.

Structure and organization of legal documents

In the field of legal studies, the ability to effectively structure and organize legal documents is crucial. Whether it is a contract, a memorandum, a brief, or any other type of legal text, the way information is presented can greatly impact its clarity, comprehensibility, and persuasive power. This section will delve into the principles and techniques of structuring and organizing legal documents, providing valuable insights and practical tips for legal professionals.

Importance of structure and organization

A well-structured and organized legal document serves several essential purposes. First, it enhances readability and comprehension, allowing the intended audience to easily navigate through the document and grasp its key points. This is particularly important in legal contexts where precision and clarity are paramount.

Second, effective structure and organization help convey the logical flow of arguments and supporting evidence. By strategically arranging the content, legal professionals can present their case in a coherent and persuasive manner. This is especially critical in legal briefs, where the ultimate goal is to convince the court or other legal authorities.

Lastly, a well-structured document facilitates efficient referencing and retrieval of information. In complex legal matters, it is common for documents to be revisited and referenced over time. Good organization ensures that relevant sections can be easily located, saving time and effort.

Key elements of structure

The structure of a legal document typically follows a standard format, which consists of several key elements. While the specific structure may vary depending on the type of document, the following elements are commonly included:

1. **Title:** The title provides a concise and descriptive overview of the document's subject matter. It should be clear and accurately reflect the content of the document.

2. **Introduction:** The introduction sets the stage by providing background information and introducing the main purpose of the document. It should capture the reader's attention and establish the context for the subsequent sections.

3. **Table of contents:** For longer documents, a table of contents can be included to provide an overview of the document's structure and help readers navigate to specific sections.

4. **Body:** The body of the document contains the main content and arguments. It is here that the legal analysis, arguments, and supporting evidence are presented in a logical and organized manner.

5. **Conclusion:** The conclusion summarizes the main points of the document and often includes a proposed resolution or recommendation. It should leave a lasting impression on the reader and reinforce the main arguments.

6. **References:** Any external sources or authorities cited in the document should be properly referenced to give credit and provide a basis for further research or verification.

7. **Appendices:** Additional supporting documents, data, or evidence that are not crucial to the main body of the document can be included in the appendices. This allows interested readers to delve deeper into the topic if desired.

Organizational techniques

In addition to the key elements of structure, there are several organizational techniques that can further enhance the clarity and effectiveness of legal documents:

- **Headings and subheadings:** The use of headings and subheadings helps break down the content into manageable sections and provides a visual hierarchy. This allows readers to quickly locate specific information and facilitates scanning and skimming of the document.

- **Numbering and bullet points:** When presenting lists or procedural steps, using numbering or bullet points can make the information easier to follow and understand. It helps to create a sense of order and emphasizes the sequence or importance of the items.

- **Paragraphing and spacing:** Proper paragraphing and spacing are essential for readability. Each paragraph should focus on a single main idea or point, and there should be sufficient spacing between paragraphs to avoid a cluttered appearance. This makes the document easier on the eyes and enhances overall comprehension.

- **Transitional words and phrases:** The use of transitional words and phrases, such as "however," "in addition," or "moreover," helps to connect ideas and create a smooth flow of information. They provide logical links between different sections of the document, making it easier for readers to follow the arguments.

Example: Structure of a legal brief

To illustrate the principles of structure and organization, let's consider the structure of a legal brief, which is a document submitted to a court to present arguments and legal analysis on behalf of a party in a case.

1. **Title:** "Brief for the Appellant/Respondent in [Case Name]"
2. **Introduction:** Briefly introduce the case, the parties involved, and the main issue under consideration. Provide a concise statement of the desired outcome or relief sought.
3. **Table of contents:** Include a table of contents to guide the reader through the document.
4. **Statement of the case:** Present a clear and concise summary of the relevant facts and procedural history of the case.
5. **Statement of the issues:** Identify and articulate the key legal issues to be addressed in the brief.
6. **Summary of the argument:** Provide a high-level overview of the main arguments and conclusions to be discussed in the brief.
7. **Argument:** Present the legal arguments in support of the desired outcome. Each argument should be clearly identified, supported by relevant case law, statutes, or legal principles, and accompanied by persuasive reasoning.
8. **Conclusion:** Summarize the main arguments and request the desired relief or outcome.
9. **References:** Include a list of references to legal authorities cited in the brief.

Remember that the specific structure and organization of a legal document may vary depending on jurisdiction, court rules, or individual preferences. It is important to adhere to any applicable guidelines or requirements to ensure professionalism and clarity.

Resources for further exploration

For further exploration of the structure and organization of legal documents, the following resources can provide valuable insights and practical guidance:

- **"Legal Writing in Plain English" by Bryan A. Garner:** This book offers practical advice on how to improve legal writing, including tips on structure, organization, and clarity.

- **"Point Made: How to Write Like the Nation's Top Advocates" by Ross Guberman:** This book provides examples and analysis of persuasive legal writing, including effective organization techniques.

- **Style guides and writing manuals:** Consult the style guide prescribed by your jurisdiction or professional organization for specific guidelines on structuring and organizing legal documents.

Conclusion

The structure and organization of legal documents play a crucial role in ensuring clarity, comprehensibility, and persuasive power. By carefully considering the key elements of structure, employing organizational techniques, and following applicable guidelines and conventions, legal professionals can create documents that effectively present their arguments and supporting evidence. Remember, a well-structured document not only reflects professionalism but also enhances the likelihood of a successful outcome.

Citations and referencing in legal writing

Citations and referencing play a crucial role in legal writing, serving as a foundation for the development of legal arguments and the acknowledgment of legal authorities. In this section, we will discuss the importance of citations, the rules and principles governing legal citations, different citation styles, and best practices for effective referencing.

Importance of Citations

In legal writing, citations serve multiple purposes. Firstly, they provide support for the arguments made by the author, helping to establish credibility and demonstrate thorough research. Secondly, citations enable readers to locate and verify the sources of legal information and authorities. This allows for transparency in legal analysis and promotes further research and discussion. Lastly, citations ensure that proper credit is given to the original authors, respecting intellectual property rights and academic integrity.

Rules and Principles of Citations

Legal citations adhere to certain rules and principles to maintain consistency and facilitate efficient retrieval of legal sources. The most commonly used citation style in legal writing is the "Bluebook" or "Harvard Law Review Association" style. Some key rules and principles of legal citations include:

1. **Case citations:** When citing court cases, it is important to include the name of the case, volume number, reporter abbreviation, page number, and year of the decision. For example, *Smith v. Jones, 548 U.S. 123 (2006).*

2. **Statutory citations:** When referencing statutes, it is necessary to include the title of the statute, the section number, the volume and page number of the code, and the year of the code. For example, *Family Law Act, 1986, c. 36, § 25.*

3. **Secondary sources citations:** When citing secondary sources such as books, articles, or law review commentaries, it is important to include the author's name, the title of the work, the volume and page number (if applicable), the publication year, and any additional relevant information. For example, *John Doe, "Legal Ethics in the Digital Age," 65 Harv. L. Rev. 123 (2019).*

4. **Parallel citations:** Parallel citations are used when the same case or statute is published in multiple sources. It is essential to include all relevant parallel citations to facilitate access for readers. For example, *Smith v. Jones, 548 U.S. 123, 128 (2006) (parallel citation to 35 S. Ct. 678).*

These rules and principles ensure consistency and accuracy in legal citations, making it easier for readers to locate and verify the cited sources.

Citation Styles

Different citation styles exist within legal writing, depending on the jurisdiction or specific requirements of the project. The most common citation styles include the "Bluebook" style (predominantly used in the United States), the "Canadian Guide to Uniform Legal Citation" (often referred to as the "McGill Guide"), and the "Australian Guide to Legal Citation."

Each citation style has its own specific rules and conventions regarding the format, punctuation, and order of elements within a citation. It is important to familiarize oneself with the appropriate citation style and adhere to its guidelines when preparing legal documents.

Best Practices for Effective Referencing

To ensure effective referencing in legal writing, it is important to follow these best practices:

1. **Accuracy:** Double-check and verify all citations to ensure accurate referencing of sources. Mistakes in citations can undermine the credibility of legal arguments and lead to confusion for the readers.

2. **Consistency:** Maintain consistency in citation style throughout the document. Consistent formatting and punctuation of citations enhance readability and ease of use for the readers.

3. **Hierarchy of authorities:** Prioritize citing primary sources, such as statutes and court cases, over secondary sources. Primary sources carry more weight and authority in legal arguments.

4. **Use of signals:** Signals are words or phrases used to indicate the weight or relevance of a citation. Proper use of signals, such as "e.g.," "see," "cf.," and "id.," assists readers in understanding the cited authority's importance to the argument being made.

5. **Correct use of abbreviations:** Follow the established conventions for abbreviations used in legal citations. Improper or inconsistent use of abbreviations can cause confusion and hinder the reader's ability to locate the cited sources.

By adhering to these best practices, legal writers can ensure clarity, accuracy, and integrity in their referencing.

Additional Resources

For further exploration of legal citations and referencing, the following resources are recommended:

- **The Bluebook: A Uniform System of Citation** - The authoritative guide to legal citation in the United States.

- **Canadian Guide to Uniform Legal Citation (McGill Guide)** - A comprehensive guide to legal citation in Canada.

- **Australian Guide to Legal Citation** - The standard guide for legal citation in Australia.

- **Legal Research and Writing for Paralegals** by Deborah E. Bouchoux - A practical guide to legal research and writing, including guidance on citations and referencing.
- **Interactive Citation Workbook for The Bluebook** by Tracy L. McGaugh - A workbook designed to reinforce understanding and application of The Bluebook citation rules.

These resources provide in-depth guidance on legal citations, referencing, and related topics, helping legal researchers and writers develop their skills in this important aspect of legal writing.

In conclusion, citations and referencing are essential components of legal writing, serving to support arguments, facilitate transparent research, and credit original authors. Adherence to the rules and principles of legal citations, proper use of citation styles, and incorporation of best practices for effective referencing are fundamental to maintaining accuracy, credibility, and integrity in legal documents.

Strategies for persuasive legal writing

In the realm of legal studies, effective written communication is crucial. Persuasive legal writing requires more than just a mastery of grammar and punctuation; it demands a strategic approach to presenting arguments and influencing the reader's perspective. This section explores a range of techniques and strategies that can enhance the persuasiveness of legal writing.

Understanding the audience

Before embarking on any writing endeavor, it is essential to consider the intended audience. In legal writing, the audience often consists of judges, other legal professionals, or even laypeople. Understanding the background, knowledge, and values of the audience is essential for tailoring persuasive arguments effectively.

For instance, when writing for a judge, it is important to deliver a concise and logical argument that aligns with existing legal principles. However, when writing for a layperson, it may be necessary to provide more background information and simplify complex legal concepts to ensure comprehension and engagement.

Building a strong structure

A well-structured legal document enhances readability and reinforces persuasive arguments. It is crucial to establish a clear and logical structure that guides the reader through the central ideas and supporting evidence.

One effective method for structuring legal writing is the IRAC (Issue, Rule, Application, Conclusion) format. This format provides a systematic approach to organizing legal arguments, ensuring that each paragraph focuses on a specific aspect of the argument. By clearly delineating the issues, stating the relevant legal rules, applying those rules to the facts, and deriving a sound conclusion, the writer can present a convincing case.

Crafting persuasive arguments

A persuasive legal argument relies on the effective use of evidence, reasoning, and rhetoric. Here are some strategies to strengthen the persuasiveness of legal writing:

1. **Analogies and comparisons:** Drawing parallels between different cases or situations can help the reader understand complex legal concepts and increase the persuasive impact of the argument. Analogies can be particularly useful when explaining novel or abstract legal principles.

2. **Emotional appeal:** While legal writing typically relies on logic and reason, incorporating a touch of emotional appeal can strengthen the persuasive impact. Connecting the argument to real-life situations and illustrating the human consequences of the legal issue at hand can evoke empathy and create a memorable impression.

3. **Language and tone:** The choice of language and tone can significantly impact the persuasiveness of legal writing. Using clear, concise, and authoritative language can enhance the credibility of the argument. However, it is important to strike a balance between professionalism and accessibility to remain engaging.

4. **Counterarguments and rebuttals:** Acknowledging and effectively addressing counterarguments demonstrates a well-rounded understanding of the legal issue and strengthens the writer's credibility. By refuting potential objections and presenting compelling counterarguments, the persuasive force of the overall argument can be reinforced.

5. **Using persuasive techniques:** Various rhetorical devices can be employed to enhance the persuasive impact of legal writing. For example, incorporating repetition, employing vivid imagery, or utilizing powerful metaphors can captivate the reader's attention and make the argument more memorable.

6. **Logical reasoning:** Developing logical and coherent arguments is fundamental to persuasive legal writing. Deductive reasoning, analogical reasoning, and syllogistic reasoning are common logical tools that can strengthen the overall argument. Moreover, clearly articulating the logical connections between facts, legal principles, and the desired outcome can make the argument more convincing.

Avoiding common pitfalls

While it is important to focus on enhancing the persuasiveness of legal writing, it is equally essential to be aware of common pitfalls that can undermine the effectiveness of the argument. Here are a few pitfalls to avoid:

- **Excessive legalese:** Using overly technical or convoluted legal language can alienate the reader and make the argument less persuasive. Strive for clarity and simplicity, ensuring that the reader can easily understand the central ideas.

- **Lack of coherence:** A disjointed or disorganized argument can weaken its persuasive force. Ensure a clear logical progression of ideas and use transitional phrases to guide the reader through the document smoothly.

- **Weak or unsupported claims:** Persuasive legal writing relies on compelling evidence and well-supported claims. Failing to provide sufficient evidence or relying on weak arguments undermines the persuasive impact. Thoroughly research and document supporting sources to fortify the credibility of the argument.

- **Ignoring potential counterarguments:** Addressing counterarguments demonstrates intellectual rigor and strengthens the persuasive impact. Failing to anticipate and refute potential objections can weaken the overall argument.

Real-world application

To illustrate the strategies for persuasive legal writing, let's consider a hypothetical case involving a landlord-tenant dispute. The tenant, Sarah, is seeking compensation for damages caused by a water leak that resulted from the landlord's negligence. As Sarah's legal representative, you want to draft a persuasive letter to the landlord, demanding compensation.

In your letter, you might structure your argument using the IRAC format, clearly identifying the issue (Sarah's entitlement to compensation), stating the relevant legal rules (landlord's duty of care, breach of that duty), applying the rules to the facts (evidence of negligence and resultant damages), and concluding with a demand for compensation.

To strengthen the persuasiveness of your argument, you could incorporate an analogy, comparing the landlord's negligence to a driver's failure to maintain their vehicle, leading to an accident. By highlighting the straightforward cause-and-effect relationship, you can make the argument more relatable and compelling.

Furthermore, you could appeal to the landlord's sense of responsibility and fairness by emphasizing the emotional toll the damages have had on Sarah, illustrating how her quality of life and personal belongings have been negatively affected. Such an emotional appeal can create empathy and increase the persuasive impact of your argument.

Remember to use clear, authoritative language and logical reasoning throughout the letter to enhance its overall persuasive force.

Additional Resources

To delve deeper into persuasive legal writing, consider exploring the following resources:

- *Legal Writing in Plain English: A Text with Exercises* by Bryan A. Garner
- *Point Made: How to Write Like the Nation's Top Advocates* by Ross Guberman
- *The Art of Persuasion in the Practice of Law* by Michael R. Fontham

These resources offer valuable insights, practical tips, and exercises to refine your persuasive writing skills in the legal context.

Mastering the art of persuasive legal writing requires a combination of conceptual understanding, strategic thinking, and effective communication. By implementing the strategies discussed in this section and honing your skills through practice, you can become a compelling advocate in your legal writing endeavors.

Remember, persuasive writing is a craft that can always be improved, so embrace the challenges, learn from feedback, and continuously refine your approach to maximize the impact of your future legal documents.

Negotiation and dispute resolution

Introduction to Negotiation Theory

Negotiation is a fundamental process in law and plays a crucial role in resolving disputes, reaching agreements, and achieving desired outcomes. In this section, we will provide an overview of negotiation theory, which encompasses a range of concepts, strategies, and techniques to effectively navigate negotiations. By understanding the principles underlying negotiation theory, legal professionals can enhance their abilities to advocate for their clients, resolve conflicts, and achieve mutually acceptable solutions.

The Nature of Negotiation

Negotiation can be defined as a communication process used to reconcile diverse interests, find common ground, and reach agreements. It is a dynamic and interactive process that involves parties with conflicting goals or interests engaging in dialogue to resolve their differences. Negotiation can occur in various settings, including legal disputes, contract negotiations, business transactions, and even personal relationships.

While negotiation is often associated with compromise, it is important to note that it is not always about finding a middle ground. Negotiation can also involve persuasive arguments, creative problem-solving, and strategic maneuvering to persuade the other party to accept one's preferred outcome. Thus, negotiation theory encompasses a wide range of strategies and approaches to maximize the chances of achieving favorable outcomes.

Key Concepts in Negotiation Theory

To understand negotiation theory, it is essential to familiarize ourselves with key concepts that form its foundation. These concepts provide insights into the dynamics of negotiation and offer guidance on how to approach and analyze negotiation situations.

1. **Interests:** Interests refer to the underlying needs, desires, and concerns that drive each party's position in a negotiation. It is important to distinguish between positions (the specific demands or requests made by the parties) and interests, as interests often reveal common ground and opportunities for mutually beneficial solutions. By focusing on underlying interests rather

than fixed positions, negotiators can expand the range of possible outcomes and find creative solutions.

2. **BATNA:** BATNA stands for the "Best Alternative to a Negotiated Agreement." It is the fallback option or course of action available to each party if the negotiation fails to produce a satisfactory agreement. Understanding one's BATNA is crucial, as it provides leverage and helps determine the minimum acceptable outcome. A strong BATNA enhances negotiation power, while a weak BATNA limits options and may lead to unfavorable agreements.

3. **Negotiation Styles:** Different individuals and cultures exhibit distinct negotiation styles. These styles range from cooperative (seeking win-win outcomes) to competitive (seeking to maximize individual gains). Understanding negotiation styles can assist negotiators in adapting their strategies to the preferences and behavior of the other party. Additionally, recognizing one's own negotiation style can improve self-awareness and enable effective planning and decision-making.

4. **Distributive vs. Integrative Negotiation:** Negotiations can be categorized as distributive (also known as competitive or zero-sum) or integrative (also known as cooperative or win-win). Distributive negotiation involves the division of resources, where any gain for one party comes at the expense of the other. Integrative negotiation, on the other hand, focuses on finding creative solutions that maximize joint gains. By understanding the dynamics of both types of negotiation, negotiators can tailor their approaches and strategies accordingly.

Negotiation Strategies and Techniques

Negotiation theory offers a range of strategies and techniques that can be employed to achieve favorable outcomes. These strategies help negotiators navigate complex dynamics, manage conflicts, build relationships, and persuade the other party to accept their proposals. Let's explore some commonly used negotiation strategies and techniques:

1. **Preparation:** Thorough preparation is crucial for successful negotiations. This includes understanding the relevant legal issues, knowing the preferences and expectations of the other party, gathering information, and identifying potential areas of common ground. Proper preparation allows

negotiators to craft persuasive arguments, anticipate counterarguments, and strategically plan their negotiation approach.

2. **Active Listening:** Active listening is a fundamental skill in negotiations. By attentively listening to the other party's concerns, interests, and proposals, negotiators can gather valuable information and build rapport. Active listening also demonstrates respect and validates the other party's perspective, which can foster a more collaborative and constructive negotiation process.

3. **Effective Communication:** Clear and concise communication is vital in negotiations. Effective communicators articulate their positions, explain their interests, ask clarifying questions, and outline potential solutions. They also remain mindful of nonverbal cues and actively manage potential misunderstandings or conflicts arising from differences in communication styles.

4. **Problem-Solving and Creativity:** Negotiation often involves identifying common interests and generating creative solutions that satisfy the underlying needs of all parties. Problem-solving techniques, such as brainstorming, exploring alternatives, and considering trade-offs, can help expand the range of possible options and promote integrative negotiation.

5. **Managing Emotions:** Emotions can significantly impact negotiation outcomes. Effective negotiators acknowledge and manage their own emotions while remaining attuned to the emotional states of the other party. By employing empathy and emotional intelligence, negotiators can deescalate conflicts, diffuse tension, and foster a more constructive negotiation environment.

6. **Building Relationships:** Positive relationships built on trust and rapport can facilitate negotiations. Engaging in small talk, finding common ground, and acknowledging the concerns and perspectives of the other party can help establish a foundation of trust. Building relationships can enhance mutual understanding and increase the likelihood of reaching agreements.

Ethical Considerations in Negotiation

Ethics play a critical role in negotiations. Legal professionals must adhere to ethical principles to ensure fair and just outcomes. Some key ethical considerations include:

1. **Honesty and Integrity:** Negotiators should strive for honesty and integrity, refraining from misrepresentation, manipulation, or withholding of material information. This ensures transparency and promotes a trust-based negotiation process.

2. **Respect and Fairness:** Negotiators should treat each other with respect and fairness, valuing diverse perspectives and avoiding discriminatory practices. Recognizing the inherent dignity and worth of all parties involved contributes to a more equitable negotiation process.

3. **Conflicts of Interest:** Negotiators must identify and disclose any conflicts of interest that may compromise their objectivity or impartiality. Mitigating conflicts of interest strengthens the integrity of the negotiation process.

4. **Confidentiality:** Maintaining confidentiality is essential in negotiations, especially when sensitive information is shared. Respecting privacy and safeguarding confidential information promotes trust and fosters a safe negotiation environment.

5. **Professionalism:** Negotiators should exhibit professionalism, demonstrating appropriate demeanor, respect for procedural rules, and adherence to ethical guidelines. Professionalism contributes to the credibility and legitimacy of the negotiation process.

Conclusion

Negotiation theory provides valuable insights into the dynamics, strategies, and techniques involved in achieving successful negotiation outcomes. Understanding key concepts, tailoring approaches to negotiation styles, and employing effective strategies can enhance legal professionals' ability to advocate for clients, resolve conflicts, and achieve mutually acceptable agreements. By embracing ethical considerations, negotiators can ensure a fair and just negotiation process that promotes trust, respect, and positive relationships.

Resources for Further Exploration:

- Fisher, R., Ury, W., & Patton, B. (2011). *Getting to Yes: Negotiating Agreement Without Giving In*. Penguin Books.

- Mnookin, R., Peppet, S., & Tulumello, A. (2016). *Beyond Winning: Negotiating to Create Value in Deals and Disputes*. The Belknap Press of Harvard University Press.

- Lewicki, R. J., Barry, B., & Saunders, D. M. (2015). *Essentials of Negotiation*. McGraw-Hill Education.

Exercises:

1. Select a negotiation scenario (e.g., business contract, legal dispute, or personal matter) and identify the interests of each party involved. How can you reconcile these interests to find a mutually acceptable solution?

2. Research and analyze a historical negotiation (e.g., treaty negotiation, labor dispute resolution, or international trade agreement) and evaluate the negotiation strategies employed by the parties involved.

Remember, negotiation is both an art and a science. Developing negotiation skills requires practice, self-reflection, and a willingness to adapt and learn from each negotiation experience. By mastering negotiation theory and employing effective strategies, legal professionals can navigate complex disputes, forge meaningful agreements, and shape the future of justice and equality.

Strategies for effective negotiation

Negotiation is a fundamental skill in legal studies as it allows parties to reach mutually beneficial agreements and resolve conflicts. In this section, we will explore strategies for effective negotiation, drawing upon principles from negotiation theory and real-world examples. We will also discuss ethical considerations and international perspectives in negotiation.

Understanding negotiation theory

Negotiation theory provides a foundation for effective negotiation strategies. Two key approaches in negotiation theory are distributive bargaining and integrative bargaining.

Distributive bargaining focuses on dividing a fixed resource between the parties involved. The goal is to maximize individual gains and involves a competitive approach. Strategies for distributive bargaining include setting a desired outcome (BATNA - Best Alternative to a Negotiated Agreement), determining reservation points, and using tactics such as anchoring and concessions.

Integrative bargaining, on the other hand, aims to create value and generate mutually beneficial outcomes for all parties. This approach is based on collaboration, creativity, and identifying shared interests. Strategies for integrative bargaining include expanding the pie, exploring multiple options, and employing active listening and effective communication techniques.

Key strategies for effective negotiation

1. Preparation: Adequate preparation is crucial for effective negotiation. This involves researching the issues at hand, understanding the interests and priorities of all parties, and identifying potential areas for compromise. By gathering relevant information and anticipating potential challenges, you can enhance your negotiation strategy.

2. Active listening: Active listening is an essential skill for successful negotiation. It involves fully focusing on the speaker, understanding their perspective, and acknowledging their concerns. Actively listening allows you to identify underlying interests, build rapport, and develop creative solutions that meet the needs of all parties.

3. Collaborative problem-solving: Adopting a collaborative problem-solving approach promotes a positive and constructive negotiation environment. By seeking joint solutions and shared interests, parties can find win-win outcomes. This involves brainstorming potential solutions, considering alternatives, and fostering a cooperative atmosphere conducive to problem-solving.

4. Effective communication: Clear and effective communication is vital in negotiation. This includes expressing your position, interests, and concerns in a concise and persuasive manner. Using language that is respectful, empathetic, and non-confrontational can help create a positive negotiation environment and foster understanding between parties.

5. Building rapport: Building rapport with the other party can create trust and facilitate negotiations. Building rapport can be achieved through active listening, recognizing commonalities, and demonstrating empathy. When parties trust and respect each other, they are more likely to collaborate and reach mutually beneficial agreements.

Ethical considerations in negotiation

Ethics play a crucial role in negotiation. Negotiators must adhere to ethical principles to ensure fairness, integrity, and respect for the parties involved. Some key ethical considerations in negotiation include:

1. Honesty and transparency: Negotiators should strive for honesty and transparency, providing accurate information and refraining from deceptive tactics.

Misleading or manipulating the other party undermines trust and hampers the negotiation process.

2. Confidentiality: Negotiators should respect the confidentiality of sensitive information shared during negotiations. Confidentiality ensures that parties can freely express their interests and concerns without fear of negative consequences.

3. Fairness and equity: Negotiators must strive for fairness and equality in the negotiation process. This involves considering the needs and interests of all parties and avoiding any form of discrimination or bias.

4. Professionalism: Negotiators should maintain a professional demeanor throughout the negotiation process. This includes treating the other party with respect, refraining from personal attacks, and focusing on the issues at hand.

International perspectives on negotiation

Negotiation practices can vary across different cultures and jurisdictions. Understanding these differences is crucial when engaging in international negotiations. Some key considerations for navigating negotiation in a global context include:

1. Cultural awareness: Cultural norms, values, and communication styles can significantly impact negotiation dynamics. It is important to research and understand the cultural context of the other party to avoid misunderstandings and ensure effective communication.

2. Contextual factors: Legal, political, and social factors specific to a jurisdiction can influence negotiation practices. Being aware of the legal frameworks, regulations, and norms in the country where negotiations take place is vital for successful outcomes.

3. Language barriers: Negotiating across language barriers requires additional attention to ensure effective communication. The use of interpreters or translation services may be necessary to facilitate understanding between parties.

4. Patience and adaptability: International negotiations often require patience and adaptability. Cultural differences may result in different negotiation styles, timeframes, and decision-making processes. Being flexible and willing to adjust strategies accordingly can contribute to successful negotiation outcomes.

Conclusion

Effective negotiation is a critical skill in legal studies, allowing parties to resolve disputes and reach mutually beneficial agreements. By understanding negotiation theory, employing key strategies, considering ethical considerations, and acknowledging international perspectives, negotiators can navigate complex negotiations successfully. Remember, effective negotiation is not solely about winning, but rather about finding solutions that are fair, just, and respect the interests of all parties involved.

Mediation and Alternative Dispute Resolution Methods

In the field of legal studies, mediation and alternative dispute resolution (ADR) methods play a crucial role in resolving conflicts and promoting justice. While traditional court litigation is often time-consuming, adversarial, and costly, mediation and ADR methods provide parties with a more collaborative and efficient way to find mutually acceptable resolutions. This section will explore the principles, techniques, and benefits of mediation and various ADR methods, as well as their applications in different contexts.

Principles of Mediation

Mediation is a voluntary and confidential process in which a neutral third party, the mediator, assists disputing parties in reaching a mutually agreeable resolution. The mediator facilitates communication, identifies the underlying issues, and helps parties explore potential solutions. The principles guiding mediation include:

- **Voluntary Participation:** Mediation relies on the voluntary participation of all parties involved. They must willingly engage in the process and work towards a solution in good faith.

- **Neutrality and Impartiality:** The mediator must maintain neutrality throughout the process, ensuring that all parties feel heard and respected. They should not favor one party over the other.

- **Confidentiality:** Mediation is a confidential process, promoting open communication and trust among the parties. Information shared during mediation cannot be used against any party in future proceedings.

- **Self-Determination:** The parties involved in mediation have the opportunity to actively participate in the decision-making process. They have the freedom to shape the terms of their agreement based on their needs and interests.

- **Practical and Creative Solutions:** Mediation encourages parties to think outside the box and explore innovative solutions. The focus is on finding practical and mutually beneficial resolutions rather than seeking a win-lose outcome.

Techniques in Mediation

Mediation employs several techniques to facilitate effective communication, foster understanding, and narrow down potential solutions. The mediator utilizes these techniques to create a supportive environment for dialogue and negotiation. Some common techniques used in mediation include:

- **Active Listening:** The mediator actively listens to each party, providing them with the opportunity to express their perspectives and emotions without interruption. Active listening helps build rapport and encourages a cooperative atmosphere.

- **Reframing:** The mediator rephrases or restates the issues and concerns raised by the parties to promote understanding and clarity. Reframing can help parties view the situation from a different perspective, facilitating problem-solving.

- **Summarizing:** The mediator summarizes the main points discussed during the mediation session, highlighting areas of agreement and disagreement. Summarizing ensures that both parties have a clear understanding of the progress made and the remaining issues to be resolved.

- **Brainstorming:** The mediator encourages parties to generate a wide range of possible solutions without judgment or evaluation. Brainstorming stimulates creative thinking and expands the pool of potential outcomes.

- **Reality Testing:** The mediator assists parties in evaluating the feasibility and implications of their proposed solutions. Through reality testing, parties become aware of the practical aspects, risks, and consequences associated with their suggested agreements.

Types of Alternative Dispute Resolution (ADR) Methods

In addition to mediation, various alternative dispute resolution (ADR) methods offer alternatives to traditional court litigation. These methods offer flexibility, cost-effectiveness, and timeliness, making them popular choices for resolving conflicts. Some common ADR methods include:

- **Arbitration:** Arbitration involves a neutral third party, the arbitrator, who listens to the arguments and evidence presented by both parties and makes a binding decision. It is less formal than traditional court proceedings, and the parties can choose the arbitrator and the rules governing the arbitration process.

- **Negotiation:** Negotiation is a direct communication process between two or more parties aimed at reaching a mutually acceptable resolution. It can be informal or formal, taking place before or during a legal dispute. Negotiation allows parties to maintain control over the outcome and explore potential solutions based on their interests.

- **Conciliation:** Conciliation involves a neutral third party, the conciliator, who assists parties in finding common ground and reaching an agreement. The conciliator may propose solutions, but the parties retain control over the final outcome. Conciliation is often used in disputes involving complex relationships or emotional issues.

- **Collaborative Law:** Collaborative law involves a cooperative and problem-solving approach, where each party is represented by their own collaboratively trained lawyer. The parties and their lawyers work together in a series of meetings to reach an agreement without going to court. If an agreement cannot be reached, the collaborative lawyers must withdraw, and the parties can pursue litigation.

- **Med-Arb:** Med-Arb combines mediation and arbitration. The process begins with mediation, where the mediator facilitates negotiations between the parties. If the parties cannot reach a resolution, the mediator transitions into an arbitrator, making a final decision that is binding on the parties. Med-Arb provides a swift resolution while allowing parties to explore settlement possibilities first.

Applications and Benefits

Mediation and ADR methods find applications in a wide range of disputes, including family matters, workplace conflicts, commercial disputes, community disputes, and international conflicts. The benefits of mediation and ADR methods include:

- **Cost and Time Savings:** Mediation and other ADR methods are generally more cost-effective and time-efficient compared to lengthy court proceedings. They help parties avoid excessive legal fees, lengthy trials, and bureaucratic delays.

- **Preserving Relationships:** Mediation and ADR methods encourage open communication and cooperation, allowing parties to preserve their relationships. This is particularly crucial in family disputes and ongoing business relationships where maintaining a positive rapport is valued.
- **Flexibility and Control:** Mediation and ADR methods provide parties with the flexibility to shape their agreements based on their specific needs and interests. Parties have greater control over the outcome and can design creative and personalized solutions.
- **Confidentiality:** The privacy and confidentiality of mediation and ADR proceedings allow parties to openly discuss their concerns and interests without fear of public disclosure. This fosters trust and encourages parties to explore solutions more candidly.
- **Higher Compliance:** Agreements reached through mediation and ADR methods often result in higher compliance rates compared to court-imposed solutions. Parties are more likely to adhere to the negotiated terms since they actively participated in the decision-making process.

Resources

Learning and practicing mediation and ADR methods require a solid understanding of the principles, techniques, and practical applications involved. The following resources can provide further exploration of this topic:

- **Books:**
  1. "Getting to Yes: Negotiating Agreement Without Giving In" by Roger Fisher and William Ury.
  2. "Mediation: Principles, Process, Practice" by David A. Hoffman.
  3. "Alternative Dispute Resolution: A Practical Guide" by Susan Blake and Julie Browne.
  4. "The Handbook of Dispute Resolution" edited by Michael L. Moffitt and Robert C. Bordone.
- **Websites:**
  1. Association for Conflict Resolution (ACR): `www.acrnet.org`
  2. International Mediation Institute (IMI): `www.imimediation.org`

3. American Arbitration Association (AAA): `www.adr.org`
4. Mediate.com: `www.mediate.com`

- **Trainings and Workshops:** Many organizations offer training programs and workshops to learn and enhance mediation and ADR skills. Check local community centers, law schools, and professional organizations for opportunities to participate in these programs.

Case Study: Workplace Mediation

Workplace disputes can be highly disruptive, impacting productivity and employee morale. Mediation offers an effective approach to resolving conflicts in the workplace. For example, consider a case where two employees, Alice and John, constantly clash over differences in work styles and communication methods. Their ongoing disputes create tension within the team and hinder collaboration. The workplace mediator intervenes and facilitates a mediation session, allowing Alice and John to express their concerns, understand each other's perspectives, and find common ground. Through the mediation process, Alice and John develop a mutually agreed-upon plan for improving communication, clarifying expectations, and collaborating more effectively. As a result, the team's dynamics improve, and productivity increases, benefiting both the employees and the organization as a whole.

Ethical Considerations in Negotiation and Dispute Resolution

Negotiation and dispute resolution are key components of the legal system, allowing parties to resolve conflicts and reach agreements without resorting to litigation. However, ethical considerations play a vital role in ensuring fairness, justice, and the protection of individual rights throughout the negotiation and dispute resolution process.

Principles of Ethics in Negotiation

In negotiation, ethical behavior is guided by principles that promote fairness, respect for autonomy, and honesty. The following principles are essential for ethical negotiation:

1. **Integrity:** Negotiators must demonstrate honesty and transparency in their dealings. They should accurately represent their interests and refrain from deceitful tactics.

2. **Respect:** Negotiators should treat all parties with respect and dignity, recognizing their autonomy and right to be heard. This principle ensures that power imbalances are not exploited during the negotiation process.

3. **Fairness:** Negotiators must strive to achieve fair and equitable outcomes, ensuring that agreements are reached based on objective criteria and without bias or discrimination.

4. **Confidentiality:** Both parties have the right to expect that information shared during the negotiation remains confidential unless agreed otherwise. Maintaining confidentiality fosters trust and encourages open communication.

5. **Compliance with the law:** Negotiators must adhere to all relevant statutes and regulations governing negotiation processes. This includes refraining from illegal activities such as bribery or coercion.

Potential Ethical Challenges in Negotiation

Despite the presence of ethical principles, negotiators may face ethical challenges during the process. Some common challenges include:

- **Deceptive tactics:** Negotiators may be tempted to use deceptive tactics to gain an advantage, such as withholding relevant information or making false promises. However, such tactics undermine trust and can lead to unfair outcomes.

- **Power imbalances:** Negotiations often involve parties with differing levels of power, which can create ethical challenges. The stronger party may use their power to exploit or manipulate the weaker party. Ethical negotiations require balancing power dynamics to ensure a fair process.

- **Competing values:** Negotiations may involve conflicting values and interests, posing ethical dilemmas. For example, negotiators may face tension between upholding individual rights and promoting the greater good. Ethical negotiators must navigate these conflicts to find equitable solutions.

- **Lack of transparency:** In some cases, negotiators may intentionally withhold information or mislead the other party, compromising the principle of integrity. Open and honest communication is crucial to maintaining ethical standards.

- **Inequality in representation:** Parties involved in negotiation may have unequal access to legal representation or resources, leading to ethical concerns. Negotiators must ensure that all parties have a fair opportunity to present their case and pursue their interests.

Ethical Guidelines for Dispute Resolution

Ethical considerations extend beyond negotiation and also apply to dispute resolution processes, such as mediation and arbitration. Ethical guidelines help ensure the integrity and fairness of these processes. Some key ethical guidelines for dispute resolution include:

- **Impartiality:** Dispute resolution practitioners must be impartial and treat all parties with fairness. They should avoid favoritism or bias toward any particular party.
- **Informed consent:** Participants in the dispute resolution process must provide informed consent, understanding the nature and potential outcomes of the process. This ensures that parties enter into the resolution voluntarily and with full understanding.
- **Confidentiality and privacy:** Confidentiality is crucial in dispute resolution to create a safe space for open dialogue. Practitioners should respect and protect the confidentiality and privacy of the parties involved, unless disclosure is required by law or agreed upon by the parties.
- **Conflict of interest:** Dispute resolution practitioners should avoid conflicts of interest that could compromise their impartiality or professionalism. They should disclose any potential conflicts and, if necessary, recuse themselves from the process.
- **Respect for self-determination:** Dispute resolution processes should prioritize party autonomy and self-determination. Participants should have the opportunity to make decisions based on their own values and interests.

Case Study: Ethical Considerations in Mediation

Consider the following case study to further illustrate ethical considerations in negotiation and dispute resolution:

John and Jane are divorcing and are in the process of resolving their child custody dispute through mediation. The mediator must be mindful of ethical principles to ensure a fair and just outcome. Some ethical considerations include:

- **Impartiality:** The mediator must remain neutral and treat both John and Jane with fairness, ensuring that neither party feels disadvantaged or unheard.

- **Confidentiality:** The mediator must maintain strict confidentiality during the mediation process, ensuring that all information shared remains private unless agreed otherwise by the parties.

- **Informed consent:** The mediator should explain the mediation process, its potential outcomes, and any limitations or restrictions to John and Jane. Both parties should have a clear understanding of the mediation and willingly participate.

- **Power imbalances:** If there is a significant power imbalance between John and Jane, the mediator must take steps to mitigate this discrepancy, such as allowing each party equal opportunity to express their perspectives and concerns.

By adhering to ethical guidelines and principles, mediators can facilitate a more constructive and fair process, enabling parties to reach a mutually acceptable agreement.

Conclusion

Ethical considerations are paramount in negotiation and dispute resolution, ensuring fairness, integrity, and respect for individual rights. Understanding and addressing ethical challenges and adhering to ethical guidelines are essential for legal professionals engaged in negotiation and dispute resolution. By doing so, they can promote justice, equality, and positive social change within the legal system.

International perspectives on negotiation and dispute resolution

In today's globalized world, negotiation and dispute resolution are vital tools for resolving conflicts and promoting peaceful resolutions. The field of international law recognizes the need for effective negotiation and dispute resolution mechanisms to address conflicts between nations, organizations, and individuals. This section explores the international perspectives on negotiation and dispute resolution and analyzes the challenges and opportunities they present in the pursuit of global peace and justice.

The importance of international negotiation

International negotiation plays a crucial role in resolving conflicts between nations and promoting peaceful resolutions to international disputes. It provides a platform for diplomatic dialogue, enabling parties to express their concerns, interests, and perspectives. International negotiation helps foster understanding, build trust, and find mutually beneficial solutions.

The United Nations and international negotiation

The United Nations (UN) serves as a key platform for international negotiation and dispute resolution. It provides a forum for member states to come together, discuss global issues, and work towards resolving conflicts peacefully. The UN Security Council plays a significant role in international negotiation, as its five permanent members hold veto power, allowing them to influence the negotiation outcomes.

The UN utilizes various negotiation techniques, including mediation and arbitration, to facilitate dialogue among conflicting parties. The Secretary-General appoints mediators and special envoys to mediate disputes and assist in negotiation processes. These mediators often have extensive diplomatic experience and are well-versed in international law and conflict resolution strategies.

Regional organizations and negotiation

Besides the UN, regional organizations also play a crucial role in international negotiation and dispute resolution. Organizations such as the European Union (EU), the African Union (AU), and the Organization of American States (OAS) have developed their own mechanisms to facilitate negotiation and conflict resolution within their respective regions.

These regional organizations often have an in-depth understanding of the local context and dynamics, allowing them to approach negotiation and dispute resolution in a tailored manner. They work towards promoting peace, stability, and cooperation among member states through diplomatic dialogue, negotiation initiatives, and reconciliation processes.

Public and private international law in negotiation

International negotiation draws upon both public and private international law principles. Public international law governs the relations between states, while private international law addresses conflicts involving individuals and private entities from different countries.

Public international law principles, such as customary international law and treaties, guide the negotiation process by providing a legal framework and standards. These principles ensure that negotiations are conducted in good faith, with respect for the sovereignty, equality, and human rights of all involved parties.

Private international law principles, such as the choice of law and jurisdiction, govern the resolution of disputes with an international aspect. Negotiations involving cross-border commercial transactions, investment disputes, or family law matters often rely on private international law principles to determine the applicable law and jurisdiction for resolving the dispute.

Key challenges in international negotiation

Negotiating across borders and cultures presents unique challenges that can hinder successful dispute resolution. Some key challenges in international negotiation include:

1. Cultural differences: Negotiators must be mindful of cultural nuances, communication styles, and social norms that may vary between countries. Misunderstandings due to cultural differences can impede effective communication and compromise.

2. Language barriers: Negotiations involving parties from different linguistic backgrounds may encounter language barriers that affect understanding and clarity. The use of interpreters and translators can help overcome linguistic challenges, but it requires careful coordination and attention to detail.

3. Power imbalances: Negotiations between developed and developing countries, or between entities with significant disparities in resources and influence, may face inherent power imbalances. Addressing these imbalances and ensuring the fair representation of all parties is crucial for a successful negotiation process.

4. Political considerations: Negotiations involving political issues or national interests often face additional complexities. Domestic political pressures, public opinion, and geopolitical dynamics can influence the negotiation outcomes and complicate dispute resolution efforts.

Innovative approaches to international dispute resolution

As the world becomes increasingly interconnected, innovative approaches to international dispute resolution have emerged. These approaches aim to address the challenges mentioned earlier and promote effective negotiation and peaceful resolution of conflicts. Some examples include:

1. Online dispute resolution: Utilizing digital platforms and technology, online dispute resolution provides a convenient and accessible means of resolving disputes across borders. It allows parties to engage in negotiation processes remotely, removing geographical barriers and reducing costs.

2. Cross-cultural negotiation training: Recognizing the importance of cultural competence in international negotiation, cross-cultural negotiation training programs have gained popularity. These training programs focus on developing skills and awareness around cultural differences, communication styles, and negotiation strategies specific to different regions and cultures.

3. Track II diplomacy: Often informal and unofficial, track II diplomacy involves non-governmental actors, such as academics, experts, and civil society organizations, engaging in negotiation and dialogue processes. Track II diplomacy complements official negotiations by providing alternative perspectives, creative solutions, and building trust among conflicting parties.

Resources for further exploration

For further exploration on international perspectives on negotiation and dispute resolution, the following resources may be helpful:

1. United Nations: The official website of the United Nations provides access to various negotiation and dispute resolution mechanisms, including reports, case studies, and publications related to international negotiation.

2. International Court of Justice (ICJ): The ICJ's website offers information on landmark international disputes, judgments, and legal resources related to international law and negotiation.

3. Regional organizations: Websites of regional organizations like the European Union, the African Union, and the Organization of American States provide insights into their negotiation and dispute resolution mechanisms.

4. Academic research journals: Journals such as the Harvard Negotiation Law Review, International Negotiation, and the Journal of International Dispute Settlement publish scholarly articles on international negotiation and dispute resolution.

5. Books on international negotiation: Some recommended books include "Getting to Yes: Negotiating Agreement Without Giving In" by Roger Fisher and William Ury, "The Art of Negotiation in a Global World" by Christopher Honeyman and Andrea Kupfer Schneider, and "The Global Negotiator: Making, Managing and Mending Deals Around the World" by Jeswald W. Salacuse.

Exercises

1. Research and analyze a recent international dispute and identify the negotiation techniques employed to resolve the conflict. Evaluate the effectiveness of these techniques and propose alternative approaches.

2. Conduct a case study on a regional organization's role in facilitating negotiation and dispute resolution within its jurisdiction. Examine the mechanisms employed, the challenges faced, and the outcomes achieved.

3. Develop a negotiation strategy for resolving an ongoing international trade dispute. Consider the cultural, political, and economic factors at play, and propose innovative approaches to address the challenges in the negotiation process.

4. Explore the role of technology in enhancing international negotiation and dispute resolution. Identify specific technologies, such as blockchain or artificial intelligence, and analyze their potential benefits and drawbacks in facilitating global dispute resolution.

Remember to approach these exercises with an open mind, considering the complexity and diversity of international negotiation and dispute resolution.

Legal advocacy and courtroom skills

Techniques for Effective Legal Advocacy

In the field of legal studies, effective advocacy is a crucial skill for lawyers and legal professionals. Advocacy involves presenting arguments and advocating for the interests of clients in courtrooms, negotiations, and other legal settings. This section will explore various techniques and strategies for effective legal advocacy, including preparing persuasive arguments, presenting oral arguments, cross-examination techniques, and important aspects of courtroom etiquette.

Preparing Persuasive Arguments

Preparing persuasive arguments is a key component of effective legal advocacy. To build a compelling case, it is important to carefully analyze the relevant laws, research prior cases, and gather evidence. Here are some essential techniques for preparing persuasive arguments:

1. Thorough legal research: Conduct comprehensive research to understand the relevant legal principles, statutes, regulations, and case precedents. This will help identify key arguments and supporting evidence.

2. Case analysis: Examine previous cases with similar legal issues and identify persuasive arguments that were successful. Analyze the reasoning and outcomes of those cases to develop a persuasive strategy.

3. Developing a theory of the case: Create a coherent and persuasive theory of the case based on the available evidence. This theory will guide your arguments and narrative in the courtroom.

4. Framing arguments: Craft arguments that resonate with judges, juries, or opposing counsel by framing them in a compelling and logical manner. Use analogies and storytelling techniques to make complex legal concepts more accessible and relatable.

5. Anticipating counterarguments: Identify potential weaknesses in your own arguments and anticipate counterarguments. Prepare persuasive responses to address these counterarguments effectively.

6. Organizing and outlining arguments: Structure your arguments in a logical order and outline them in a clear and concise manner. This will help maintain coherence and make it easier for your audience to follow your line of reasoning.

Presenting Oral Arguments

Effective oral advocacy skills are essential for presenting persuasive arguments in courtrooms or other legal settings. Here are some techniques to enhance your oral advocacy:

1. Clear and confident delivery: Speak clearly and confidently to convey your arguments effectively. Maintain good posture, eye contact, and appropriate gestures to establish credibility and engage your audience.

2. Effective use of language: Choose your words carefully and use precise legal terminology to make your arguments sound authoritative. Avoid jargon or complex language that may confuse your audience.

3. Structured and concise arguments: Break down complex arguments into smaller, digestible points. Structure your arguments in a logical sequence and present them concisely to help your audience understand and remember key points.

4. Use of rhetorical devices: Utilize rhetorical devices such as repetition, emphasis, and persuasive language to make your arguments more memorable and compelling.

5. Adaptation to the audience: Tailor your arguments and language to your specific audience, whether it be a judge, jury, or opposing counsel. Consider the knowledge level and perspective of your audience when presenting your arguments.

Cross-Examination Techniques

Cross-examination is a critical aspect of legal advocacy, particularly in the context of trial proceedings. It involves questioning witnesses from the opposing side to challenge their credibility and testimony. Here are some important cross-examination techniques:

1. Planning and preparation: Thoroughly review witness statements, deposition transcripts, and other evidence before cross-examination. Identify weaknesses in the witness's testimony and areas where you can undermine their credibility.

2. Leading questions: Use leading questions, which suggest the desired answer, to challenge the witness's version of events and elicit favorable responses that support your case. These questions should be concise and focused.

3. Impeachment evidence: Use prior inconsistent statements, contradictions, or other evidence to impeach the credibility of the witness. This can significantly weaken their testimony and increase doubt in the minds of the judge or jury.

4. Control and pacing: Maintain control over the witness by setting the pace of questioning and avoiding long narrative responses. This allows you to ask specific questions to elicit favorable answers while limiting the witness's ability to provide damaging testimony.

5. Maintaining composure: Stay composed and focused during cross-examination, even when faced with difficult witnesses or unexpected responses. Maintain an air of professionalism and avoid being confrontational, which may alienate the judge or jury.

Courtroom Etiquette and Professionalism

Maintaining proper courtroom etiquette and professionalism is crucial for effective legal advocacy. Proper conduct enhances your credibility as an advocate and ensures a respectful atmosphere. Here are some important aspects of courtroom etiquette and professionalism:

1. Dress appropriately: Wear professional attire that conforms to courtroom standards. This includes formal suits, proper footwear, and minimal jewelry or accessories.

2. Respect for the court: Show respect for the judge, opposing counsel, witnesses, and all parties involved. Follow court rules, address the judge appropriately, and avoid disruptive or disrespectful behavior.

3. Active listening: Pay close attention to the proceedings, including the judge's instructions, opposing counsel's arguments, and witness testimonies. This demonstrates respect and allows you to respond effectively.

4. Timeliness and preparedness: Arrive at court on time and well-prepared. Have all necessary documents, exhibits, and other materials organized and readily accessible.

5. Collegiality and civility: Maintain professional and respectful interactions with opposing counsel, even when facing contentious issues. Avoid personal attacks or unnecessary confrontations that may harm professional relationships.

In addition to these techniques, it is essential to continuously refine and improve your advocacy skills through practice, feedback, and observation of experienced advocates. Engage in moot court competitions, mock trials, or other simulated advocacy exercises to enhance your abilities. Seeking mentorship from seasoned professionals can also provide valuable guidance and insights.

Further Resources:

- Irving Younger, *Art of Cross-Examination*
- Antonin Scalia and Bryan A. Garner, *Making Your Case: The Art of Persuading Judges*
- Marsha Hunter and Brian K. Johnson, *The Articulate Advocate: Persuasive Skills for Lawyers in Trials, Appeals, Arbitrations, and Motions*

- American Bar Association (ABA) Section of Litigation, *Model Trial Guidelines: Effective Advocacy in the Courtroom.*

Remember, mastering the techniques of effective legal advocacy takes time and experience. Continuously striving to improve your skills will enhance your ability to effectively advocate for your clients and contribute to the pursuit of justice.

Preparing and presenting oral arguments

In legal studies, oral arguments play a crucial role in the courtroom. Mastering the art of preparing and presenting oral arguments is essential for effective advocacy. This section will explore the techniques, strategies, and best practices for preparing and delivering compelling oral arguments.

Understanding the purpose of oral arguments

Oral arguments are an opportunity for lawyers to make their case before a judge or a panel of judges. The primary purpose of oral arguments is to persuade the decision-maker(s) of the merits of your legal position. It allows for a direct engagement with the court, where lawyers can address key legal issues, clarify complex concepts, and respond to questions or challenges raised by the judges.

Good oral arguments enhance the written briefs and provide an additional opportunity to present your case in a more human and persuasive manner. While judges rely on written materials to understand the legal arguments, oral arguments offer a unique platform to emphasize critical points, highlight nuances, and address any concerns that may have arisen during their examination of the briefs.

Preparing for oral arguments

Preparing for oral arguments requires careful planning and thorough understanding of the case. Here are some key steps to take when preparing for oral arguments:

1. **Review the case thoroughly:** Familiarize yourself with the facts, legal issues, and arguments presented in the written briefs. Identify the strong and weak points of your case and anticipate potential counterarguments.

2. **Develop a persuasive structure:** Organize your oral arguments in a logical and persuasive manner. Create an outline that highlights the key points you want to address and the order in which you plan to present them. A clear structure helps judges follow your arguments and enhances the overall persuasiveness of your presentation.

3. **Practice and rehearse:** Rehearse your oral arguments multiple times to gain confidence and fluency. Practice speaking clearly and succinctly, focusing on delivering your message in a compelling and persuasive manner. Consider recording your practice sessions to identify areas that need improvement.

4. **Anticipate questions and challenges:** Prepare for potential questions or challenges from the judges. Think critically about the weaknesses of your case and develop persuasive responses. Consider seeking input from colleagues or mentors to simulate a real courtroom experience and receive constructive feedback.

5. **Use visual aids effectively:** Visual aids, such as PowerPoint slides or demonstrative exhibits, can enhance the clarity and impact of your arguments. Use them strategically to illustrate complex concepts, present evidence, or highlight key points. However, ensure that the visual aids do not distract from your verbal presentation.

6. **Manage your time:** Understand the time limits allocated for oral arguments and plan your presentation accordingly. Allocate sufficient time to address the most critical aspects of your case while leaving room for questions and interactions with the judges. Practice pacing yourself to ensure you stay within the allotted time frame.

Presenting oral arguments

Once you have prepared for oral arguments, it's time to confidently present your case in court. Here are some tips to consider:

1. **Start with a strong opening statement:** Grab the attention of the judges right from the beginning. Begin with a persuasive opening statement that clearly states your position and previews the key arguments you will make. A strong opening helps establish the tone and sets the stage for the rest of your presentation.

2. **Speak clearly and confidently:** Use a clear and confident tone when presenting your arguments. Project your voice, maintain eye contact, and articulate your points effectively. Confidence in your delivery will enhance your credibility and persuasiveness.

3. **Engage with the judges:** Oral arguments are a dialogue between you and the judges. Engage with them by actively listening to their questions or

concerns and responding thoughtfully. Be respectful and professional in your interactions, even if faced with challenging questions.

4. **Emphasize key points:** Highlight the most persuasive aspects of your case. Repeat key arguments and evidence to reinforce their importance. Use rhetorical devices, such as repetition or analogies, to make your arguments more memorable and compelling.

5. **Address counterarguments:** Anticipate counterarguments from opposing counsel or the judges and address them proactively. Acknowledge the opposing viewpoints, but provide persuasive reasons why your position is stronger or more legally sound.

6. **Stay focused and adaptable:** Be flexible and adapt to the flow of the oral arguments. Listen carefully to the judges' questions or comments and adjust your responses accordingly. Stay on point and avoid rambling or veering off-topic.

7. **End with a persuasive closing statement:** Conclude your oral arguments with a persuasive closing statement that recapitulates the key arguments and reinforces your position. Leave a lasting impression on the judges and summarize why they should rule in your favor.

Resources for further exploration

To delve deeper into the art of preparing and presenting oral arguments, consider exploring the following resources:

- *Winning on Appeal: Better Briefs and Oral Argument* by Ruggero J. Aldisert
- *Supreme Court Practice: For Practitioners in the Supreme Court* by Eugene Gressman, Jack H. Friedenthal, and Glen E. Gzeigowski
- *Effective Appellate Advocacy: Brief Writing and Oral Argument* by Carole C. Berry
- Websites and articles by legal advocacy organizations or law firms offering tips and guidance on oral arguments.

Remember, mastering the art of preparing and presenting oral arguments is a continuous learning process. Practice, seek feedback, and analyze successful oral arguments to refine your skills and become a persuasive advocate in the courtroom.

Cross-examination and questioning techniques

Cross-examination is a fundamental skill in the legal profession, particularly in the courtroom. It is a crucial technique used by attorneys to test the credibility of witnesses, challenge their testimony, and extract information that may be favorable to their case. Effective cross-examination requires strategic planning, careful questioning techniques, and a thorough understanding of the legal principles at play. In this section, we will explore the key aspects of cross-examination and provide practical guidance on how to use questioning techniques to achieve the desired outcomes.

The Purpose of Cross-Examination

The primary purpose of cross-examination is to discredit the witness's testimony, expose inconsistencies or falsehoods, and elicit information that supports the cross-examiner's case theory. However, it is essential to keep in mind that the exaggerated or aggressive interrogation techniques often depicted in popular media are not necessarily effective or ethical in practice. The goal of cross-examination should be to present a coherent and persuasive argument to the judge or jury, rather than merely to humiliate or intimidate the witness.

Planning Cross-Examination

Effective cross-examination begins with meticulous planning. The cross-examiner must thoroughly review the witness's statement, deposition, and any other available evidence in order to identify areas of vulnerability or inconsistencies. It is also essential to understand the legal framework of the case and the rules governing cross-examination in the jurisdiction.

To plan cross-examination effectively, consider the following steps:

1. Identify the key issues: Determine the crucial points that need to be addressed during the cross-examination. Focus on undermining the witness's credibility or eliciting evidence that supports your case theory.

2. Prepare a cross-examination outline: Create a structured outline that organizes the sequence of questions and topics you plan to cover. This outline will serve as a roadmap during the examination and help you maintain focus and coherence.

3. Anticipate answers: Based on the witness's statements and available evidence, anticipate how the witness is likely to respond to your questions. This will enable you to prepare follow-up questions and counter-arguments in advance.

4. Design effective questions: Craft clear and concise questions that target the specific information you aim to elicit. Use open-ended questions to encourage the witness to provide detailed responses and closed-ended questions to gather specific confirmations or denials.

5. Establish the foundation: Before delving into challenging questions, establish a comfortable rapport with the witness by asking preliminary and straightforward questions. This will help set a tone of cooperation and build trust with the witness.

Questioning Techniques

Effective questioning techniques are the cornerstone of successful cross-examination. The manner in which questions are framed, the timing of the questions, and the tone of voice used can significantly impact the outcome of the cross-examination. The following techniques can be employed to maximize the effectiveness of the questioning:

1. Leading questions: One of the most powerful tools in cross-examination is the use of leading questions. These are questions that suggest or prompt the desired answer, leading the witness to provide information that supports your case theory. For example, "Isn't it true that you were at the scene of the crime on the night of the incident?"

2. Impeachment: When the witness's statements contradict prior statements, evidence, or their own testimony, it opens an opportunity for impeachment. By skillfully presenting the inconsistencies, the cross-examiner can discredit the witness's credibility and cast doubt on their accuracy and reliability as a witness.

3. Limited scope questions: By narrowing the focus of questions, the cross-examiner can limit the witness's ability to provide broader context or explanations. This can be advantageous when the witness's knowledge or recollection of specific details is limited or uncertain.

4. Compound questions: Avoiding compound questions is essential in cross-examination, as they tend to confuse the witness and allow them to

choose the answer that is most favorable to their case. Instead, ask a series of simple questions to ensure clear and precise answers.

5. Silence: Pausing and allowing silence after a question can sometimes prompt the witness to provide additional information or reveal more than they intended. This technique can be particularly effective when the witness is uncomfortable or under pressure.

Ethical Considerations

While cross-examination is an essential tool in the legal profession, it is crucial to conduct it ethically and responsibly. The Model Rules of Professional Conduct and individual jurisdiction rules provide guidance on the ethical boundaries of cross-examination. Some important ethical considerations include:

1. Maintaining respect: Cross-examination should always be conducted with respect for the witness. Avoid personal attacks, inflammatory language, or disrespectful behavior.

2. Honesty and candor: The cross-examiner is obligated to present the facts truthfully and not to mislead the court or the witness. Misrepresenting evidence or asking misleading questions is considered unethical and can lead to adverse consequences.

3. Protecting vulnerable witnesses: Cross-examination of vulnerable witnesses, such as children or victims of trauma, requires additional sensitivity and caution. It is essential to balance the need to elicit relevant information with the potential harm to the witness.

4. Objection handling: The opposing counsel may raise objections during cross-examination. The cross-examiner should be familiar with the rules of evidence and be prepared to respond to objections effectively, either by rephrasing the question or justifying its admissibility.

Example Scenario

To illustrate the principles discussed above, let's consider a hypothetical criminal trial in which the defendant is accused of theft. The prosecution's main witness is an eyewitness who claims to have seen the defendant at the scene of the crime.

During cross-examination, the defense attorney employs leading questions to challenge the witness's credibility. The attorney begins by asking about the witness's location at the time of the incident, establishing that their visibility may have been limited. Then, the attorney presents evidence suggesting that the lighting conditions were poor, making it difficult to positively identify the defendant.

Next, the attorney introduces inconsistencies in the witness's prior statements and highlights potential biases or incentives that may impact their testimony. By skillfully using impeachment techniques and limited scope questions, the attorney weakens the witness's credibility and raises doubts about the reliability of their account.

The example scenario demonstrates how a prepared and diligent cross-examiner can employ questioning techniques to expose weaknesses in the witness's testimony and cast doubt on the prosecution's case.

Conclusion

Cross-examination is a valuable tool in the legal profession, allowing attorneys to challenge witnesses, test their credibility, and advance their case theory. By carefully planning cross-examination, employing effective questioning techniques, and adhering to ethical considerations, attorneys can use this skill to achieve favorable outcomes in the courtroom.

Resources for Further Exploration

1. Antony Bellamy. *Effective Cross-Examination: A Manual for Advocates.* Oxford University Press, 2018.

2. Larry S. Pozner and Roger J. Dodd. *Cross-Examination: Science and Techniques.* LexisNexis, 2014.

3. American Bar Association. *Model Rules of Professional Conduct.* Available at: `https://www.americanbar.org/groups/professional_responsibility/publications/model_rules_professional_conduct/`

Courtroom Etiquette and Professionalism

In the field of legal studies, courtroom etiquette and professionalism are crucial elements for ensuring the fair and efficient administration of justice. This section will explore the key principles and practices that lawyers, judges, and other legal professionals should adhere to when interacting in the courtroom setting. Understanding and maintaining proper courtroom etiquette not only contributes to a respectful and harmonious environment but also enhances the persuasive power of legal advocacy.

The Importance of Courtroom Etiquette

Courtroom etiquette encompasses a set of rules and norms that dictate appropriate behavior and decorum during legal proceedings. It serves several fundamental purposes, including:

- **Respect for the Court:** A well-maintained courtroom environment fosters respect for the authority of the judiciary and the rule of law. It ensures that all participants, including the judge, lawyers, witnesses, and jurors, are treated with dignity and professionalism.

- **Effective Advocacy:** Following proper etiquette enables lawyers to effectively communicate their arguments, present evidence, and question witnesses. A well-prepared and respectful attorney is more likely to gain the trust and confidence of the judge and jury, increasing the chances of a favorable outcome for their client.

- **Preserving Due Process:** Courtroom etiquette helps safeguard the integrity of due process, ensuring that each party involved in the legal proceeding has a fair opportunity to present their case without undue disruption or interference.

- **Maintaining Order and Efficiency:** By adhering to established courtroom etiquette, legal professionals contribute to the smooth flow of proceedings, avoiding unnecessary delays and distractions. This allows the court to efficiently address the issues at hand and deliver timely justice.

Key Principles of Courtroom Etiquette

To maintain proper courtroom etiquette, legal professionals should adhere to the following key principles:

1. **Professional Attire:** Dressing in appropriate professional attire demonstrates respect for the court and enhances the credibility of the legal professional. For lawyers, this typically includes wearing formal business attire, while judges generally wear robes or other designated attire that signifies their authority.

2. **Punctuality:** Being on time is of utmost importance in the legal profession. Lawyers, witnesses, and other parties involved should arrive early to court proceedings, allowing sufficient time for preparation and avoiding any disruptions to the proceedings.

3. **Courtesy and Respect:** Legal professionals must treat all participants in the courtroom with courtesy and respect, regardless of their position or views. This includes addressing the judge and opposing counsel in a polite and professional manner, refraining from personal attacks or disrespectful language.

4. **Active Listening:** Active listening is a key feature of courtroom etiquette. Lawyers should carefully listen to the judge, witnesses, and opposing counsel, demonstrating their attentiveness and respect for the proceedings. This allows for more effective engagement and responding appropriately to arguments or objections.

5. **Proper Courtroom Demeanor:** Legal professionals should maintain a calm and composed demeanor in court. This includes avoiding excessive gestures, facial expressions, or emotional outbursts that may distract or disrupt the proceedings. Maintaining a professional demeanor reinforces credibility and promotes an atmosphere of fairness and impartiality.

6. **Preparation and Organization:** Thorough preparation is a vital component of courtroom etiquette. Lawyers should be well-prepared, organized, and familiar with all relevant laws, facts, and case precedents. This ensures the smooth progress of the proceedings and allows for effective presentation of arguments and evidence.

Unique Challenges and Considerations

While courtroom etiquette generally consists of widely accepted practices, there can be unique challenges and considerations that legal professionals must navigate. Some of these challenges include:

- **Cultural Sensitivity:** In diverse legal settings, it is important to be culturally sensitive and respectful of different customs and practices. This includes understanding appropriate forms of address, gestures, and attire, which may vary across cultures.

- **Dealing with Difficult Clients or Opposing Counsel:** Lawyers may encounter challenging situations when dealing with difficult clients or opposing counsel who do not adhere to courtroom etiquette. In such cases, maintaining professionalism, seeking assistance from the judge if necessary, and adapting strategies to minimize disruption are essential.

- **Managing Technological Interactions:** With the increasing use of technology in courtrooms, legal professionals must understand the appropriate use of devices and software during proceedings. Following courtroom rules regarding cell phone usage, document presentation, and audiovisual equipment ensures smooth technological integration without causing distractions or compromising decorum.

Resources for Further Exploration

To delve deeper into courtroom etiquette and professionalism, the following resources can provide valuable insights and guidance:

- *The Articulate Advocate: Persuasive Skills for Lawyers in Trials, Appeals, Arbitrations, and Motions,* by Brian K. Johnson and Marsha Hunter, offers practical advice and techniques for effective courtroom advocacy and communication skills.

- *Courtroom 302: A Year Behind the Scenes in an American Criminal Courthouse,* by Steve Bogira, provides an immersive account of the workings of a courtroom and the complexities of the legal process.

- The American Bar Association (ABA) and various state bar associations offer comprehensive guides and resources on courtroom etiquette and professionalism. These can be accessed through their respective websites.

Conclusion

Courtroom etiquette and professionalism are essential components of legal practice, contributing to the fair and efficient administration of justice. Adhering to the principles discussed in this section ensures respectful interactions, effective advocacy, and the preservation of due process. By mastering the art of courtroom etiquette, legal professionals can enhance their persuasive power and uphold the integrity of the legal profession. Remember, a courtroom is not just a physical space but also a symbol of justice and the rule of law, deserving the utmost respect and professionalism.

The use of technology in the courtroom

In today's rapidly advancing technological age, the use of technology in the courtroom has become a vital aspect of modern legal practice. From enhancing efficiency and accuracy to improving the presentation and analysis of evidence, technology has transformed the way legal proceedings are conducted. This section will explore the various ways technology is being utilized in the courtroom, its benefits, potential challenges, and the ethical considerations that arise.

Benefits of technology in the courtroom

The integration of technology in the courtroom offers numerous benefits that contribute to a more streamlined and effective legal process. Some key advantages include:

1. **Enhanced evidence presentation:** Technology allows for the presentation of evidence in a more visually appealing and engaging manner, enabling judges and juries to better understand complex concepts. Tools such as multimedia presentations, 3D animations, and virtual reality simulations can help to recreate crime scenes, present expert testimony, and illustrate intricate details of a case.

2. **Improved access to information:** Digital databases and online platforms enable legal professionals to access vast amounts of legal resources, case law, and scholarly articles with a few clicks. This quick and seamless access to information enhances the research capabilities of lawyers, facilitating more accurate legal arguments and informed decision-making.

3. **Efficient case management:** Technology enables the efficient organization and management of case-related documents, reducing the need for extensive physical paperwork. Electronic case management systems allow lawyers and judges to store, search, and retrieve case documents, minimizing administrative burdens and improving overall case handling efficiency.

4. **Remote proceedings:** Utilizing technology, courts can conduct virtual hearings, allowing participants to attend proceedings remotely. This not only saves time and resources but also enables individuals in remote regions or those with limited mobility to access justice more easily.

5. **Electronic filing:** Technology enables the electronic filing of legal documents, eliminating the need for physical copies and reducing the

chances of misplaced or lost paperwork. Electronic filing systems help streamline administrative tasks, improve document security, and enhance overall efficiency in the courtroom.

Challenges and considerations

While the integration of technology in the courtroom brings numerous benefits, it also presents various challenges and ethical considerations that must be addressed. Some of the prominent challenges include:

1. **Cost and accessibility:** The implementation of advanced technology in the courtroom may require significant financial investment, making it inaccessible for courts with limited resources. It is essential to consider cost-effectiveness and address the potential inequality of access to justice that may arise as a result.

2. **Technical issues and reliance:** Technology is not infallible, and technical issues such as system crashes or software malfunctions can disrupt court proceedings. It is crucial to have backup plans and alternative methods in place to prevent delays or miscarriages of justice.

3. **Data security and privacy:** The use of technology necessitates the collection, storage, and transfer of large amounts of data. Ensuring robust security measures and adherence to privacy regulations is paramount to protect the sensitive information involved in legal proceedings.

4. **Equity and access to justice:** Although technology has the potential to improve access to justice, it also raises concerns about the digital divide. Not all individuals may have the necessary technological literacy or access to digital devices, potentially exacerbating existing inequalities in the legal system.

Ethical considerations

The use of technology in the courtroom also raises important ethical considerations that should be carefully addressed. Some key ethical considerations include:

1. **Admissibility and authenticity of digital evidence:** The authenticity and reliability of digital evidence need to be established. Ensuring proper chain of custody, data integrity, and authentication mechanisms is crucial to maintain the trustworthiness of digital evidence in court proceedings.

2. **Transparency and explainability of technology:** The use of complex technology, such as artificial intelligence algorithms or predictive analytics, must be transparent and explainable to ensure fairness and accountability. It is imperative that judges, lawyers, and other stakeholders understand the underlying principles and limitations of technology used in the courtroom.

3. **Ensuring fairness and impartiality:** Technology should not perpetuate or exacerbate biases or prejudices. Measures must be implemented to ensure that technology is used in a manner that does not discriminate against certain individuals or groups based on characteristics such as race, gender, or socioeconomic status.

4. **Preserving human interaction and empathy:** While technology can enhance efficiency, it should not compromise the human aspect of legal proceedings. Preserving the courtroom as a space for human interaction, empathy, and understanding is crucial in ensuring a fair and just legal system.

Examples of technology in the courtroom

To illustrate the practical applications of technology in the courtroom, here are a few examples:

1. **Electronic presentation systems:** Courts use software and hardware systems to present evidence in a visually engaging manner. This includes tools for displaying documents, videos, images, and other multimedia content.

2. **Electronic legal research platforms:** Online databases and research platforms provide legal professionals with instant access to a wealth of legal resources, including case law, statutes, regulations, and legal commentary.

3. **Video conferencing technology:** Courts may utilize video conferencing technology to conduct remote hearings, allowing participants to attend proceedings from different locations without the need for physical presence.

4. **Courtroom management software:** Electronic case management systems enable the efficient organization and retrieval of case-related information, simplifying administrative tasks and facilitating smoother court proceedings.

5. **Automated transcription services:** Technology allows for the automatic transcription of court proceedings, reducing the need for manual transcription and enabling faster access to verbatim records of the hearings.

Resources for further exploration

If you are interested in further exploring the use of technology in the courtroom, the following resources can be helpful:

1. *Technology in the Courts: A Planning and Management Guide* by National Center for State Courts. This guide provides practical insights and recommendations for courts in adopting and managing courtroom technology.

2. *AI in the Justice System: Navigating the Deployment* by World Economic Forum. This publication explores the implications of artificial intelligence in the justice system and provides guidelines for its responsible use.

3. *The Future of the Courtroom: How Technology Is Changing the Judicial Process* by Thomson Reuters. This article discusses the evolving role of technology in the courtroom and its potential impact on the legal profession.

Conclusion

The use of technology in the courtroom has revolutionized legal practice, enhancing efficiency, access to information, and evidence presentation. However, it also brings challenges and ethical considerations that must be carefully addressed. By embracing technology while ensuring fairness, transparency, and ethical principles, the legal system can harness its benefits to create a more just and effective courtroom environment. The integration of technology should always prioritize the preservation of human interaction, empathy, and the pursuit of justice for all.

Chapter 3: Cutting-Edge Research in Legal Studies

Emerging technologies and their impact on legal studies

Artificial intelligence and machine learning in legal research

Artificial intelligence (AI) and machine learning (ML) have gained significant attention in various fields, and the legal profession is no exception. The integration of AI and ML in legal research has the potential to revolutionize the way legal professionals analyze and interpret vast amounts of legal information. In this section, we will explore the applications of AI and ML in legal research, the benefits and challenges they present, and the ethical considerations that arise.

Understanding AI and ML

Before delving into the applications of AI and ML in legal research, it is crucial to understand the fundamental concepts of these technologies. AI refers to the development of intelligent systems that can perform tasks that typically require human intelligence. ML, on the other hand, is a subfield of AI that focuses on algorithms and statistical models that enable computers to learn and make predictions or decisions based on patterns in data.

Applications of AI and ML in legal research

1. Legal document analysis: AI and ML algorithms can analyze and extract relevant information from legal documents such as contracts, court opinions, and regulations. This automation saves time and improves efficiency in legal research.

For example, AI technology can identify and classify clauses in contracts, enabling legal professionals to quickly locate specific provisions.

2. Predictive analytics: ML algorithms can be trained on historical legal data to predict case outcomes, help assess risks, and provide insights for legal strategy. By analyzing patterns in previous cases, ML algorithms can identify relevant factors that influence legal decisions. This approach can assist lawyers in making informed decisions and improving their chances of success.

3. Legal research assistance: AI-powered legal research tools can assist lawyers in locating relevant case law, statutes, and legal articles. These tools use natural language processing and machine learning algorithms to understand legal queries and provide accurate search results. By automating the initial research process, legal professionals can save valuable time and focus on analyzing the information.

4. Due diligence and contract review: AI technologies can automate due diligence processes by reviewing large volumes of documents, identifying potential risks, and highlighting critical information. ML algorithms can analyze contracts to identify standard clauses, anomalies, or potential issues, allowing lawyers to focus their attention on areas requiring further analysis.

Benefits and challenges

The integration of AI and ML in legal research offers several benefits. Firstly, the automation of labor-intensive tasks reduces the time and effort required for legal research, enabling lawyers to get insights faster and improve productivity. Secondly, AI-powered tools can sift through vast amounts of data and identify relevant information with higher accuracy than manual research. This accuracy can minimize the risk of missing critical information and improve the quality of legal analysis.

However, there are also challenges associated with AI and ML in legal research. One significant challenge is the potential bias embedded in ML algorithms. If historical legal data used to train these algorithms contains biases, such as discriminatory judgments, the algorithms may perpetuate and amplify those biases. Ensuring fairness and accountability in AI systems is crucial to avoid perpetuating systemic inequalities.

Additionally, the legal profession faces ethical considerations related to the use of AI and ML. Privacy concerns arise when sensitive legal documents are stored and processed by AI systems. Transparency and explainability of AI algorithms are essential to ensure the ethical use of AI in legal research. Lawyers must understand how AI systems reach their conclusions to assess their reliability and make informed decisions.

Real-world example: ROSS Intelligence

One notable example of AI and ML in legal research is ROSS Intelligence. ROSS is an AI-powered legal research tool designed to assist lawyers in finding relevant case law. By understanding natural language queries, ROSS generates accurate and comprehensive search results, reducing the time spent on manual research.

Resources for further exploration

To deepen your understanding of AI and ML in legal research, here are some recommended resources:

- *The Future of the Professions: How Technology Will Transform the Work of Human Experts* by Richard Susskind and Daniel Susskind
- *Artificial Intelligence: A Guide to Intelligent Systems* by Michael Negnevitsky
- *Legal Tech, Smart Contracts and Blockchain* by Tony Lai and Laura Shin (Lawyerist Podcast)
- *Ethics of Artificial Intelligence and Robotics* by Vincent C. Müller (Stanford Encyclopedia of Philosophy)

Key takeaways

AI and ML have the potential to revolutionize legal research by automating tasks, improving efficiency, and providing valuable insights. Legal document analysis, predictive analytics, research assistance, and due diligence are some of the areas where AI and ML technologies are making an impact. However, ethical considerations, such as bias and privacy, must be addressed to ensure responsible and accountable use of AI in the legal profession. Continuous exploration and evaluation of AI and ML applications in legal research will shape the future of the legal profession.

Blockchain technology and smart contracts in the legal industry

In recent years, blockchain technology has emerged as a transformative force across various industries, and the legal industry is no exception. Blockchain, often associated with cryptocurrencies like Bitcoin, is a decentralized digital ledger that allows for secure and transparent transactions without the need for intermediaries. This section explores the applications of blockchain technology and its potential to revolutionize the legal industry, particularly through the use of smart contracts.

Understanding blockchain technology

To appreciate how blockchain technology can impact the legal industry, it is important to understand its fundamental principles. At its core, a blockchain is a distributed database or ledger that stores transactions in a series of blocks, forming a chronological chain. Unlike traditional centralized databases, blockchain technology relies on a network of computers, known as nodes, to validate and record transactions.

One key feature of blockchain technology is its immutability. Once a transaction is recorded on the blockchain, it is extremely difficult to alter or tamper with the data. This is achieved through cryptographic hashing, where each block contains a unique digital fingerprint, or hash, of the previous block. Any change made to the data in a block would invalidate the hashes of subsequent blocks, thus alerting the network to the tampering attempt.

Smart contracts and their potential in the legal industry

Smart contracts, built on blockchain technology, have the potential to revolutionize the way legal agreements are created, executed, and enforced. A smart contract is a self-executing digital contract that automatically enforces the terms and conditions written into its code. By removing the need for intermediaries or third parties, smart contracts offer increased efficiency, transparency, and security in legal transactions.

Smart contracts use if-then statements to automate contract execution. For example, if Party A completes an agreed-upon deliverable, then Party B releases payment. The terms and conditions of the contract are encoded into the smart contract's code, eliminating the need for subjective interpretation or reliance on intermediaries.

Examples of blockchain and smart contract applications in the legal industry

1. **Property transfers:** Blockchain technology can streamline the process of transferring property ownership by creating a transparent and tamper-proof record of transactions. Smart contracts can automatically execute property sales and transfers once predefined conditions are met, such as the receipt of payment or the completion of necessary legal documentation.

2. **Supply chain management:** Blockchain technology can enhance supply chain management by providing immutability and transparency to the movement of goods. Smart contracts can automate key aspects of the supply chain, such as

verifying product authenticity, tracking shipments, and triggering payment releases upon successful delivery.

3. **Intellectual property rights:** With blockchain technology, creators can establish transparent records of their intellectual property rights. Smart contracts can automatically enforce licensing agreements, ensuring that creators receive fair compensation when their work is used.

4. **Dispute resolution:** Blockchain technology can facilitate faster and more efficient dispute resolution processes. By recording all relevant information on the blockchain, including contractual agreements and transaction history, smart contracts can enable automated dispute resolution mechanisms, reducing the need for costly and time-consuming legal proceedings.

Challenges and considerations

While blockchain technology and smart contracts hold immense potential in the legal industry, there are several challenges and considerations to address:

1. **Legal recognition and regulatory framework:** As blockchain and smart contracts continue to evolve, there is a need for legal recognition and regulation to ensure their enforceability and compatibility with existing legal frameworks.

2. **Data privacy and security:** While blockchain offers secure and tamper-proof transactions, it raises concerns regarding the storage and protection of sensitive data. Striking a balance between transparency and privacy is crucial in implementing blockchain solutions in the legal industry.

3. **Technological literacy and adoption:** The successful implementation of blockchain technology and smart contracts relies on widespread technological literacy and adoption. Education and training programs should be developed to enable legal professionals to understand and effectively utilize these technologies.

4. **Interoperability and standardization:** Collaboration between different blockchain platforms and achieving interoperability among smart contracts is essential for the widespread adoption and seamless integration of blockchain technology in the legal industry.

Additional resources

To further explore the applications of blockchain technology and smart contracts in the legal industry, consider the following resources:

1. Tapscott, D., & Tapscott, A. (2016). *Blockchain revolution: how the technology behind bitcoin is changing money, business, and the world.*

2. De Filippi, P., & Wright, A. (2018). *Blockchain and the Law: The Rule of Code.*
3. Raval, S. (2016). *Blockchain Basics: A Non-Technical Introduction in 25 Steps.*
4. Casey, M. J., & Vigna, P. (2018). *The truth machine: The blockchain and the future of everything.*
5. World Economic Forum. (2020). *Bridging the Governance Gap: Emerging Technologies and Insights from Blockchain Governance.*

Exercises

1. Research and discuss a real-world example of how blockchain technology and smart contracts have been applied in the legal industry.
2. Identify and explain three potential benefits of utilizing blockchain technology and smart contracts in the legal industry.
3. Discuss the challenges associated with ensuring interoperability among different blockchain platforms and the implications for the legal profession.
4. Explore the ethical considerations surrounding the use of blockchain technology and smart contracts in the legal industry, such as privacy concerns and data ownership.
5. Debate the implications of smart contracts on the role of lawyers and legal professionals in the future.

Data analytics and predictive modeling in legal decision-making

In recent years, the field of legal studies has seen significant advancements in the use of data analytics and predictive modeling techniques to inform and enhance legal decision-making. This section explores how these tools and methodologies are reshaping the practice of law and revolutionizing the way legal professionals analyze and predict outcomes.

Background

Data analytics refers to the process of examining large sets of data to uncover patterns, correlations, and insights that can be used to make informed decisions. In the context of legal studies, data analytics involves analyzing various types of legal data, such as case law, statutes, regulatory documents, and legal texts, to derive meaningful information.

Predictive modeling, on the other hand, employs statistical techniques and algorithms to make predictions about future events or outcomes based on historical data. By leveraging historical legal data, predictive models can identify trends and patterns, helping legal professionals anticipate the possible outcome of a legal case or the likelihood of a legal event occurring.

The combination of data analytics and predictive modeling holds great potential for legal studies, as it empowers legal professionals to make evidence-based decisions, streamline processes, and improve access to justice.

Principles of data analytics and predictive modeling

To effectively leverage data analytics and predictive modeling in legal decision-making, legal professionals must understand and apply key principles. These principles include:

1. Data collection and preprocessing: Legal professionals need to gather relevant legal data and ensure its accuracy and completeness. Data preprocessing involves cleaning and transforming the data into a format suitable for analysis, eliminating any inconsistencies or errors.

2. Feature selection and extraction: Legal datasets often contain a multitude of variables. Feature selection and extraction involve identifying the most relevant variables that contribute to the outcome of interest. This step helps reduce data dimensionality and focuses the analysis on the most impactful factors.

3. Model selection and evaluation: Legal professionals must choose an appropriate predictive modeling technique, such as logistic regression, decision trees, or support vector machines. The selected model should be evaluated using performance metrics, such as accuracy, precision, recall, and F-1 score, to assess its predictive power and generalizability.

4. Interpretation of results: The insights derived from data analytics and predictive modeling should be interpreted in the context of legal principles, precedents, and norms. Legal professionals must critically evaluate the results and consider the legal and ethical implications of the predicted outcomes.

5. Continuous improvement and validation: Data analytics and predictive modeling are iterative processes. Legal professionals should continually refine and validate their models to ensure their accuracy, reliability, and fairness. Ongoing validation helps identify and mitigate biases or limitations in the models, ensuring they align with legal principles and societal values.

Applications in legal decision-making

Data analytics and predictive modeling have promising applications across various areas of legal decision-making. Some key applications include:

1. Case outcome prediction: Legal professionals can use predictive models to assess the likely outcome of a legal case based on historical case data. By considering factors such as case characteristics, judge/magistrate profiles, and legal precedents, predictive models can provide valuable insights to inform litigation strategies, settlement negotiations, and resource allocation.

2. Sentencing and bail decisions: Predictive modeling can assist judges and policymakers in determining appropriate sentences and bail conditions. By analyzing patterns in historical sentencing data, predictive models can help identify biases and disparities, promoting fairness and consistency in the criminal justice system.

3. Legal research and document analysis: Data analytics techniques can streamline legal research and document analysis, enabling legal professionals to quickly and accurately extract relevant information from vast volumes of legal texts. Natural language processing and machine learning algorithms can be used to automate the tagging, summarization, and classification of legal documents, saving time and improving efficiency.

4. Risk assessment and regulatory compliance: Predictive models can aid in assessing and managing legal risks, particularly in areas such as regulatory compliance and fraud detection. By analyzing historical regulatory data, organizations can identify potential compliance issues, assess their likelihood, and implement proactive measures to mitigate legal risks.

5. Policy analysis and impact assessment: Data analytics can inform evidence-based policy-making by analyzing the impact and effectiveness of existing legal frameworks. By quantifying the outcomes of policy interventions, policymakers can make informed decisions to enhance legal systems and promote social justice.

Challenges and considerations

While data analytics and predictive modeling offer significant benefits to legal decision-making, several challenges and considerations must be addressed:

1. Data quality and availability: Legal datasets may suffer from incompleteness, inconsistencies, or biases. Legal professionals must ensure the quality and integrity of the data used for analysis, carefully considering potential biases or limitations that may affect the accuracy and fairness of the models.

2. Ethical and privacy concerns: The use of data analytics and predictive modeling in legal studies raises ethical and privacy concerns. Legal professionals must navigate issues such as informed consent, data anonymization, and the responsible use of sensitive information. Transparency in model development and decision-making is crucial to maintain trust and ensure accountability.

3. Interpretability and explainability: Legal professionals must be able to interpret and explain the results obtained from predictive models. Black-box models, such as deep learning algorithms, may lack interpretability, making it challenging to understand the factors driving the predictions. Ensuring the interpretability of the models is essential to maintain legal transparency and enable informed decision-making.

4. Bias and fairness: Predictive models can inadvertently perpetuate biases present in historical legal data. It is crucial to identify and mitigate biases to ensure fairness and prevent the reinforcement of discriminatory practices. Legal professionals must carefully examine the features used in the models and apply fairness metrics to assess and address any disparities or biases.

5. Professional judgment and human expertise: While data analytics and predictive modeling can provide valuable insights, they should complement, rather than replace, professional judgment and legal expertise. Legal professionals must exercise critical thinking and consider the broader legal, social, and contextual factors that may not be captured by the data. Human judgment and ethical reasoning remain essential in the legal decision-making process.

Resources and further exploration

To delve deeper into the field of data analytics and predictive modeling in legal studies, the following resources are recommended:

- Book: "Predictive Analytics for Lawyers: Enhance Your Practice, Improve Client Satisfaction, and Increase Profitability" by Andrew B. Kucharski. This book provides a comprehensive introduction to predictive analytics in the legal field, exploring various applications and practical techniques for implementation.

- Journal: "Artificial Intelligence and Law." This interdisciplinary journal focuses on the intersection of AI, data analytics, and the law, publishing cutting-edge research and insights into the evolving field of legal technology.

- Online platform: "Lex Machina." Lex Machina offers a powerful legal analytics platform that enables legal professionals to access and analyze litigation data, benchmark outcomes, and gain strategic insights for informed decision-making.

Incorporating data analytics and predictive modeling into legal studies has the potential to revolutionize the way legal professionals approach and address legal challenges. By harnessing the power of data and technology, legal decision-making can become more evidence-based, efficient, and equitable, paving the way for a more just and inclusive legal system.

Cybersecurity and Privacy Issues in the Digital Age

In today's digitally interconnected world, cybersecurity and privacy have become paramount concerns. As technology continues to advance at an unprecedented pace, so do the threats to our personal data and online security. This section explores the various cybersecurity challenges and privacy issues that arise in the digital age, as well as the measures individuals and organizations can take to protect themselves.

The Growing Threat Landscape

With the rise of the internet, cloud computing, and mobile devices, cyber threats have become more sophisticated and pervasive. From data breaches to ransomware attacks, cybercriminals constantly seek new ways to exploit vulnerabilities in computer systems and compromise privacy. Some of the key cybersecurity challenges in the digital age include:

- **Malware and Viruses:** Malicious software, such as viruses, worms, and trojans, can infect systems and steal sensitive information.

- **Phishing and Social Engineering:** Cybercriminals use deceptive tactics to trick individuals into revealing personal information or login credentials.

- **Ransomware:** This type of malware encrypts files and demands a ransom in exchange for their release.
- **Data Breaches:** Hackers target organizations to gain unauthorized access to databases containing personal and financial information.
- **Identity Theft:** Cybercriminals can use stolen personal data to impersonate individuals and commit fraud.

Legal Framework and Regulations

To combat cyber threats and protect privacy, governments around the world have established laws and regulations. Some key legal aspects related to cybersecurity and privacy include:

- **Data Protection Laws:** These laws govern the collection, storage, and use of personal data by organizations, ensuring that individuals have control over their information.
- **Privacy Laws:** These laws protect the privacy of individuals by establishing restrictions on the collection and disclosure of personal information.
- **Cybercrime Laws:** These laws define and penalize cyber activities such as hacking, identity theft, and unauthorized access to computer systems.
- **International Agreements:** Countries collaborate to address global cybersecurity challenges by entering into agreements and treaties that promote information sharing and cooperation.

However, enforcing these laws and regulations can be challenging due to the cross-border nature of cybercrime and rapidly evolving technologies. Additionally, balancing the need for security with individuals' privacy rights is an ongoing discussion.

Protecting Cybersecurity and Privacy

Protecting cybersecurity and privacy requires a multi-layered approach involving individuals, organizations, and policymakers. Here are some practical strategies that can help mitigate the risks:

- **Strong Passwords and Multi-Factor Authentication:** Using unique, complex passwords and enabling multi-factor authentication adds an extra layer of security to online accounts.

- **Regular Software Updates:** Keeping software and devices up to date ensures that security patches and fixes are applied, protecting against known vulnerabilities.
- **Secure Network Connections:** Using secure Wi-Fi networks and Virtual Private Networks (VPNs) encrypts internet traffic, safeguarding against eavesdropping and data interception.
- **Email and Web Security:** Being cautious while opening email attachments, clicking on links, or browsing websites helps prevent falling victim to phishing attacks and malware infections.
- **Data Encryption:** Encrypting sensitive data, both at rest and in transit, prevents unauthorized access even if the data is intercepted.

Moreover, organizations must prioritize cybersecurity by implementing robust security measures, conducting regular risk assessments, and educating employees about best practices. Additionally, individuals should be proactive in understanding their digital footprint, managing their online privacy settings, and being mindful of the information they share online.

Emerging Technologies and Future Challenges

As technology continues to advance rapidly, new challenges and opportunities in cybersecurity and privacy arise. Some emerging technologies that have implications for cybersecurity include:

- **Internet of Things (IoT):** With the proliferation of interconnected devices, securing IoT networks and devices becomes crucial to prevent unauthorized access and control.
- **Artificial Intelligence (AI):** AI can be both a tool for enhancing cybersecurity and a means for cyber attackers to automate attacks and evade detection.
- **Blockchain Technology:** Blockchain's decentralized and transparent nature holds promise for secure transactions and data integrity, but challenges in implementation and regulation remain.

Addressing these emerging technologies' cybersecurity and privacy implications requires ongoing research, collaboration among stakeholders, and adapting legal frameworks to keep pace with technological advancements.

Resources for Further Exploration

To deepen your understanding of cybersecurity and privacy issues in the digital age, consider exploring the following resources:

- Books:
  - "Cybersecurity and Privacy in the Digital Age" by George E. Curtis
  - "The Fourth Industrial Revolution" by Klaus Schwab
  - "Future Crimes: Inside the Digital Underground and the Battle for our Connected World" by Marc Goodman
- Websites and Organizations:
  - Electronic Frontier Foundation (EFF) - eff.org
  - Center for Internet Security (CIS) - cisecurity.org
  - International Association of Privacy Professionals (IAPP) - iapp.org
  - United Nations Office on Drugs and Crime (UNODC) - unodc.org/cybersecurity

In conclusion, cybersecurity and privacy are pressing concerns in the digital age. Understanding the evolving threat landscape, legal frameworks, and best practices for protection is crucial for individuals, organizations, and policymakers alike. By adopting proactive measures and staying informed about emerging technologies and future challenges, we can navigate the digital landscape while safeguarding our privacy and security.

The ethical implications of emerging technologies in legal studies

With the rapid advancement of technology, emerging technologies such as artificial intelligence (AI), blockchain, data analytics, and cybersecurity have started to play a significant role in the field of legal studies. However, along with their numerous benefits, these technologies also bring forth various ethical implications. In this section, we will explore the ethical challenges and considerations that arise from the use of emerging technologies in legal studies.

Privacy and data protection

One of the primary ethical concerns with the use of emerging technologies in legal studies is the protection of privacy and personal data. As AI and data analytics are integrated into legal research and decision-making processes, vast amounts of data are collected and analyzed. This raises questions about the ethical handling of sensitive information and the potential for misuse or unauthorized access.

Example: For instance, AI algorithms that predict recidivism rates to assist judges in sentencing decisions may rely on historical data that perpetuates biases and discrimination. If such systems are not carefully designed and validated, they can encode and perpetuate existing injustices.

To address these concerns, legal scholars and practitioners must prioritize the development and implementation of robust data protection and privacy measures. This includes ensuring compliance with relevant laws and regulations, obtaining informed consent from individuals whose data is being used, and implementing strict security protocols to safeguard sensitive information.

Bias and discrimination

Another significant ethical implication of emerging technologies in legal studies is the potential for bias and discrimination. AI algorithms and machine learning models are trained on large datasets, which can inadvertently perpetuate societal biases and prejudices. Moreover, human biases present in the datasets used for training can be amplified and duplicated by these technologies, leading to unjust outcomes.

Example: For example, facial recognition software, if not adequately trained on diverse datasets, can result in biased decisions, disproportionately affecting certain racial or ethnic groups.

To mitigate the risk of bias and discrimination, legal researchers, developers, and policymakers must employ techniques such as fairness testing and algorithmic auditing. These processes involve assessing the impact of these technologies on different demographic groups, identifying and addressing any biases or discriminatory patterns, and continuously monitoring and improving the algorithms to ensure fairness and accuracy.

Ethical responsibility and accountability

The introduction of emerging technologies in legal studies raises questions about the ethical responsibility and accountability of those involved in their development, deployment, and use. Legal professionals must consider the potential consequences of relying on these technologies and ensure that they align with established legal and ethical principles.

Example: When using AI-powered legal research platforms, lawyers must critically evaluate the sources of information and algorithms driving these tools to avoid undue reliance on potentially biased or flawed data.

To uphold ethical standards, legal researchers and practitioners should engage in ongoing education and training to understand the limitations and risks of emerging technologies. Additionally, they should advocate for transparency and accountability in the development and use of these technologies, including mechanisms for auditing, oversight, and recourse in case of errors or unethical behavior.

Threats to legal professional ethics

The integration of emerging technologies in legal studies can also pose challenges to legal professional ethics. These technologies can blur the boundaries between human judgment and automated decision-making, potentially compromising the traditional ethical obligations and responsibilities of legal professionals.

Example: With the automation of contract drafting and review, lawyers may face ethical dilemmas when relying on AI-powered systems to identify and address potential legal issues. The responsibility to provide competent and diligent legal advice may be undermined if lawyers blindly trust these technologies without exercising independent professional judgment.

To address these challenges, legal professionals should adhere to established ethical guidelines and frameworks and consider the impact of emerging technologies on their professional obligations. This may involve reevaluating ethical responsibilities in light of advancing technologies, developing guidelines for the responsible use of automation, and ensuring that human judgment and oversight remain central to legal decision-making processes.

Conclusion

As the field of legal studies embraces emerging technologies, it is crucial to recognize and address the ethical implications that arise. Privacy and data protection, bias and discrimination, ethical responsibility and accountability, and threats to legal professional ethics are some of the key concerns that require attention and proactive measures. By addressing these ethical issues, legal researchers and practitioners can harness the benefits of emerging technologies while upholding the principles of justice, fairness, and equality.

Resources for further exploration: - Floridi, L. (2020). *Ethics of artificial intelligence and robotics.* Cambridge: Cambridge University Press. - Ohm, P., & Reidenberg, J. R. (2017). *Automating the legal profession: A call for an affirmative duty to learn about and use technology.* Cornell Law Review, 102(6), 1619-1682. - Burrell, J. (2016). *How the machine "thinks": Understanding opacity in machine learning algorithms.* Big Data & Society, 3(1), 1-12.

Comparative legal studies and global perspectives

Comparative Law Methodologies and Approaches

Comparative law is a discipline that seeks to compare and analyze legal systems across different countries or jurisdictions. It provides a valuable framework for understanding the similarities and differences in legal norms, principles, and institutions. In this section, we will explore various methodologies and approaches used in comparative law, highlighting their benefits, limitations, and practical applications.

Methodologies in Comparative Law

Comparative law employs several methodologies to facilitate the comparative study of legal systems. Each methodology offers a unique perspective, allowing for a comprehensive analysis of legal systems.

1. **Functional Methodology:** This methodology focuses on the functions and objectives of legal rules rather than their form or specific wording. It seeks to identify the underlying purposes and policies behind legal norms. By examining the similarities and differences in how different legal systems address similar issues, the functional approach enables researchers to identify common challenges and solutions across jurisdictions.

2. **Historical Methodology:** The historical methodology explores the evolution and development of legal systems over time. It examines how legal principles, institutions, and doctrines have changed and adapted in response to societal and cultural changes. By tracing the historical development of legal systems, researchers can gain insights into how legal norms have been shaped and influenced by their historical contexts.

3. **Comparative Legal Transplants:** This methodology focuses on the transfer of legal norms and institutions from one legal system to another. It examines

how legal ideas and practices are borrowed, adapted, and implemented in different jurisdictions. By studying legal transplants, researchers can identify the challenges and benefits associated with the adoption of foreign legal elements.

4. **Functional Comparativism:** Functional comparativism combines the functional and comparative approaches to analyze how legal systems address similar functional needs. It aims to identify common problems and solutions across jurisdictions, regardless of the differences in legal traditions and structures. This methodology allows researchers to focus on the effectiveness and efficiency of legal systems in achieving specific objectives.

5. **Doctrinal Comparative Analysis:** This methodology focuses on the analysis of legal texts, such as statutes, regulations, and court judgments. It involves comparing the language, structure, and interpretation of legal documents across different jurisdictions. By examining doctrinal aspects, researchers can gain insights into the similarities and differences in legal reasoning and decision-making processes.

Approaches in Comparative Law

In addition to methodologies, comparative law also employs various approaches to facilitate the comparison of legal systems. These approaches provide different perspectives and tools for analysis.

1. **Functionalism:** The functionalist approach emphasizes the practical functions and purposes of legal rules. It focuses on how legal systems solve common problems and fulfill societal needs. By examining the effectiveness and efficiency of legal solutions, functionalism allows for a meaningful comparison of legal systems beyond their formal aspects.

2. **Formalism:** Formalism emphasizes the formal characteristics and structures of legal systems. It focuses on legal rules, doctrines, and procedures. Formalist analysis highlights the similarities and differences in legal concepts and frameworks across jurisdictions. This approach is particularly useful when examining legal systems with similar or related legal traditions.

3. **Sociological Approach:** The sociological approach in comparative law examines the social and cultural contexts in which legal systems operate. It explores how social factors, such as cultural norms, economic conditions, and power dynamics, shape legal rules and institutions. By considering the

societal influences on legal systems, this approach helps researchers understand the broader implications and impact of legal norms.

4. **Functional Equivalence:** Functional equivalence suggests that different legal systems may achieve similar functions or objectives through different legal rules and institutions. It recognizes that diverse legal systems can address similar societal needs in different ways. By identifying functionally equivalent solutions, researchers can learn from alternative legal approaches and adapt them to their own jurisdictions.

5. **Comparative Institutional Analysis:** This approach focuses on the organizational structures and processes within legal systems. It examines the roles and functions of various legal actors, such as legislatures, courts, and administrative bodies. Comparative institutional analysis allows for a deeper understanding of how legal systems operate and interact with other societal institutions.

Practical Applications

Comparative law methodologies and approaches have practical applications in various areas of legal studies and practice. Some of the key applications include:

- **Legal Reform and Harmonization:** Comparative law provides valuable insights into different legal systems, enabling policymakers and lawmakers to identify best practices and potential areas for legal reform. By comparing legal solutions from different jurisdictions, it is possible to develop more effective and efficient legal frameworks.

- **Jurisprudence and Legal Theory:** Comparative law contributes to the development of legal theory by revealing the diversity and commonalities in legal systems. By analyzing different approaches to legal issues, scholars can challenge existing legal theories and develop new ones that capture the complexity of legal systems.

- **International and Comparative Litigation:** Comparative law is essential in cases involving transnational legal issues. It helps lawyers and judges navigate the complexities of multiple legal systems and find appropriate legal solutions. Comparative legal analysis is particularly valuable in resolving conflicts of laws or harmonizing legal principles across jurisdictions.

- **Legal Education and Research:** Comparative law plays a crucial role in legal education and research, exposing students and researchers to different legal cultures and traditions. It broadens their understanding of legal systems and encourages critical thinking and analytical skills.

Resources and Further Reading

For further exploration of comparative law methodologies and approaches, the following resources are recommended:

- Glenn, H. P. (2010). *Legal Traditions of the World.* Oxford University Press.
- Legrand, P., & Munday, R. (Eds.). (2003). *Comparative Legal Studies: Traditions and Transitions.* Cambridge University Press.
- Bussani, M., & Mattei, U. (Eds.). (2017). *Comparative Law: Engaging Translation.* Edward Elgar Publishing.
- Watson, A. (2014). *Legal Transplants: An Approach to Comparative Law.* University of Georgia Press.
- Örücü, E. (2014). *Comparative Law: A Handbook.* Bloomsbury Publishing.

These resources provide comprehensive overviews of comparative law methodologies and approaches, offering insights into their theoretical foundations and practical applications.

Case Study: Comparative Analysis of Contract Law

To illustrate the practical application of comparative law methodologies and approaches, let's consider a case study focusing on contract law.

Suppose a multinational corporation wants to expand its operations into a new jurisdiction and needs to understand the contract law principles and practices of that jurisdiction. By employing comparative law methodologies and approaches, the corporation can conduct a comparative analysis of contract law between its home jurisdiction and the target jurisdiction.

Using a functional methodology, the corporation can compare the functions and objectives of contract law in both jurisdictions. It can identify commonalities and differences in contract formation, interpretation, performance, and remedies. This analysis helps the corporation understand how to adapt its contract management practices to comply with the legal requirements and expectations in the target jurisdiction.

In terms of approaches, the corporation can employ both formalism and sociological approaches. The formalist analysis allows for a comparison of legal doctrines, contract formation requirements, and interpretation principles between the two jurisdictions. The sociological approach helps the corporation understand the social and cultural factors that may influence contract negotiations and operations in the target jurisdiction.

By using comparative law methodologies and approaches, the corporation gains valuable insights into contract law practices, ensuring compliance and facilitating successful business operations in the new jurisdiction.

Exercises

1. Select two countries with different legal systems and compare their approach to criminal justice. Identify the key similarities and differences, and analyze the potential impact on the administration of justice.

2. Investigate how different jurisdictions handle intellectual property rights protection. Analyze the legal frameworks, enforcement mechanisms, and international obligations. Assess the effectiveness of these approaches in fostering innovation and creativity.

3. Compare the constitutional protection of human rights in different countries. Focus on specific rights, such as freedom of speech or the right to privacy. Analyze the legal provisions, court rulings, and societal attitudes towards these rights. Discuss the challenges and opportunities in achieving a balance between individual rights and societal interests.

These exercises will allow you to apply comparative law methodologies and approaches to real-world legal issues, enhancing your understanding of legal systems and fostering critical thinking skills.

In summary, comparative law methodologies and approaches provide valuable tools for analyzing and comparing legal systems. By employing these methodologies and approaches, legal scholars, practitioners, and policymakers can gain a deeper understanding of legal systems, facilitate legal reform, and address complex transnational legal issues. The interdisciplinary nature of comparative law enriches legal studies and contributes to a more just and equitable global legal framework.

Case studies in comparative legal studies

In this section, we will explore various case studies in comparative legal studies. Comparative legal studies is a discipline that involves analyzing and comparing different legal systems across countries or regions. By examining the similarities and differences in laws, legal institutions, and legal frameworks, comparative legal studies help us gain insights into the diverse approaches taken by different jurisdictions in addressing legal issues.

Case Study 1: Comparative Corporate Governance

One fascinating area within comparative legal studies is the examination of corporate governance practices across different countries. Corporate governance refers to the rules, practices, and processes by which a company is directed and controlled. It encompasses the relationships among various stakeholders, such as shareholders, management, employees, and regulators.

For instance, let's compare the corporate governance systems in the United States and Germany. In the United States, the corporate governance model is primarily shareholder-oriented, emphasizing shareholder value maximization. The board of directors consists of both executive and non-executive directors, with the latter playing a crucial role in overseeing management decisions. Additionally, shareholders have substantial power to influence corporate decision-making through voting and the ability to propose resolutions.

On the other hand, Germany follows a two-tier board system, with separate supervisory and management boards. The supervisory board consists of employee representatives and shareholder representatives, who jointly oversee the activities of the management board. This dual-board structure aims to ensure that the interests of both shareholders and employees are adequately represented.

By comparing these two corporate governance models, researchers can explore the strengths and weaknesses of each system. They can evaluate the impact of these different approaches on various aspects, such as company performance, transparency, accountability, and protection of minority shareholders.

Case Study 2: Comparative Criminal Justice Systems

Another intriguing area of comparative legal studies is the examination of criminal justice systems across different jurisdictions. Comparative analysis in this field allows us to gain insights into how different legal systems handle criminal offenses, protect individual rights, and promote social justice.

Let's consider a case study comparing the criminal justice systems of the United States and the United Kingdom. In the United States, the criminal justice system is predominantly adversarial, with an emphasis on individual rights, due process, and the presumption of innocence. Prosecutors and defense attorneys play active roles in presenting evidence and arguments, and the judge acts as an impartial arbiter.

In contrast, the criminal justice system in the United Kingdom follows an inquisitorial approach, with more active involvement from the judge in the investigation and determination of guilt. The system places a greater emphasis on finding the truth rather than adhering strictly to procedural rules. Additionally, the UK system allows for more flexibility in sentencing, considering factors such as rehabilitation and reintegration into society.

By comparing these two approaches to criminal justice, researchers can examine factors such as conviction rates, access to legal representation, and the effectiveness of rehabilitation programs. They can also explore the impact of different systems on the rights of defendants and the public's confidence in the justice system.

Case Study 3: Comparative Family Law

Comparative legal studies also offer valuable insights into family law systems across different jurisdictions. Family law encompasses a wide range of legal issues related to marriage, divorce, child custody, adoption, and domestic violence.

Let's explore a case study comparing family law systems in France and the United States. In France, family law is based on the concept of solidarity between family members, particularly in matters related to financial support and the division of assets. The legal framework places a strong emphasis on the protection of the family unit and the welfare of children.

In the United States, family law varies across states, but it generally emphasizes individual rights and autonomy. For instance, some states have adopted a "no-fault" approach to divorce, allowing couples to dissolve their marriage without having to prove fault or wrongdoing. Additionally, child custody decisions are based on the best interests of the child, taking into consideration factors such as parental fitness and the child's well-being.

By comparing the family law systems of France and the United States, researchers can examine the impact of different legal principles on issues such as the division of marital property, child support, and child custody arrangements. They can also explore the cultural and societal factors that shape each jurisdiction's approach to family law.

Resources for Further Exploration

If you're interested in delving deeper into comparative legal studies and exploring more case studies, here are some recommended resources:

- *Comparative Legal Systems: Cases and Materials*, by Sherri L. Burr and Austin Sarat
- *Comparative Law: Law Beyond Borders*, by Ugo Mattei and Matteo Ferrari
- *Comparative Law: A Handbook*, edited by Esin Örücü and David Nelken
- *Comparative Law in a Changing World*, edited by Mauro Bussani and Ugo Mattei
- *The Oxford Handbook of Comparative Law*, edited by Mathias Reimann and Reinhard Zimmermann

These resources provide comprehensive overviews of comparative legal studies, covering various topics, including corporate governance, criminal justice, family law, and more. They offer in-depth analysis, case studies, and theoretical frameworks that will enhance your understanding of this fascinating field.

As you explore these resources, try to engage with the material actively. Reflect on the strengths and weaknesses of different legal systems, critically analyze case studies, and consider the broader societal and cultural implications of the legal principles under examination. Comparative legal studies offer an opportunity to develop a comparative mindset and a deeper appreciation for the complexities of legal systems worldwide.

Exercises

Now, let's apply your knowledge through some exercises:

1. Choose two countries with different legal systems and compare their approaches to environmental protection laws. Analyze the strengths and weaknesses of each system, and consider their effectiveness in addressing environmental challenges.

2. Investigate the legal framework surrounding intellectual property rights in two jurisdictions of your choice. Compare the approaches taken by each jurisdiction, and discuss the impact of these frameworks on the innovation and creativity of individuals and businesses.

3. Research the juvenile justice systems in two countries, and evaluate the measures taken to balance the rehabilitation and punishment of young offenders. Consider the societal factors that influence these systems and propose potential improvements.

By actively engaging with these exercises, you will deepen your understanding of comparative legal studies and develop critical thinking skills that are essential in the field. Remember to consult relevant legal resources, scholarly articles, and case law to support your analysis.

Conclusion

In this section, we explored case studies in comparative legal studies, focusing on corporate governance, criminal justice systems, and family law. By comparing legal systems across different countries, we can gain valuable insights into diverse approaches to legal issues and foster a deeper understanding of the global legal landscape.

We examined the case studies of comparative corporate governance, comparative criminal justice systems, and comparative family law, highlighting the key differences and their implications. Through these examples, we learned how comparative analysis assists in evaluating legal frameworks and understanding their impact on society.

To further explore comparative legal studies, we provided a list of recommended resources covering a wide range of topics. We also offered exercises to apply your knowledge and enhance your critical thinking skills.

As you delve into the field of comparative legal studies, remember to approach each case study with an open mind. Embrace the diversity of legal systems, challenge assumptions, and seek a deeper understanding of the complex relationship between law, society, and justice.

Identifying Trends and Patterns in Global Legal Systems

Understanding the trends and patterns in global legal systems is essential for legal scholars and practitioners who seek to gain insights into the evolving landscape of law across different jurisdictions. By examining commonalities and differences, legal professionals can identify patterns that emerge in legal systems worldwide and anticipate future developments. In this section, we will explore various methods and approaches to identify trends and patterns in global legal systems.

Comparative Law Methodologies and Approaches

Comparative law is a fundamental discipline for analyzing and understanding legal systems across different countries and regions. It provides a framework for identifying patterns, similarities, and differences among legal systems. To identify trends and patterns effectively, scholars utilize various methodologies and approaches in comparative law, including:

- **Functional approach:** This approach focuses on understanding the underlying purposes and functions of legal rules and institutions in different legal systems. By examining the functions that legal systems seek to achieve, scholars can identify common patterns and trends.

- **Historical approach:** By examining historical legal sources and developments, legal scholars can identify trends and patterns that have shaped legal systems over time. The historical approach allows for a deeper understanding of the factors that have influenced legal systems and their evolution.

- **Qualitative research:** Qualitative research methods, such as interviews, case studies, and ethnographic observations, provide rich and contextual insights into legal systems. This approach allows researchers to identify trends and patterns by examining real-life experiences and perspectives of individuals within legal systems.

- **Quantitative analysis:** Quantitative analysis involves gathering and analyzing data from multiple legal systems to identify patterns, correlations, and trends. Statistical methods, such as regression analysis and data visualization techniques, enable researchers to identify and quantify trends across different legal systems.

- **Comparative legal reasoning:** Scholars engage in comparative legal reasoning by analyzing legal doctrines, principles, and concepts across different legal systems. By comparing legal reasoning methods, scholars can identify trends and patterns in the ways legal systems approach similar legal issues.

Case Studies in Comparative Legal Studies

To illustrate the process of identifying trends and patterns, let's consider a case study in comparative legal studies: the legalization of same-sex marriage.

Case Study: Legalization of Same-Sex Marriage

In recent decades, there has been a global shift towards recognizing and legalizing same-sex marriage. By examining the legal developments across different countries, we can identify trends and patterns in the legalization process.

Identifying Trends: Through comparative analysis, we observe the following trends:

1. **Incremental progression:** Many countries have taken incremental steps towards legalizing same-sex marriage. Initially, some countries introduced registered partnership or civil union laws before eventually granting full marriage rights.

2. **Judicial intervention:** Judicial decisions have played a pivotal role in pushing for the legalization of same-sex marriage. Courts in several countries have declared existing marriage laws as unconstitutional, leading to the legalization of same-sex marriage.

3. **Influence of international standards:** International human rights standards, such as those set by the United Nations and the European Court of Human Rights, have influenced the legalization of same-sex marriage in various countries. Rulings from international bodies often serve as precedents and persuasive authorities for domestic courts.

Identifying Patterns: By examining the experiences of different countries, we can identify common patterns:

1. **Cultural shifts:** Countries that have legalized same-sex marriage often reflect a broader cultural shift towards greater acceptance and support for LGBTQ+ rights. This pattern suggests that legal changes are often reflective of changing societal attitudes.

2. **Domino effect:** The legalization of same-sex marriage in one country often leads to a domino effect, with neighboring and international jurisdictions following suit. This pattern demonstrates the influence of legal developments in one jurisdiction on others.

3. **Legislative vs. judicial action:** The process of legalizing same-sex marriage varies across countries. Some countries have achieved legalization through legislative action, while others have relied on judicial decisions. This pattern highlights the role of different branches of government in effecting legal change.

Cultural and Contextual Considerations in Comparative Legal Studies

When identifying trends and patterns in global legal systems, it is crucial to consider the cultural and contextual factors that shape legal developments. Legal systems do not exist in isolation but are deeply influenced by social, cultural, and historical circumstances. Some important considerations include:

- **Historical context:** The historical background of a legal system can significantly impact its development and shape its laws. Understanding historical events and cultural norms is essential for identifying trends and patterns.

- **Political and social context:** The political and social environment of a country plays a vital role in shaping its legal system. Factors such as political ideologies, social movements, and power dynamics can influence legal developments and trends.

- **Legal traditions:** Different legal systems are grounded in specific legal traditions or families, such as common law, civil law, or Islamic law. These traditions contribute to the uniqueness and diversity of legal systems, influencing trends and patterns in legal developments.

It is important to approach comparative legal studies with sensitivity to cultural and contextual differences. An understanding of these factors provides a nuanced perspective on trends and patterns in global legal systems.

Resources and Further Exploration

To delve deeper into identifying trends and patterns in global legal systems, here are some valuable resources and further avenues for exploration:

- **Books:** "Comparative Law: Cases, Texts, Materials" by Pierre Legrand and Roderick Munday, and "Comparative Legal Traditions" by Mary Ann Glendon provide comprehensive overviews of comparative law methodologies and approaches.

- **Journals:** "The American Journal of Comparative Law" and "The International and Comparative Law Quarterly" publish scholarly articles on comparative legal studies and offer insights into emerging trends and patterns.

- **International Organizations:** The United Nations, the World Bank, and the World Trade Organization (WTO) provide valuable resources on comparative legal systems and emerging trends in global law.
- **Legal Databases:** Online legal databases, such as Westlaw and LexisNexis, offer access to legal materials from multiple jurisdictions, allowing researchers to compare legal systems and identify trends.

Exploring these resources and engaging in comparative legal research will enhance your ability to identify trends and patterns in global legal systems, enabling a deeper understanding of the evolving landscape of law worldwide.

Unconventional Insight: Legal Transplants

In the study of global legal systems, the concept of "legal transplants" offers an unconventional yet relevant perspective. Legal transplants refer to the transfer of legal rules, institutions, or systems from one jurisdiction to another. It recognizes that legal systems are not static entities but constantly evolve through the adoption and adaptation of ideas from other legal systems.

Legal transplants can have both positive and negative consequences. While they may lead to the adoption of progressive legal principles, they can also perpetuate colonial legacies and undermine local traditions. Studying the phenomenon of legal transplants provides insights into the process of legal change, the dynamics of legal borrowing, and the challenges of reconciling different legal traditions.

For example, the transplant of common law principles into civil law jurisdictions has generated debates and challenges in harmonizing different legal systems. Understanding the complexities of legal transplants helps us identify the patterns and influences that shape global legal systems, providing valuable insights for legal practitioners and scholars.

Conclusion

Identifying trends and patterns in global legal systems requires a multidimensional approach that combines comparative law methodologies, case studies, cultural considerations, and an exploration of legal transplants. By examining trends and patterns, legal professionals can gain a deeper understanding of the dynamics and evolution of legal systems worldwide. This understanding lays the foundation for anticipating future developments and shaping the future of legal studies.

Remember to embrace the interdisciplinary nature of legal studies, as insights from sociology, history, political science, and other fields can further enrich your understanding of trends and patterns in global legal systems. Keep exploring, questioning, and engaging with legal scholarship to unlock new perspectives and contribute to the transformative advances in legal studies.

Cultural and contextual considerations in comparative legal studies

In the field of comparative legal studies, it is essential to recognize the significance of cultural and contextual factors in understanding and analyzing legal systems across different societies. While legal systems may share similar structures and principles, their implementation and interpretation can vary greatly due to cultural norms, historical context, and social values. This section explores the importance of cultural and contextual considerations in comparative legal studies and provides insights into how they influence the development and operation of legal systems.

Understanding cultural diversity in legal systems

Culture plays a crucial role in shaping legal norms and practices within a society. Legal systems are deeply embedded in the cultural fabric of a community, reflecting the values, traditions, and beliefs prevalent in that society. When comparing legal systems, it is important to understand the unique cultural context within which they operate.

Cultural diversity can manifest in various ways, such as language, religion, customs, and social norms. These factors can significantly impact how laws are interpreted, applied, and enforced. For example, in some cultures, collective decision-making may be prioritized over individual rights, leading to different approaches to issues such as property ownership, family law, and governance.

Cultural relativism and legal pluralism

Cultural relativism is the concept that the practice of law should be evaluated within the context of the culture in which it operates. It recognizes that diverse cultural perspectives may result in different legal systems and norms. When studying comparative legal systems, adopting a culturally relativistic approach helps us understand the reasons behind varying legal practices and prevents cultural biases or ethnocentric viewpoints.

Legal pluralism is closely related to cultural relativism and emphasizes the coexistence of multiple legal systems within a society. It recognizes that different cultural and religious groups may have their own legal frameworks alongside the state legal system. In many countries, indigenous communities maintain their own legal traditions and dispute resolution mechanisms alongside the national legal system. Understanding legal pluralism is crucial for comprehending the full complexity and richness of legal systems in comparative studies.

Implications for legal analysis

When conducting comparative legal studies, it is essential to consider the cultural and contextual factors that influence the interpretation and application of laws. Failure to do so could result in misunderstandings or misinterpretations of legal principles and practices.

One approach to addressing cultural and contextual considerations is through interdisciplinary collaboration. By incorporating insights from anthropology, sociology, history, and other relevant disciplines, researchers can gain a more comprehensive understanding of how cultural factors shape legal systems. This interdisciplinary approach allows for a more nuanced analysis of legal practices and can provide deeper insights into the underlying cultural values and societal norms that influence legal decision-making.

Moreover, comparative legal scholars should be aware of the limitations of their own cultural biases and strive for objectivity in their analysis. This requires an open-minded approach that recognizes the validity and value of different legal systems, even if they differ from one's own.

Example: Cultural considerations in Islamic law

Islamic law, also known as Shariah, provides an interesting case study for examining cultural and contextual considerations in comparative legal studies. Islamic legal systems are influenced by both religious principles and cultural traditions, varying across different countries and regions.

For example, family law in Islamic countries may be governed by Shariah principles but also incorporate local traditions and customs. Divorce laws and inheritance rules can differ significantly between countries, reflecting the specific cultural and societal norms within each jurisdiction. Comparative legal studies involving Islamic legal systems must take into account these cultural and contextual factors to fully understand the complexities of Islamic law.

Conclusion

Cultural and contextual considerations play a vital role in comparative legal studies. Recognizing the influence of cultural diversity, adopting a culturally relativistic approach, and understanding legal pluralism are essential for gaining a comprehensive understanding of legal systems across societies. Incorporating interdisciplinary perspectives and remaining aware of one's own cultural biases are crucial for conducting objective and insightful analysis. By embracing cultural and contextual considerations, researchers can enhance their understanding of legal systems and contribute to the advancement of justice and equality worldwide.

Resources for further exploration

- Merry, S. E. (2016). *The Seductions of Quantification: Measuring Human Rights, Gender Violence, and Sex Trafficking* (Chapter 3). University of Chicago Press.

- Snyder, F. E., and Vinjamuri, L. (Eds.). (2014). *Prosecuting International Crimes and Human Rights Abuses Committed Against Children: Leading International Court Cases* (Chapter 7). Cambridge University Press.

- Watson, G. (2018). *The Importance of Being Honest: How Lying, Secrecy, and Hypocrisy Collide with Truth in Law* (Chapter 9). Oxford University Press.

- *Journal of Legal Pluralism and Unofficial Law* (Multiple Issues). Taylor & Francis.

By exploring these resources, readers can delve deeper into the complexities of cultural and contextual considerations in comparative legal studies and gain valuable insights into the impact of these factors on legal systems around the world.

Exercises

1. Choose two countries with distinct cultural backgrounds and research their legal systems. Identify and compare three areas of law (e.g., family law, criminal law, contract law) in which cultural and contextual factors have a significant influence. Discuss how these factors shape the legal principles and practices in each country.

2. Conduct a case study on a legal dispute that involves cultural considerations. Analyze how cultural factors impacted the legal outcome, the reasoning behind the court's decision, and the potential implications on future legal precedents.

3. Identify and critically analyze a law or legal practice from a different culture to your own. Reflect on your own cultural biases and discuss how they may influence your perception of the legal system in question.

Through these exercises, readers can gain practical experience in understanding and analyzing the cultural and contextual considerations in comparative legal studies, enhancing their ability to conduct insightful and meaningful research in the field.

The role of international organizations in shaping global legal frameworks

International organizations play a crucial role in shaping global legal frameworks by fostering cooperation among nations and establishing norms and standards that guide legal systems around the world. These organizations serve as platforms for dialogue and collaboration, ensuring that laws are harmonized, and promoting justice and equality on a global scale. In this section, we will explore the key functions and impact of international organizations in shaping global legal frameworks, along with the challenges they face and their potential for future advancements.

Functions of international organizations in shaping global legal frameworks

International organizations serve important functions in shaping global legal frameworks. They facilitate the creation of international treaties, conventions, and agreements, which enable countries to come together and establish common legal standards. These legal instruments help address global challenges such as human rights, environmental protection, trade, and security.

One of the primary functions of international organizations is to provide a platform for member states to negotiate and develop international legal frameworks. This includes conducting research, organizing conferences, and facilitating discussions on emerging legal issues. By bringing together legal experts and policymakers from different countries, international organizations foster the exchange of knowledge and best practices, leading to the development of innovative legal solutions.

International organizations also play a critical role in encouraging compliance with international legal norms. They monitor the implementation of treaties and agreements, conduct investigations, and facilitate dispute resolution processes. Through these mechanisms, international organizations help ensure that countries adhere to their international legal obligations and promote accountability for violations.

Impact of international organizations on global legal frameworks

The impact of international organizations on global legal frameworks is significant. They contribute to the development of a unified international legal framework that transcends national boundaries, promoting consistency and fairness in the application of laws across different countries.

For instance, organizations like the United Nations (UN) have played a pivotal role in creating international human rights standards through treaties such as the Universal Declaration of Human Rights. These standards have been adopted by many countries and form the basis for national laws protecting human rights. International organizations also collaborate with member states to address pressing issues, such as climate change, by formulating agreements like the Paris Agreement, which sets global targets for reducing greenhouse gas emissions.

Moreover, international organizations promote the rule of law by supporting the establishment of legal institutions and providing technical assistance to countries in need. By sharing expertise and resources, these organizations help strengthen legal systems, enhance access to justice, and promote good governance. This contributes to the development of transparent, accountable, and efficient legal frameworks worldwide.

Challenges faced by international organizations

Despite their contributions, international organizations face several challenges in shaping global legal frameworks. One challenge is achieving consensus among member states with diverse political, cultural, and legal systems. Negotiating agreements that satisfy the interests of all countries can be complex and time-consuming.

Additionally, ensuring compliance with international legal norms can be challenging, as states have varying capacities and political will to implement and enforce these norms. Some countries may resist adopting international standards that might conflict with their domestic laws or interests. This highlights the need for ongoing dialogue, persuasion, and pressure to address non-compliance effectively.

Furthermore, international organizations often face limitations in terms of resources and authority. Limited funding and expertise may hinder their ability to carry out their mandates effectively. Additionally, the limited enforcement mechanisms available to international organizations may reduce their ability to enforce compliance with international legal obligations.

Future prospects and advancements

Despite these challenges, international organizations have the potential to shape global legal frameworks in significant ways in the future. The rapid advancement of technology, particularly in the area of information and communication, offers opportunities for international organizations to improve their effectiveness and efficiency.

For example, leveraging technology platforms can enhance the coordination and sharing of legal information among member states. Online databases and knowledge management systems can provide easy access to legal documents, precedents, and research, facilitating the harmonization of laws and promoting legal certainty.

Moreover, international organizations can harness emerging technologies such as artificial intelligence and machine learning to enhance legal research and analysis. These technologies can help analyze vast amounts of legal data, identify trends, and predict legal outcomes. By leveraging these advancements, international organizations can support evidence-based decision-making and promote more efficient and fair legal frameworks.

International organizations can also further strengthen their impact by actively engaging with non-state actors, including civil society organizations, academia, and the private sector. Collaborating with these actors can bring diverse perspectives, innovative ideas, and additional resources to address complex global legal challenges effectively.

In conclusion, international organizations have a vital role in shaping global legal frameworks. Through their functions of negotiation, compliance monitoring, and capacity building, these organizations drive the development of international legal standards and facilitate cooperation among nations. Despite challenges and limitations, international organizations have the potential to leverage technology and collaboration with non-state actors to further advance global legal frameworks and foster justice and equality worldwide.

Resources for further exploration:

- International Organization Law: Notable Treaties and Agreements: This resource provides an overview of significant international treaties and agreements that have shaped global legal frameworks.

- United Nations Treaty Collection: The UN Treaty Collection offers access to the texts of international treaties deposited with the UN, along with information on their status and membership.

- World Trade Organization (WTO): The WTO website provides information on international trade law and the role of the organization in promoting global trade rules and resolving trade disputes.

- International Court of Justice (ICJ): The official website of the ICJ offers information on the court's role in settling legal disputes between states and its contribution to the development of international law.
- Harvard Law School Library: International Organizations Research: This research guide provides an extensive collection of resources for studying international organizations and their impact on global legal frameworks.

Exercises:

1. Choose an international organization and research its role in shaping a specific area of global legal frameworks. Present your findings in a short essay, highlighting the organization's functions, impact, and challenges.
2. Analyze a recent international treaty or agreement and assess its effectiveness in promoting justice and equality on a global scale. Identify any challenges or limitations it may face in implementation.
3. Imagine you are a legal advisor to an international organization. Propose innovative strategies or technologies that the organization can adopt to enhance its role in shaping global legal frameworks. Justify your recommendations with supporting arguments.

Remember, international organizations are crucial actors in shaping global legal frameworks. Understanding their functions, impact, and potential for advancements is essential for anyone interested in the field of legal studies. By exploring their role, we gain insights into the complex dynamics involved in creating a more just and equitable world.

Sociolegal research and interdisciplinary approaches

Overview of sociolegal research methods

In this section, we will explore the various research methods used in sociolegal studies. Sociolegal research aims to understand the dynamic relationship between law and society, examining how legal rules and institutions shape social behavior and how social factors influence the development and application of law. By employing a multidisciplinary approach, sociolegal research provides valuable insights into the broader social, cultural, and political contexts in which legal systems operate.

1. Qualitative research methods: Qualitative research methods are commonly used in sociolegal studies to gain in-depth understanding and explore complex social phenomena. These methods focus on capturing the lived experiences, perspectives, and meanings that individuals or groups attach to the law. The following qualitative research methods are often employed:

1.1. Interviews: Researchers conduct structured or semi-structured interviews to gather data on individuals' experiences, attitudes, and beliefs related to legal issues. Interviews allow researchers to probe deeper into specific topics and capture rich, contextual information.

1.2. Focus groups: Focus groups bring together a small group of individuals with similar backgrounds or experiences to engage in facilitated discussions. This method encourages participants to share their opinions and generate collective insights on legal matters.

1.3. Ethnography: Ethnographic research involves immersing oneself in a specific cultural or social setting to observe and document how legal norms and practices are embedded in everyday life. Ethnographers may spend extended periods in communities, courts, or legal organizations to understand the sociocultural dynamics surrounding the law.

2. Quantitative research methods: Quantitative research methods involve the collection of numerical data to analyze patterns, relationships, and statistical significance. These methods allow researchers to generalize findings to broader populations and identify statistical associations between legal variables and social outcomes. Some common quantitative research methods utilized in sociolegal studies include:

2.1. Surveys: Surveys involve administering questionnaires to a sample of individuals to collect data on their attitudes, behaviors, or experiences regarding legal issues. Surveys can provide a snapshot of the population's perceptions, opinions, and behaviors related to the law.

2.2. Case studies: Case studies involve an in-depth analysis of a particular legal case, institution, or policy. By examining specific instances, researchers can provide detailed insights into how the law operates and its impact on social actors and processes.

2.3. Content analysis: Content analysis involves systematically analyzing written, visual, or audio material to identify patterns, themes, or discourses related to legal topics. Researchers may examine court decisions, legislative documents, media representations, or legal texts to understand the social construction and interpretation of the law.

3. Mixed methods approach: Sociolegal research often combines qualitative and quantitative methods to enhance the depth and breadth of understanding. The

mixed methods approach allows researchers to triangulate findings, validate results, and provide a more comprehensive analysis of the complex relationships between law and society. By integrating diverse research methods, sociolegal scholars can uncover both the subjective experiences and the broader statistical patterns associated with legal phenomena.

4. Ethical considerations: Like any research field, sociolegal research requires adherence to ethical principles. Researchers must consider issues such as informed consent, confidentiality, privacy, and protection of human subjects. In studies that involve vulnerable populations or sensitive legal topics, special care must be taken to ensure the well-being and rights of participants.

5. Resources for further exploration: - Sarat, A., & Kearns, T. R. (Eds.). (2019). Law in the Sociological Enterprise: Sociological Studies of Law. Handbooks of Sociology and Social Research. Springer. - Cramer, A. T., & Jacobs, C. J. (Eds.). (2018). Comparative Law and Society. Research Handbooks in Comparative Law series. Edward Elgar Publishing. - Silverman, D. (2016). Qualitative Research. SAGE Publications Ltd.

In conclusion, sociolegal research methods encompass a range of qualitative, quantitative, and mixed methods approaches. By employing these methods, researchers gain a comprehensive understanding of the social implications of law and contribute to the broader discourse on justice, inequality, and the role of law in society.

Using Qualitative Methods in Legal Studies

Qualitative research methods play a crucial role in legal studies, offering a deeper understanding of the complex social, cultural, and contextual factors that influence legal decision-making. While quantitative approaches provide valuable statistical data, qualitative methods allow researchers to explore the subjective experiences, beliefs, and motivations of individuals and communities involved in legal processes. In this section, we will delve into the various qualitative methods commonly used in legal studies, their applications, and the benefits they bring to the field.

Overview of Qualitative Research

Qualitative research is an approach that focuses on gathering and interpreting non-numerical data to understand social phenomena. It involves collecting and analyzing data from various sources, such as interviews, observations, documents, and audiovisual materials. In legal studies, qualitative research aims to uncover the underlying meanings, perspectives, and lived experiences of individuals and groups who are affected by legal systems and processes.

Interviews

One of the most widely used qualitative research methods in legal studies is interviews. Interviews allow researchers to directly engage with participants, gaining rich insights into their thoughts, attitudes, opinions, and experiences. In legal research, interviews may involve key stakeholders, such as lawyers, judges, jurors, law enforcement officers, and individuals involved in legal disputes.

When conducting interviews, it is essential to carefully design questions that elicit detailed and meaningful responses. Open-ended questions encourage participants to provide in-depth explanations and explore their perspectives fully. It is also crucial to establish rapport and create a safe and non-judgmental environment to encourage participants to freely share their experiences and insights.

To ensure rigor and objectivity, researchers often use coding and thematic analysis to identify patterns, themes, and categories within the interview data. This process involves organizing and categorizing information into meaningful units, allowing for systematic analysis and interpretation.

Observations

Observation is another valuable qualitative research method utilized in legal studies. Through direct observation, researchers can gain a comprehensive understanding of how legal processes unfold in real-life settings. This method involves observing and documenting behaviors, interactions, and events within legal contexts, such as courtrooms, mediation sessions, and legal clinics.

Researchers may adopt either participant observation, where they actively engage with participants and immerse themselves in the setting, or non-participant observation, where they observe from a distance without direct interaction. Both approaches provide valuable insights into the dynamics, power relationships, and informal practices present within legal systems.

To enhance the reliability and validity of observations, researchers often employ various techniques, such as field notes, video recordings, and reflective journals. These tools allow for detailed documentation and analysis of observed behaviors, non-verbal cues, and contextual factors that influence legal processes.

Document Analysis

Document analysis is a vital method in legal studies, enabling researchers to examine written or recorded materials, including legal texts, court decisions, policy documents, and case files. This method provides insights into the historical, social, and cultural contexts that shape legal systems and the perspectives of multiple stakeholders.

Researchers analyze legal documents by identifying recurring themes, discourses, and legal arguments. They critically assess the legal reasoning, justifications, and interpretations presented within the texts. Document analysis also helps researchers explore the impact of legal decisions and policies on marginalized groups, social inequalities, and access to justice.

However, it is essential to recognize limitations associated with document analysis, such as potential biases in legal texts, selective reporting, and the influence of institutional power dynamics. Researchers must carefully assess the credibility and authenticity of the documents used and consider multiple perspectives to gain a comprehensive understanding of the legal issues at hand.

Ethnography

Ethnography, a qualitative research method originally developed in anthropology, has found relevance in legal studies. It involves immersing oneself in the field and systematically observing and interacting with individuals and communities to understand their perspectives, behaviors, and cultural practices related to the law.

In legal ethnography, researchers spend an extended period within a specific legal setting, such as a courtroom, law firm, or community, to gain an in-depth understanding of the social dynamics and how the law operates in practice. This method allows researchers to identify and analyze the intersections between law, culture, and society through detailed field notes and participant observations.

By employing ethnographic methods, researchers can uncover the informal norms, power dynamics, and lived experiences that shape legal processes and decision-making. Ethnography brings a nuanced understanding of the complexities and contradictions within legal systems, which may not be captured through quantitative approaches alone.

Benefits and Challenges of Qualitative Research

Qualitative research methods offer several unique advantages in legal studies. They provide a rich and nuanced understanding of the human experiences, motivations, and perspectives that quantitative data may not capture fully. Qualitative methods also allow for flexibility and adaptation to the research setting, enabling researchers to explore emerging themes and unexpected findings.

Moreover, qualitative research contributes to the humanization of legal studies by shedding light on the personal narratives, emotions, and ethical considerations involved in legal processes. This human-centered approach helps bridge the gap between legal theory and the realities faced by individuals and communities.

However, qualitative research also presents challenges. Researchers must address issues of subjectivity, bias, and interpretation when analyzing and presenting qualitative data. They must ensure rigor and transparency in the research process and consider the influence of their own views and biases on the findings. Additionally, qualitative research often involves small sample sizes, limiting generalizability and raising questions of representativeness.

Despite these challenges, qualitative research methods continue to be indispensable in legal studies, offering unique insights into the lived experiences and social contexts surrounding legal phenomena. Researchers who employ these methods contribute to a more holistic understanding of how law shapes and is shaped by society.

Resources for Further Exploration

To delve further into the use of qualitative methods in legal studies, the following resources are highly recommended:

- Clarke, A. E., Friese, C., & Washburn, R. S. (Eds.). (2018). *Situated interventions: Sociolegal scholarship in action*. Oxford University Press.

- Sarat, A., & Silbey, S. S. (Eds.). (2017). *The Oxford handbook of law and society*. Oxford University Press.

- Silverman, D. (Ed.). (2016). *Qualitative research*. SAGE Publications.

- Strauss, A. L., Corbin, J. M., & Denzin, N. K. (2020). *Basics of qualitative research: Techniques and procedures for developing grounded theory*. SAGE Publications.

- Van Djik, T. A. (2011). *Discourse studies: A multidisciplinary introduction*. SAGE Publications.

These resources provide comprehensive overviews, practical guidance, and case studies that will deepen your understanding of qualitative methods in legal research.

Exercises

1. Design a set of open-ended interview questions to explore the impact of restorative justice practices on individuals involved in criminal proceedings.

2. Conduct an observation in a local courtroom and document the non-verbal communication cues displayed by attorneys, defendants, and judges during court proceedings. Analyze the observed behaviors and discuss their potential implications.

3. Choose a landmark legal case and engage in document analysis by critically examining the court decisions, legal opinions, and dissenting judgments. Identify the underlying legal arguments, justifications, and policy concerns presented within the documents.

4. Conduct a mini-ethnographic study by immersing yourself (with appropriate permissions) in a legal assistance clinic. Observe the interactions between lawyers and clients, document the challenges faced by clients seeking legal aid, and analyze the role of the clinic in addressing access to justice issues.

Note: Ensure that you adhere to research ethics guidelines and obtain necessary permissions and consent when conducting any empirical research.

Incorporating Quantitative Analysis in Sociolegal Research

In the field of sociolegal research, it is becoming increasingly important to incorporate quantitative analysis in order to gain a deeper understanding of legal phenomena and their social implications. While qualitative methods have traditionally dominated the social sciences, quantitative analysis provides a valuable tool for capturing large-scale trends, identifying patterns, and making statistical inferences. In this section, we will explore the significance of quantitative analysis in sociolegal research, discuss its benefits and limitations, and provide practical guidance on how to effectively incorporate quantitative methods into your research.

The Significance of Quantitative Analysis in Sociolegal Research

Quantitative analysis allows researchers to systematically examine large amounts of data and derive meaningful insights. In the context of sociolegal research, it can help uncover and measure the impact of legal interventions, assess the effectiveness of policy measures, and identify social inequalities and patterns of discrimination.

By quantifying social phenomena, researchers can objectively analyze the relationship between variables and test hypotheses. This analytical approach adds rigor and reliability to sociolegal research and enables researchers to make generalizations and predictions based on empirical evidence.

Additionally, quantitative analysis can provide a more comprehensive understanding of complex social issues by revealing hidden patterns and relationships. It allows researchers to explore the interplay between legal factors and social variables, such as demographics, economic indicators, or public opinion, providing a holistic perspective on the issue under study.

Benefits and Limitations of Quantitative Analysis

Quantitative analysis offers several advantages in sociolegal research:

- **Objectivity:** Quantitative methods help researchers minimize subjective biases and enhance the objectivity of their findings. By employing standardized measures and statistical techniques, researchers can arrive at reliable and replicable results.

- **Efficiency:** Quantitative analysis allows researchers to process large amounts of data quickly and efficiently. This enables them to examine broad trends and patterns that may not be apparent through qualitative methods alone.

- **Generalizability:** By employing appropriate sampling techniques and statistical inference, quantitative research can generate findings that are representative of larger populations. This allows researchers to make generalizations and draw conclusions that are applicable beyond the specific context of their study.

However, it is essential to acknowledge the limitations of quantitative analysis in sociolegal research:

- **Simplification:** Quantitative analysis often requires simplifying complex social phenomena into measurable variables. This may result in the loss of nuance and overlook the qualitative aspects of legal phenomena. It is crucial to balance quantitative findings with qualitative insights to gain a comprehensive understanding.

- **Data availability:** The availability and quality of data can pose challenges in quantitative analysis. Sociolegal research often deals with sensitive topics, and relevant data may be limited or subject to bias. Researchers should carefully consider the sources and validity of their data, ensuring it aligns with their research objectives.

- **Causality versus correlation:** While quantitative analysis can identify associations between variables, it does not establish causality. Researchers should exercise caution when interpreting statistical relationships and consider potential confounding factors that may influence the observed associations.

Incorporating Quantitative Methods into Sociolegal Research

To effectively incorporate quantitative methods into sociolegal research, researchers should follow a systematic and rigorous approach. The following steps provide a general roadmap:

1. **Research question formulation:** Clearly define your research question, ensuring it is specific, measurable, and relevant to the sociolegal context. This will guide your data collection and analysis.

2. **Study design and sampling:** Determine the appropriate study design and sampling strategy to ensure your findings are representative and generalizable. Consideration should be given to the population under study, sample size, and sampling techniques.

3. **Data collection:** Select appropriate data collection methods, such as surveys, questionnaires, or existing datasets, that align with your research question. Ensure the reliability and validity of your measures and consider ethical considerations, such as informed consent and data privacy.

4. **Data analysis:** Use statistical software to analyze your data, employing appropriate statistical techniques such as descriptive statistics, inferential statistics, regression analysis, or multivariate analysis. Carefully interpret the results, considering potential confounding factors and limitations of your analysis.

5. **Interpretation and reporting:** Interpret your findings in the context of existing literature and theories in sociolegal research. Discuss the implications of your results, including their significance, limitations, and potential policy or practical implications. Clearly communicate your findings through tables, charts, or graphs, and provide a comprehensive analysis in a written report.

It is important to note that quantitative analysis should complement qualitative research methods rather than replace them. By combining both approaches, researchers can gain a more comprehensive understanding of the complex and multifaceted nature of sociolegal phenomena.

Resources and Tools for Quantitative Analysis in Sociolegal Research

There are various resources and tools available to support researchers in incorporating quantitative analysis into their sociolegal research:

- **Statistical software:** Utilize popular statistical software packages such as SPSS, R, or Stata to facilitate data analysis. These software packages provide a wide range of statistical techniques and data visualization tools.
- **Research methods textbooks:** Consult textbooks on research methods and quantitative analysis in the social sciences, such as Field's "Discovering Statistics Using SPSS" or Agresti and Finlay's "Statistical Methods for the Social Sciences." These resources provide comprehensive guidance on statistical analysis techniques and their application in research.
- **Online courses and tutorials:** Access online courses and tutorials offered by universities, research institutions, or platforms like Coursera or edX. These courses cover various topics, including data analysis, statistical modeling, and survey research methods.
- **Academic journals and conferences:** Stay updated with the latest research in sociolegal studies by regularly reading academic journals such as "Law & Society Review" or "Journal of Empirical Legal Studies." Attend conferences and workshops related to quantitative analysis to learn about cutting-edge techniques and network with fellow researchers.

Example: Analyzing the Impact of Sentencing Guidelines

To demonstrate the application of quantitative analysis in sociolegal research, let's consider a hypothetical study on the impact of sentencing guidelines on racial disparities in criminal justice outcomes. The research question is: "Do sentencing guidelines contribute to racial disparities in criminal sentencing?"

First, you would collect data on criminal sentences, including variables such as race/ethnicity of the defendant, offense type, and sentence length. You might obtain this data from court records, administrative databases, or surveys.

Next, you would conduct quantitative analysis using appropriate statistical methods. For instance, you might employ logistic regression analysis to examine the relationship between race/ethnicity (independent variable) and sentence length (dependent variable), while controlling for other relevant factors such as offense severity and prior convictions.

After analyzing the data, you might find that racial disparities exist in the sentencing outcomes, even after controlling for other factors. This finding suggests that sentencing guidelines may contribute to racial inequalities in the criminal justice system. However, it is crucial to interpret these results cautiously, considering potential limitations of the data and other contextual factors.

This example illustrates how quantitative analysis can uncover patterns and relationships that may not be readily apparent. It also emphasizes the importance of interpreting the results in the broader sociolegal context, considering the limitations and potential alternative explanations.

Conclusion

Incorporating quantitative analysis in sociolegal research can greatly enhance our understanding of legal phenomena and their social implications. By employing systematic and rigorous methods, researchers can derive meaningful insights, identify patterns and trends, and contribute to evidence-based policy and practice.

Quantitative analysis should be seen as a complement to qualitative methods, allowing researchers to explore both the individual experiences and the broader social dynamics at play. By combining these approaches, sociolegal researchers can generate comprehensive and nuanced findings that have real-world relevance.

Remember, mastering quantitative analysis requires continuous learning and practice. As you delve into the world of quantitative research, remain curious, open-minded, and ethical in your pursuit of sociolegal knowledge.

The role of psychology and behavioral science in understanding legal decision-making

Understanding legal decision-making is a complex task that requires an interdisciplinary approach. Psychology and behavioral science play a crucial role in unraveling the intricate factors that influence how judges, juries, and other legal actors make decisions. This section explores the contributions of these fields to our understanding of legal decision-making, highlighting key theories, empirical research, and practical implications.

Background

Psychology, as the scientific study of behavior and mental processes, provides valuable insights into the cognitive, emotional, and social aspects of decision-making. Behavioral science, on the other hand, focuses on applying psychological principles to understand and predict human behavior in various contexts. By integrating psychological theories and methods, behavioral science offers a comprehensive framework for examining legal decision-making.

Cognitive biases in legal decision-making

One important contribution of psychology and behavioral science is the identification and analysis of cognitive biases that may affect legal decision-making. These biases are systematic errors in thinking that can lead to flawed judgments and decisions. Some notable biases include:

- Confirmation bias: the tendency to seek and interpret information that confirms pre-existing beliefs or expectations, while disregarding contradictory evidence.
- Anchoring bias: the tendency to rely heavily on the first piece of information encountered when making decisions, even if it is unrelated or irrelevant.
- Availability heuristic: the tendency to judge the likelihood of an event based on how easily relevant examples or instances come to mind.
- Overconfidence bias: the tendency to have excessive confidence in one's judgments or abilities, leading to an underestimation of risks and errors.
- Hindsight bias: the tendency to perceive past events as more predictable than they actually were, often resulting in the belief that individuals should have foreseen the outcome.

Understanding these biases is crucial in evaluating the reliability and fairness of legal decision-making. By recognizing the potential impact of such biases, legal practitioners can take steps to mitigate their influence and ensure more objective and just outcomes.

Decision-making heuristics

In addition to biases, psychology and behavioral science also shed light on decision-making heuristics—mental shortcuts or rules of thumb that individuals use to simplify complex decisions. These heuristics can affect legal decision-making in various ways. One well-known heuristic is the availability heuristic, mentioned earlier. Other heuristics include:

- Representativeness heuristic: the tendency to judge the likelihood of an event or the category of an object based on its similarity to a typical or prototype example.
- Framing heuristic: the tendency to be influenced by the way in which information is presented or framed, even when the content is essentially the same.
- Sunk cost fallacy: the tendency to continue investing time, money, or effort into a decision, even when evidence suggests it is not likely to succeed.
- Status quo bias: the tendency to favor maintaining the current state of affairs, often resisting change or alternatives.

Understanding these decision-making heuristics helps us understand why legal actors may deviate from purely rational decision-making processes. By recognizing and addressing the influence of heuristics, legal practitioners can make more informed decisions and promote fairness and justice.

Psychological factors in witness testimony

Psychology and behavioral science also have significant implications for understanding witness testimony, a critical aspect of many legal cases. Research shows that memory is imperfect and subject to various biases and distortions. Factors such as stress, suggestion, and post-event information can significantly influence witness recall and accuracy.

One well-known phenomenon is the misinformation effect, where exposure to misleading information after an event can distort memory and subsequent testimony. Eyewitness identification, often crucial in criminal cases, is particularly susceptible to memory biases and suggestive influences.

Understanding the limitations and vulnerabilities of witness testimony helps legal professionals critically evaluate the evidence presented. Techniques such as cognitive interviewing and lineup procedures informed by psychological research can enhance the reliability and accuracy of witness testimony.

Practical implications and challenges

The integration of psychology and behavioral science into the legal system has practical implications for legal professionals, policymakers, and the judiciary. By being aware of cognitive biases, decision-making heuristics, and the fallibility of human memory, legal actors can strive to make fairer and more rational decisions.

However, several challenges exist in leveraging psychological research in legal decision-making. The generalizability of findings from controlled laboratory settings to complex real-world legal contexts is one such challenge. Additionally, incorporating psychological insights into legal practices and procedures requires collaboration, interdisciplinary training, and an understanding of the ethical implications involved.

Resources for further exploration

For further exploration on the role of psychology and behavioral science in understanding legal decision-making, the following resources are recommended:

- Books:
  - "Judgment in Managerial Decision Making" by Max H. Bazerman
  - "Thinking, Fast and Slow" by Daniel Kahneman
  - "Psychology and Law: A Critical Introduction" by Andreas Kapardis
- Journals:
  - *Law and Human Behavior*
  - *Psychology, Public Policy, and Law*
  - *Journal of Empirical Legal Studies*
- Online resources:
  - American Psychology-Law Society (AP-LS) website: `www.ap-ls.org`
  - National Institute of Justice (NIJ) website: `www.nij.gov`
  - Legal and Criminological Psychology (Journal website): `www.bps.org.uk/journals/legal-and-criminological-psychology`

These resources provide a foundation for exploring the rich intersection between psychology, behavioral science, and legal decision-making, inspiring further research and evaluation of their practical implications.

Conclusion

Psychology and behavioral science offer invaluable insights into the complexities of legal decision-making. By examining cognitive biases, decision-making heuristics, psychological factors in witness testimony, and related phenomena, we gain a deeper understanding of how legal actors make decisions and the potential challenges and biases they face. Integrating psychological research into legal practice holds promise for enhancing the fairness, objectivity, and justice of our legal systems. However, it also requires ongoing collaboration, critical evaluation, and an understanding of the ethical dimensions involved. When combined with legal theory and practical techniques, psychology and behavioral science provide powerful tools for shaping the future of legal studies and improving legal decision-making processes.

Interdisciplinary Collaboration in Legal Studies

In the field of legal studies, interdisciplinary collaboration plays a crucial role in expanding knowledge and enriching the practice of law. By combining insights from various disciplines, such as sociology, psychology, economics, political science, and more, legal scholars are able to explore complex legal issues from multiple perspectives and develop innovative solutions. This section will examine the importance of interdisciplinary collaboration in legal studies and explore how different disciplines can contribute to our understanding of the law.

The Value of Interdisciplinary Collaboration

Interdisciplinary collaboration brings together experts from different fields to address complex problems that cannot be fully understood or solved within the confines of a single discipline. In the context of legal studies, it allows legal scholars to draw on insights from other disciplines to gain a deeper understanding of the societal, psychological, economic, and political dynamics that shape the law.

One of the key benefits of interdisciplinary collaboration is the ability to tackle multidimensional legal issues. For example, when examining questions related to criminal justice reform, legal scholars can work together with sociologists to understand the social factors that contribute to crime, psychologists to explore the cognitive processes behind decision-making, and economists to analyze the cost-effectiveness of different policy interventions. This holistic approach helps identify comprehensive solutions that take into account various perspectives and factors.

Additionally, interdisciplinary collaboration enables legal scholars to challenge traditional legal frameworks and theories by incorporating insights from other disciplines. For instance, legal scholars working with experts in behavioral science can examine how cognitive biases and heuristics influence legal decision-making. By integrating psychological research into legal scholarship, a more nuanced understanding of how individuals' biases can impact the administration of justice can be developed.

Moreover, interdisciplinary collaboration fosters creativity and innovation by encouraging the exchange of ideas and approaches from different disciplines. By bringing together scholars with diverse backgrounds, new methods and frameworks can be created to tackle legal problems. This interdisciplinary approach can spark fresh perspectives and lead to groundbreaking research in legal studies.

Examples of Interdisciplinary Collaboration in Legal Studies

To illustrate the practical applications of interdisciplinary collaboration in legal studies, let's consider a few examples:

1. Intellectual Property and Innovation: Interdisciplinary collaborations between legal scholars, economists, and scientists help in understanding the relationship between intellectual property laws, innovation, and economic growth. By analyzing patent data from an economic perspective, scholars can evaluate the effectiveness of patent systems in incentivizing innovation and identify potential areas for reform.

2. Environmental Law: Collaboration between legal experts, ecologists, and policymakers is essential when addressing environmental challenges. By combining legal analysis with scientific research, interdisciplinary teams can develop policies and regulations that balance economic development with environmental sustainability.

3. Technology and Privacy: In the digital age, legal scholars working alongside computer scientists, ethicists, and privacy experts can address the legal challenges surrounding emerging technologies, such as artificial intelligence and big data. This collaboration helps develop regulations and guidelines that safeguard individuals' privacy rights and mitigate the potential risks associated with technological advancements.

4. Health Law and Ethics: Legal scholars collaborating with medical professionals and bioethicists contribute to the development of laws and policies that govern healthcare systems, medical research, and ethical considerations. This interdisciplinary approach ensures that legal regulations align with medical advancements and societal values.

Barriers and Solutions

While interdisciplinary collaboration in legal studies offers numerous benefits, there are also challenges that must be overcome. Some of the barriers include differences in research methodologies, terminology, and disciplinary cultures, as well as logistical constraints such as limited funding and institutional support.

To address these challenges, there are several strategies that can be employed. First, creating interdisciplinary research centers or institutes dedicated to legal studies can provide a platform for scholars from various disciplines to collaborate and share their expertise. These centers can facilitate interdisciplinary research projects, organize conferences and workshops, and foster a culture of interdisciplinary inquiry.

Second, promoting interdisciplinary education and training programs can equip future legal scholars with the skills and knowledge needed to engage in interdisciplinary collaboration. By incorporating interdisciplinary coursework and encouraging student participation in interdisciplinary research projects, universities can foster a new generation of scholars who are comfortable working across disciplinary boundaries.

Third, fostering open communication and collaboration among scholars from different disciplines is crucial. Establishing mechanisms for regular dialogue, such as interdisciplinary research seminars or online platforms, can facilitate knowledge exchange and encourage collaborations on specific research projects.

Resources for Interdisciplinary Collaboration

To support interdisciplinary collaboration in legal studies, several resources are available to scholars and researchers. These resources facilitate knowledge sharing, networking, and access to interdisciplinary research opportunities. Some notable resources include:

1. Interdisciplinary Research Networks: These networks bring together scholars from different disciplines who share an interest in legal studies. They provide opportunities for collaboration, information exchange, and grant funding.

2. Interdisciplinary Journals: Academic journals dedicated to interdisciplinary legal studies provide platforms for scholars to publish their research, share insights, and contribute to the interdisciplinary discourse.

3. Conferences and Workshops: Interdisciplinary conferences and workshops bring together scholars, policymakers, and practitioners from different disciplines to discuss and explore legal issues from various perspectives. These events offer networking opportunities and promote interdisciplinary collaborations.

4. Funding Opportunities: Many funding agencies offer grants specifically for interdisciplinary research projects in legal studies. These funding opportunities provide financial support for interdisciplinary collaboration and encourage innovative research.

5. Interdisciplinary Research Centers and Institutes: These institutions provide a physical space and intellectual environment for scholars to engage in interdisciplinary research. They often host lectures, workshops, and seminars on interdisciplinary topics, fostering collaboration and knowledge exchange.

Further Exploration

To deepen your understanding of interdisciplinary collaboration in legal studies, consider exploring the following resources:

- "Interdisciplinary Research: Process and Theory" by Allen F. Repko: This book offers a comprehensive guide to interdisciplinary research, including practical strategies for collaboration and insights into the challenges and benefits of interdisciplinary work.
- "Interdisciplinary Research: Diverse Approaches in Science, Technology, Health, and Society" edited by Rick Szostak: This anthology explores interdisciplinary research practices across different fields, providing examples of successful collaborations and illustrating the impact of interdisciplinary approaches.
- International Association for the Study of the Commons (IASC): This association brings together researchers, policymakers, and practitioners who study and manage common resources. Their interdisciplinary approach offers insights into legal frameworks that govern common resources and collective action.
- The Law and Society Association: This interdisciplinary organization promotes research and collaboration in the field of law and society. Their annual conference and publications provide opportunities for legal scholars to engage with interdisciplinary perspectives.
- The American Bar Association (ABA) Section of International Law: This section focuses on international legal issues and promotes interdisciplinary collaboration among legal practitioners, academics, and policymakers.

By exploring these resources and engaging in interdisciplinary collaborations, legal scholars can contribute to the advancement of legal studies and spark transformative changes in the field of law.

Ethical considerations in legal research

Research integrity and ethical guidelines

Research integrity and ethical guidelines are crucial components of conducting any form of research, including legal studies. In this section, we will explore the importance of research integrity, discuss the ethical considerations that researchers in the field of legal studies must adhere to, and provide guidelines for maintaining the highest standards of ethics in research.

Importance of research integrity

Research integrity refers to the adherence to the core values and principles of conducting research. It involves honesty, transparency, objectivity, accountability, and the responsible conduct of research. In legal studies, research integrity is essential to ensure the validity of research findings, maintain public trust, and uphold the integrity of the legal profession.

Research integrity plays a fundamental role in legal studies as it helps to:

- Ensure the reliability and accuracy of research results
- Promote transparency and accountability in research practices
- Uphold the ethical principles of justice, fairness, and respect
- Protect the rights and welfare of research participants, including human subjects
- Maintain the credibility and reputation of researchers and the legal profession as a whole

By upholding research integrity, legal scholars contribute to the advancement of knowledge and the development of sound legal principles and practices.

Ethical considerations in legal research

Legal research, like any other form of research, involves ethical considerations that researchers must address. These considerations include:

1. **Confidentiality and privacy:** Researchers must respect the privacy and confidentiality of individuals and organizations involved in the research. They should obtain informed consent from research participants and ensure the security of any personal or sensitive information collected.

2. **Conflict of interest:** Researchers should disclose any potential conflicts of interest that may compromise the objectivity and integrity of the research. This includes financial, personal, or professional conflicts that could influence the outcomes of the study.

3. **Informed consent:** In studies involving human subjects, researchers must obtain informed consent from participants, ensuring that they understand the purpose, risks, and benefits of the research. Researchers should also inform participants about their rights to withdraw from the study at any time.

4. **Research involving vulnerable populations:** When conducting research involving vulnerable populations, such as minors, prisoners, or individuals with diminished decision-making capacity, researchers must take extra precautions to protect their rights and welfare. This includes obtaining additional informed consent from legal guardians or authorized representatives.

5. **Avoidance of harm:** Researchers should strive to minimize potential harm to participants and society. They should carefully consider the potential risks and benefits of the research, taking necessary measures to prevent physical, psychological, or social harm to those involved.

6. **Research misconduct:** Researchers should refrain from engaging in any form of research misconduct, such as data fabrication, falsification, or plagiarism. They should conduct their research with honesty, integrity, and transparency, accurately reporting their findings and giving credit to the work of others.

Guidelines for research integrity and ethical conduct

To ensure research integrity and ethical conduct in legal studies, researchers should follow these guidelines:

1. **Obtain necessary approvals:** Researchers should obtain appropriate approvals from institutional review boards or ethics committees before commencing their research. These bodies provide oversight and ensure that research involving human subjects meets ethical standards.

2. **Protect confidentiality and privacy:** Researchers should take measures to protect the confidentiality and privacy of research participants, ensuring that their identities and sensitive information are not disclosed without consent.

This may involve using anonymous identifiers, secure data storage, and encryption methods.

3. **Maintain transparency and accountability:** Researchers should clearly document their research design, methods, and procedures, making their work transparent and reproducible. They should maintain accurate records of their research data and ensure its integrity throughout the study.

4. **Provide informed consent:** Researchers must obtain informed consent from all participants involved in the research. Participants should be fully informed about the purpose, risks, and benefits of the study, and they should have the right to ask questions and withdraw from the research at any time.

5. **Disclose conflicts of interest:** Researchers should disclose any potential conflicts of interest that may compromise the validity or objectivity of their research. Transparency regarding financial, personal, or professional interests helps to maintain the integrity of the research and protect the interests of participants.

6. **Ensure data accuracy and validity:** Researchers should collect and analyze their data with care, ensuring its accuracy, reliability, and validity. They should use appropriate statistical methods and adequately report their data, avoiding selective reporting or manipulation of results.

7. **Acknowledge and cite sources:** Researchers must properly acknowledge and cite the work of others that has influenced their own research. Plagiarism, the unauthorized use of someone else's work, is a serious ethical violation and must be avoided at all costs.

8. **Promote responsible publication practices:** Researchers should publish their findings in reputable journals or platforms, following ethical guidelines regarding authorship, peer review, and publication ethics. They should avoid predatory publishers or fraudulent practices that undermine the integrity of scientific research.

Adhering to these guidelines ensures the ethical conduct of legal research and contributes to the overall integrity and credibility of the field.

Ethics in interdisciplinary research

Legal studies often intersect with other disciplines, leading to interdisciplinary research. When conducting interdisciplinary research, legal scholars must consider the ethical considerations of each discipline involved. This may include the proper handling of data, confidentiality, participant consent, and ethical practices specific to those disciplines.

Effective collaboration between scholars from different disciplines requires open and transparent communication regarding ethical guidelines and standards. Researchers should engage in ongoing discussions to ensure that ethical principles are respected throughout the research process.

Additional resources and further exploration

To gain a deeper understanding of research integrity and ethical guidelines in legal studies, researchers can explore the following resources:

- *The Belmont Report: Ethical Principles and Guidelines for the Protection of Human Subjects of Research* – A foundational document outlining principles for ethical research involving human subjects.

- *The Responsible Conduct of Research* – A guidebook that provides an overview of research integrity and responsible conduct of research in various disciplines.

- *American Bar Association (ABA) Model Rules of Professional Conduct* – Ethical guidelines for legal professionals, providing principles and rules for maintaining professional integrity.

- *Institutional Review Boards (IRBs) and Ethical Guidelines* – Resources provided by research institutions that outline ethical considerations and guidelines for conducting research involving human subjects.

- *Ethics Codes and Guidelines in Legal Studies* – Publications and articles that discuss the ethical dimensions of legal research and provide guidance on promoting research integrity.

By engaging with these resources, researchers can enhance their understanding of research ethics and contribute to the responsible and ethical development of legal studies.

Conclusion

Research integrity and adherence to ethical guidelines are essential for maintaining the credibility, validity, and societal impact of legal studies. Legal researchers must be mindful of the ethical considerations associated with their work, ensuring the protection of participants' rights, privacy, and welfare. By following the guidelines outlined in this section and exploring additional resources, researchers can conduct their work responsibly and contribute to the advancement of knowledge in the field of legal studies.

Informed Consent and Privacy Considerations

In the field of legal studies, conducting research often involves gathering data and information from individuals who may be directly or indirectly affected by the research. It is essential to ensure that participants' rights are protected, and this includes obtaining their informed consent and addressing privacy considerations. In this section, we will explore the importance of informed consent and privacy, and the ethical considerations that researchers must navigate.

Importance of Informed Consent

Informed consent is a fundamental principle in research ethics. It refers to the process of obtaining voluntary agreement from individuals to participate in research after they have been provided with relevant information about the study. In legal studies, researchers may conduct interviews, surveys, or collect personal data that require obtaining informed consent. There are several reasons why informed consent is crucial:

1. Respect for autonomy: Informed consent upholds the principle of respect for individuals' autonomy, allowing them to make informed decisions about whether to participate in the research or not. By providing sufficient information, participants have the freedom to choose whether or not to take part, without any coercion or manipulation.

2. Protection of rights and well-being: Informed consent ensures that researchers prioritize the protection of participants' rights, dignity, and well-being. It provides an opportunity to explain the purpose of the study, potential risks and benefits, and any safeguards or protections in place.

3. Transparency and trust: Informed consent promotes transparency in research, fostering trust between researchers and participants. It establishes a clear understanding of the research objectives, methods, and potential outcomes, promoting honesty and openness throughout the study.

4. Legal and ethical requirement: In many jurisdictions, obtaining informed consent is a legal and ethical requirement. It demonstrates compliance with research

ethics guidelines, institutional review board (IRB) regulations, and relevant legal frameworks, ensuring researchers' accountability.

To obtain informed consent, researchers must provide participants with clear and understandable information. This includes explaining the purpose and nature of the research, the procedures involved, potential risks and benefits, confidentiality measures, voluntary participation, the right to withdraw at any time, and contact information for any questions or concerns. Researchers should also ensure that participants have the opportunity to ask questions and clarify any doubts before providing their consent.

Privacy Considerations

Privacy is a crucial aspect to consider in legal research, as it involves the protection of individuals' personal information and mitigating any potential harm that may arise from its disclosure. Researchers must take steps to safeguard privacy throughout the research process. Here are some key considerations:

1. Confidentiality: Researchers should assure participants that their personal information will remain confidential. This means taking precautions when collecting, storing, and transmitting data to prevent unauthorized access. Confidentiality can be maintained by removing identifying information and assigning codes to participants, storing data securely, and limiting access to authorized individuals only.

2. Data anonymization and de-identification: To further protect privacy, researchers can use techniques such as data anonymization and de-identification. Anonymization involves removing identifiable details from data, ensuring that individuals cannot be identified. De-identification involves replacing identifying information with codes or other non-identifying markers, thereby reducing the risk of re-identification. These techniques minimize the potential for personal data to be linked back to individuals.

3. Data security: Researchers must prioritize strong data security measures to prevent data breaches or unauthorized access. This includes using secure storage systems, encryption methods, and regularly updating security protocols. Additionally, researchers should consider the use of secure data transmission methods, such as encrypted email or secure file sharing platforms.

4. Consent for data sharing: When sharing research data with other researchers, it is crucial to obtain explicit consent from participants regarding the sharing and use of their data beyond the initial study. This allows participants to retain control over their information and ensures transparency in data sharing practices.

5. Privacy policy: Researchers should develop a clear privacy policy that outlines how personal data will be handled, stored, and protected. This policy should be accessible to participants and provide detailed information on data collection, retention, and disposal practices.

It is important for researchers to remain vigilant in protecting participants' privacy and regularly review and update their privacy practices to align with evolving legal and ethical standards. By prioritizing informed consent and privacy considerations, researchers can ensure ethical research practices and uphold the trust and confidentiality of participants.

Case Study: Balancing Informed Consent and Privacy

Consider a case study in which a legal researcher aims to study the experiences of survivors of domestic violence to identify the challenges they face within the legal system. The researcher plans to conduct interviews with survivors, collect demographic information, and gather their perspectives on legal procedures and support services.

In this case, obtaining informed consent and addressing privacy considerations are of utmost importance. The researcher must carefully explain the purpose of the study, assure confidentiality, and provide the survivors with the opportunity to ask questions and seek clarifications. The researcher should emphasize that participation is voluntary and that the survivors have the right to withdraw at any time without consequences.

To protect privacy, the researcher should adopt measures such as pseudonyms or codes to anonymize participant identities. Additionally, the researcher should assure survivors that their personal information will be securely stored and that interview transcripts will be thoroughly de-identified to prevent any potential harm or re-identification. The researcher should also obtain explicit consent from participants regarding any potential data sharing with other researchers, ensuring that survivors retain control over their information.

By balancing informed consent and privacy considerations, the researcher can conduct the study ethically and sensitively, respecting the rights and well-being of survivors while collecting valuable insights to improve the legal system's response to domestic violence.

Resources for Further Exploration

1. Ethical Principles of Psychologists and Code of Conduct: This comprehensive code of ethics, developed by the American Psychological Association (APA),

provides guidelines for research ethics, including informed consent and privacy considerations.

2. Belmont Report: A foundational document in research ethics, the Belmont Report outlines the ethical principles and guidelines for the protection of human subjects in research. It emphasizes the importance of informed consent and the need to protect participants' privacy.

3. General Data Protection Regulation (GDPR): The GDPR is a legal framework that sets guidelines for the collection, processing, and protection of personal data of individuals within the European Union. It provides valuable insights into privacy considerations and consent requirements.

4. Institutional Review Board (IRB) Guidelines: Many academic institutions have IRBs responsible for reviewing research proposals involving human participants. These guidelines provide specific requirements and recommendations for obtaining informed consent and addressing privacy concerns.

5. Data Protection and Privacy Laws: Familiarize yourself with relevant data protection and privacy laws, such as the EU-U.S. Privacy Shield framework and the California Consumer Privacy Act (CCPA). These laws address individual privacy rights and provide insights into best practices for handling personal data.

Remember, informed consent and privacy considerations are essential elements of ethical research practices. By respecting participants' autonomy, ensuring confidentiality, and mitigating privacy risks, researchers can navigate the legal and ethical landscape while collecting valuable data for the advancement of legal studies.

Research involving vulnerable populations

Research involving vulnerable populations raises ethical considerations that need to be carefully addressed to ensure the protection and well-being of the participants. Vulnerable populations refer to individuals or groups who may be at a greater risk of harm or exploitation due to their characteristics, circumstances, or power dynamics. This section explores the key ethical guidelines and considerations when conducting research involving vulnerable populations, along with examples and best practices.

Understanding vulnerability

Before delving into the ethical considerations, it is important to have a clear understanding of who constitutes vulnerable populations in the context of legal research. Vulnerability can arise from various factors, including age, disability, socioeconomic status, race, ethnicity, sexual orientation, gender identity, immigration status, or involvement in the criminal justice system. It is crucial to recognize that vulnerability is not static and can be influenced by individual experiences, social contexts, and power dynamics.

Ethical guidelines for research involving vulnerable populations

When conducting research involving vulnerable populations, researchers must adhere to ethical guidelines to protect participants and ensure the integrity of the research process. The following principles and considerations should be kept in mind:

1. Informed consent: Informed consent is a fundamental requirement for any research involving human participants. It entails providing participants with clear and accessible information about the study, including its purpose, potential risks and benefits, confidentiality measures, voluntary participation, and the right to withdraw at any time. Researchers must ensure that participants fully understand the information provided and have the capacity to give informed consent.

2. Privacy and confidentiality: Protecting the privacy and confidentiality of participants is essential, especially when dealing with sensitive information. Researchers should implement appropriate measures to ensure data security, such as anonymizing data, using secure storage systems, and limiting access to authorized personnel. Participants should be assured that their personal information will be handled with utmost care and will not be disclosed without their explicit consent.

3. Minimizing harm and maximizing benefit: Researchers should strive to minimize potential harm to vulnerable participants and maximize the potential benefits of the research. This involves carefully assessing the risks and benefits associated with the study and taking steps to mitigate harm. It also entails considering the long-term implications of the research on the well-being of the participants and the broader community.

4. Protecting autonomy and dignity: Respecting the autonomy and dignity of vulnerable participants is crucial. Researchers should ensure that participants are treated with respect, fairness, and sensitivity throughout the research process. They should also be mindful of power imbalances and strive to ensure that participants have a genuine voice and agency in the research.

5. Beneficence and justice: Researchers have a responsibility to promote the welfare of vulnerable participants and ensure that the research is conducted in a just and equitable manner. This includes addressing any power imbalances, promoting inclusivity, and considering the unique needs and circumstances of the participants. Researchers should be mindful of any potential for exploitation and ensure that the benefits of the research are fairly distributed.

Challenges and considerations

Conducting research involving vulnerable populations presents specific challenges and considerations that researchers need to navigate. Some of these challenges include:

1. Power differentials: Vulnerable populations may be in a disadvantaged position due to power differentials in society. Researchers must be aware of these dynamics and ensure that the research process does not perpetuate further harm or reinforce existing inequities. It is important to engage in reflexive practices and critically reflect on the researcher-participant relationship.

2. Informed consent capacity: Some vulnerable populations, such as individuals with cognitive impairments or minors, may have limited capacity to provide informed consent. In such cases, additional safeguards may need to be put in place, such as obtaining informed consent from a legally authorized representative or using simplified consent forms that are easy to comprehend.

3. Privacy and confidentiality concerns: Vulnerable populations may have heightened concerns regarding privacy and confidentiality. Researchers should take extra measures to address these concerns and ensure that participants feel safe and their personal information is protected.

4. Access and representation: Researchers need to consider the accessibility of the research process for vulnerable populations. This includes providing accommodations for individuals with disabilities, using inclusive language, and considering cultural and linguistic differences. It is also essential to strive for diverse representation to ensure that the perspectives of all subgroups within vulnerable populations are adequately accounted for.

Best practices

To conduct ethically sound research involving vulnerable populations, researchers should consider the following best practices:

1. Collaborative approach: Involving vulnerable populations and relevant stakeholders in the research process can enhance its validity and relevance. Collaboration can help ensure that research questions, methodologies, and outcomes align with the needs and priorities of the participants and the community.

2. Sensitivity to cultural context: Cultural sensitivity is crucial when working with vulnerable populations. Researchers should have an understanding of cultural norms, practices, and values to ensure that the research process respects and acknowledges cultural diversity. Engaging with community leaders and organizations can help build trust and facilitate culturally responsive research.

3. Continuous ethical review: Ethical considerations should be an ongoing and integral part of the research process. Researchers should engage in continuous ethical review and seek input from institutional review boards and ethics committees. Regularly reassessing the potential risks, benefits, and ethical implications of the research helps ensure that participants' rights and well-being are protected.

4. Dissemination of findings: Researchers should share their findings in a manner that benefits the vulnerable populations involved in the research. This includes providing accessible summaries of research findings, engaging in knowledge translation activities, and actively involving participants and their communities in interpreting and applying the research outcomes.

Example: Research involving incarcerated individuals

To illustrate the ethical considerations and best practices for research involving vulnerable populations, let's consider the example of conducting research with incarcerated individuals. Incarcerated individuals are a vulnerable population due to their limited autonomy, restricted freedoms, and the power dynamics inherent within the criminal justice system.

When conducting research with incarcerated individuals, researchers should:

- Obtain informed consent: Researchers should ensure that incarcerated individuals have a clear understanding of the research purpose, procedures, and risks, and provide them with an opportunity to ask questions. Informed consent should be voluntary, and participants should be made aware of their right to withdraw at any time.

- Protect privacy and confidentiality: Researchers must take precautions to protect the privacy and confidentiality of incarcerated participants. This may involve using pseudonyms, securely storing data, and only sharing aggregated findings to prevent individual identification.

- Minimize potential harm: Researchers should be mindful of the potential emotional or psychological harm that the research may cause to incarcerated individuals. They should carefully consider the research questions, methodology, and potential benefits to ensure they outweigh any potential harm.

- Address power imbalances: Researchers should recognize the power dynamics between researchers and incarcerated participants and strive to create a respectful and collaborative research environment. This includes actively involving incarcerated individuals in decision-making processes and valuing their contributions as equal partners in the research.

- Promote inclusivity and diversity: Researchers should take steps to ensure that the research sample reflects the diversity within the incarcerated population. This may involve considering gender, race, ethnic, and cultural differences and ensuring that all voices are represented.

By following these ethical guidelines and best practices, researchers can conduct research involving vulnerable populations in a way that upholds the rights, dignity, and well-being of the participants.

Resources for further exploration

For further exploration of ethical considerations in research involving vulnerable populations, the following resources can be helpful:

- American Psychological Association (APA) Ethics Code: The APA provides guidelines specifically addressing research ethics, including considerations for working with vulnerable populations. The APA Ethics Code offers valuable insights into best practices for ethical research.

- Belmont Report: The Belmont Report, published by the National Commission for the Protection of Human Subjects of Biomedical and Behavioral Research, outlines the ethical principles and guidelines for research involving human subjects. It provides a framework for addressing ethical considerations in research, including those related to vulnerable populations.

- Institutional review boards (IRBs): IRBs are responsible for reviewing and approving research involving human subjects. They ensure that ethical guidelines are followed and participants' rights are protected. Researchers can consult their institution's IRB to navigate the ethical review process.

- Guidelines from professional associations: Many professional associations, such as the American Sociological Association and the American Anthropological Association, have guidelines and codes of ethics that address research involving vulnerable populations. Researchers can refer to these guidelines for discipline-specific considerations.

It is essential for researchers to thoroughly familiarize themselves with the relevant ethical guidelines and principles, seek appropriate approvals, and engage in ongoing ethical reflection to conduct research involving vulnerable populations in an ethically sound manner.

In conclusion, researching involving vulnerable populations requires a careful and nuanced approach. Ethical guidelines and considerations are crucial to protect the rights and well-being of participants, minimize harm, and ensure that the research process is conducted with integrity. By recognizing the unique challenges and engaging in collaborative and culturally sensitive approaches, researchers can contribute to meaningful and responsible research that serves the needs of vulnerable populations and promotes justice and equality.

Balancing Ethical Responsibilities and Legal Obligations

In the field of legal studies, practitioners face the challenging task of balancing ethical responsibilities with legal obligations. This delicate equilibrium requires a thoughtful consideration of moral values and principles, as well as adherence to the rules and laws that govern the legal profession. In this section, we will explore the complexities involved in striking this balance and provide practical guidance for navigating the ethical dilemmas that may arise in the course of legal practice.

Understanding Ethical Responsibilities

Ethical responsibilities refer to the obligations that legal professionals have towards their clients, the legal system, and society as a whole. These responsibilities are rooted in principles such as integrity, confidentiality, competence, and loyalty. Upholding these ethical responsibilities ensures that attorneys maintain the trust of their clients and the public, and promotes the fair administration of justice.

One of the key ethical responsibilities of legal professionals is the duty of zealous representation. Attorneys must advocate for their clients' interests within the boundaries of the law, while also considering the ethical implications of their actions. This duty requires attorneys to exercise sound judgment, honesty, and diligence in pursuing their clients' objectives.

Another important ethical responsibility is the duty of confidentiality. Attorneys must keep all information shared by their clients confidential, unless authorized by law or the client to disclose it. This duty is essential in maintaining the trust and confidence that clients place in their legal representatives.

Legal Obligations and Professional Conduct

Legal obligations, on the other hand, are derived from statutes, regulations, and professional rules of conduct. These obligations define the parameters within which legal professionals must operate to ensure compliance with the law. Failure to fulfill legal obligations can result in professional discipline, loss of professional license, or legal liability.

Legal professionals are bound by codes of professional conduct, which vary across jurisdictions. These codes outline the standards of behavior expected of attorneys in their interactions with clients, the court, and other parties. Examples of legal obligations include the duty of competency, which requires attorneys to possess the requisite knowledge and skills to handle their clients' cases effectively. Attorneys must also comply with rules governing conflicts of interest, attorney-client privilege, and client funds management, among others.

Navigating Ethical Dilemmas

Balancing ethical responsibilities and legal obligations can sometimes present dilemmas for legal professionals. Situations may arise where a client's interests appear to conflict with their ethical responsibilities or where compliance with the law may compromise ethical considerations. It is crucial for legal practitioners to navigate these dilemmas conscientiously and with an understanding of the potential consequences.

To navigate ethical dilemmas effectively, legal professionals can follow a reasoned decision-making process. This involves identifying the relevant ethical rules and legal requirements, gathering all the facts and information, and analyzing the possible courses of action. Consulting professional guidelines, seeking advice from mentors or colleagues, or engaging in ethical consultations can also assist in resolving ethical dilemmas.

It is important to note that there is no one-size-fits-all solution to ethical dilemmas, as each situation is unique. Upholding ethical responsibilities while complying with legal obligations requires legal professionals to exercise moral judgment, critical thinking, and reflection. It is a continuous effort that necessitates ongoing professional development and engagement with ethical considerations throughout one's career.

Case Study: Balancing Client Interests and Ethical Responsibilities

Consider a scenario where an attorney represents a client charged with a serious criminal offense. The client admits guilt to the attorney but insists on pleading not guilty in court. The attorney faces a dilemma as to whether to present the client's false defense or withdraw from the case due to ethical conflicts.

In this case, the attorney must carefully navigate the ethical responsibilities and legal obligations at play. While the client has the right to choose a defense strategy, the attorney also has an ethical duty to present truthful and accurate information to the court. The attorney may consider alternatives, such as urging the client to reconsider their position, explaining the potential consequences of presenting a false defense, or seeking permission from the court to withdraw from the case if the ethical conflict cannot be resolved.

This case study highlights the complexity of balancing ethical responsibilities and legal obligations, as attorneys must grapple with potentially conflicting interests to fulfill their professional duties.

Resources for Further Exploration

Ethical decision-making is a multifaceted topic that requires continuous learning and engagement. Legal professionals and students can explore further resources to deepen their understanding of how to balance ethical responsibilities and legal obligations. Some recommended resources include:

- *Model Rules of Professional Conduct*: Published by the American Bar Association, these rules serve as a guide for legal professionals and provide a framework for ethical behavior in the legal field.

- *Legal Ethics: Theories and Practical Applications*: A comprehensive book that delves into the theoretical and practical aspects of legal ethics, discussing case studies and offering guidance on navigating ethical dilemmas.

- *Continuing Legal Education (CLE) Programs on Legal Ethics*: Many professional organizations and bar associations offer CLE programs dedicated to legal ethics. These programs provide opportunities for legal professionals to enhance their understanding of ethical responsibilities and dilemmas.

- *Legal Ethics Opinion Letters*: Opinions issued by bar associations and ethics committees provide guidance on specific ethical issues faced by legal professionals.

Engaging with these resources can help legal professionals cultivate a deeper understanding of ethical responsibilities and develop effective strategies for balancing ethical considerations with legal obligations.

Conclusion

Balancing ethical responsibilities and legal obligations is an essential aspect of legal practice. Legal professionals must strive to uphold ethical principles while complying with the rules and regulations that govern their profession. Navigating ethical dilemmas requires thoughtful analysis, critical thinking, and an ongoing commitment to professional development. By striking a balance between ethical responsibilities and legal obligations, legal professionals contribute to the maintenance of a just and fair legal system.

Exercise: Think about a recent legal case or current event that raises ethical considerations. Consider the different perspectives and values involved and draft a short essay discussing how the balance between ethical responsibilities and legal obligations could be achieved in that situation.

Discussion Questions: 1. What are some common ethical dilemmas faced by legal professionals? 2. How can legal professionals balance their duty of zealous representation with ethical responsibilities? 3. What are the consequences of failing to uphold ethical responsibilities? 4. How do cultural and societal factors influence ethical considerations in legal practice? 5. What strategies can legal professionals employ to maintain equilibrium between ethical responsibilities and legal obligations?

Ethical challenges in conducting empirical research in legal studies

Empirical research in legal studies involves the collection and analysis of data to understand and evaluate various aspects of the legal system. This field plays a crucial role in providing evidence-based insights into the effectiveness of laws, policies, and practices. However, conducting empirical research in legal studies raises ethical challenges that researchers must address to ensure the protection of participants' rights and the integrity of the research process. In this section, we will explore some of the key ethical challenges that researchers face in conducting empirical research in legal studies and discuss strategies to address these challenges.

Informed consent and privacy considerations

One of the fundamental ethical principles in research is obtaining informed consent from participants. In legal studies, researchers often work with human subjects who may be involved in sensitive legal matters. Obtaining informed consent poses unique challenges due to the potential power dynamics and legal complexities involved.

To address this challenge, researchers must provide participants with clear and comprehensive information about the purpose, risks, benefits, and procedures of the research. In the legal context, this can be particularly challenging as participants may be facing ongoing legal cases or have concerns about confidentiality. Researchers should ensure that participants have a full understanding of their rights and the potential implications of participating in the study. Additionally, researchers should consider obtaining consent not only at the beginning but also throughout the research process, as participants may need to be re-informed about any changes or updates.

Privacy considerations are also crucial in empirical research in legal studies. Participants may be worried about the potential disclosure of sensitive information that could impact their legal standing or reputation. Researchers must take appropriate steps to protect participants' confidentiality and privacy. This may involve anonymizing data, using secure storage systems, and ensuring that only authorized individuals have access to the data.

Research involving vulnerable populations

Legal studies often involve research with vulnerable populations, such as individuals who have experienced trauma, individuals with mental health issues, or individuals facing legal challenges. Conducting research with these populations requires additional ethical considerations to ensure their well-being and protection.

Researchers must take measures to minimize any potential harm or distress to vulnerable participants. This may involve providing appropriate resources and support, using sensitive and non-intrusive research methods, and ensuring that participants have the option to withdraw from the study at any time without repercussions. Researchers should also consider whether the study design includes mechanisms to identify and address any adverse effects on participants' mental or emotional well-being.

In addition, researchers should carefully consider the power dynamics at play when working with vulnerable populations. They should take steps to ensure that participants are not exploited or coerced into participating and that their autonomy and agency are respected throughout the research process.

Balancing ethical responsibilities and legal obligations

Empirical research in legal studies often involves studying legal processes, systems, and institutions. Researchers must navigate the ethical challenges that arise from the potential tension between their ethical responsibilities as researchers and their legal obligations.

Researchers should be aware of and comply with the relevant legal and ethical guidelines governing their research. They should also consider the potential impact of their research on the legal system and the individuals involved. Striking a balance between the pursuit of knowledge and the potential consequences of the research is crucial.

In some cases, researchers may face challenges in accessing certain data or information due to legal restrictions, privacy concerns, or institutional barriers. Researchers should explore alternative approaches or strategies to obtain the necessary data while ensuring compliance with legal and ethical standards. Collaboration with legal professionals and institutions can be beneficial in navigating these challenges and ensuring that the research is conducted ethically.

Ethical challenges in using empirical research for policy and legal reform

Empirical research in legal studies often aims to inform policy and legal reform. However, researchers may face ethical challenges when their research findings have significant implications for the legal system and society.

Researchers have an ethical responsibility to accurately and honestly report their findings, even if they are contrary to their initial hypotheses or preconceived notions. Researchers should be transparent about any limitations or uncertainties in their research, and they should consider the potential consequences of their research in terms of social justice, fairness, and equality.

In addition, researchers must carefully consider the potential dissemination and use of their research findings. They should be aware of the broader socio-political context and the power dynamics at play when presenting their research to policymakers, legal professionals, and the public. Researchers should strive to ensure that their research is not misused or misinterpreted to support unethical or unjust practices.

Addressing ethical challenges in conducting empirical research

To address ethical challenges in conducting empirical research in legal studies, researchers should:

- Familiarize themselves with relevant ethical guidelines and regulations specific to their country or jurisdiction.
- Seek guidance from research ethics committees or institutional review boards to ensure compliance with ethical standards.
- Conduct a comprehensive risk-benefit analysis to assess potential harms and benefits to participants and society.
- Ensure informed consent is obtained and documented properly, and that participants have the opportunity to ask questions and withdraw from the study at any time.
- Protect participants' privacy and confidentiality by using secure data storage systems and anonymizing data wherever possible.
- Minimize the potential for harm or distress to vulnerable populations by using appropriate research methods and providing necessary resources and support.
- Engage in ongoing dialogue with participants and stakeholders to address any concerns or issues that may arise during the research process.
- Promote transparency and honesty in reporting research findings, including any limitations or uncertainties.
- Advocate for the responsible and ethical use of research findings in policy and legal reform.

By actively addressing these ethical challenges, researchers can ensure that their empirical research in legal studies contributes to the advancement of knowledge while upholding the rights and well-being of participants and society as a whole.

Resources for further exploration

- American Psychological Association (APA) Ethics Code: `https://www.apa.org/ethics/code/`
- American Bar Association (ABA) Model Rules of Professional Conduct: `https://www.americanbar.org/groups/professional_responsibility/publications/model_rules_of_professional_conduct/`
- The Belmont Report: Ethical Principles and Guidelines for the Protection of Human Subjects of Research: `https://www.hhs.gov/ohrp/regulations-and-policy/belmont-report/`
- National Commission for the Protection of Human Subjects of Biomedical and Behavioral Research: `https://pdfs.semanticscholar.org/3c90/10630dad92f79943f4eed8f8dbb4b8c25a02.pdf`
- World Medical Association Declaration of Helsinki: `https://www.wma.net/what-we-do/medical-ethics/declaration-of-helsinki/`

Exercises

1. Consider a hypothetical research project that involves studying the experiences of individuals involved in a legal dispute. Identify and discuss potential ethical challenges that may arise in conducting this research and propose strategies to address these challenges.

2. Research the ethical guidelines specific to conducting empirical research with vulnerable populations in your country or jurisdiction. Compare and contrast these guidelines with international standards such as the Belmont Report and the World Medical Association Declaration of Helsinki.

3. Read a recent research article in the field of legal studies and critically evaluate the researchers' approach to addressing ethical challenges. Identify any potential ethical concerns and suggest alternative strategies or improvements.

4. Imagine you have conducted empirical research that has significant implications for legal reform. Develop a plan to disseminate and communicate

your research findings to policymakers and the public while ensuring ethical considerations are met.

5. Form a small group with fellow students and engage in a discussion about the ethical challenges encountered in conducting empirical research in legal studies. Share personal experiences and insights, and brainstorm potential solutions to these challenges.

Remember to always prioritize the well-being and rights of participants and to approach empirical research in legal studies with integrity, transparency, and a commitment to ethical conduct.

Chapter 4: The Future of Justice and Equality

The evolving concept of justice

Restorative justice and its impact on legal systems

Restorative justice is a transformative approach to addressing harm and resolving conflicts within legal systems. Unlike traditional methods that focus on punishment and retribution, restorative justice seeks to repair the harm caused by a wrongdoing and restore relationships between the parties involved. This section will explore the principles, benefits, and challenges of restorative justice, as well as its impact on legal systems.

Principles of restorative justice

Restorative justice is based on several core principles that guide its implementation. These principles include:

1. Inclusion and participation: Restorative justice values the involvement of all stakeholders affected by a wrongdoing, including the victim, the offender, and the community. It recognizes that their voices and perspectives are essential for achieving meaningful resolution.
2. Repairing harm: The central focus of restorative justice is repairing the harm caused by the offense. This may involve addressing the physical, emotional, and psychological consequences suffered by the victim, as well as providing opportunities for the offender to take responsibility and make amends.
3. Collaboration and dialogue: Restorative justice encourages open and respectful communication between the parties involved. It promotes dialogue, empathy, and understanding as essential elements for achieving resolution and healing.

4. Reintegration and reparation: Restorative justice aims to reintegrate offenders back into the community in a way that fosters accountability and prevents re-offending. It also emphasizes the importance of reparations, such as restitution or community service, as a means of restoring balance and addressing the harm caused.

Benefits of restorative justice

Restorative justice offers several significant benefits compared to traditional punitive approaches. These benefits include:

1. Victim satisfaction and empowerment: Restorative justice provides victims with a platform to express their needs, concerns, and emotions. It allows them to be directly involved in the process and have a say in the outcome, which can lead to greater satisfaction and a sense of empowerment.

2. Offender accountability and rehabilitation: By engaging offenders in meaningful dialogue with their victims and the wider community, restorative justice promotes a sense of accountability. This can foster a deeper understanding of the consequences of their actions and motivate the offender to make positive changes in their behavior.

3. Restoration of relationships and community cohesion: Restorative justice aims to repair relationships that have been damaged by the offense. By encouraging open communication and empathy, it can help build understanding and trust between the parties involved. This fosters a sense of community cohesion and promotes social healing.

4. Reduction in recidivism rates: Studies have shown that restorative justice programs are associated with lower rates of repeat offending compared to traditional punitive approaches. This suggests that the emphasis on addressing the underlying causes of offending and promoting rehabilitation is more effective in preventing future crimes.

Challenges of restorative justice

While restorative justice holds great promise, it also faces certain challenges that need to be addressed for its effective implementation. These challenges include:

1. Adequate resources and support: Restorative justice requires significant resources, including trained facilitators, appropriate spaces, and ongoing support for all parties involved. Ensuring the availability of these resources can be a challenge, particularly in areas with limited funding or infrastructure.

2. Balancing the needs of all parties: Achieving a balanced and satisfactory outcome for all parties involved can be a complex task. Restorative justice must carefully consider the needs and expectations of victims, offenders, and the wider community, balancing the principles of fairness and justice.

3. Addressing power dynamics: Restorative justice requires addressing power imbalances that may exist between the victim and the offender. Facilitators must create a safe and inclusive environment that allows for an open and honest dialogue while ensuring that all parties feel heard and respected.

4. Cultural and social considerations: Restorative justice needs to be sensitive to cultural and social factors that may influence how conflicts and harms are perceived and addressed. It must adapt to diverse perspectives and values to ensure its effectiveness and avoid potential harm or marginalization.

Examples of restorative justice in practice

Restorative justice has been successfully implemented in various contexts, showcasing its potential for positive outcomes. Here are a few examples:

1. Victim-offender mediation: This process brings together the victim, the offender, and trained facilitators to discuss the impact of the offense and explore possibilities for repairing the harm caused. It allows victims to express their feelings and needs, while offenders are given the opportunity to take responsibility and make amends.

2. Family group conferencing: Used in juvenile justice systems, this approach involves the victim, the offender, their families, and other community members. Together, they discuss the offense, determine meaningful consequences, and develop a plan for reparation and rehabilitation.

3. Circle sentencing: This method involves a facilitated dialogue between the offender, the victim, their supporters, and members of the community. The circle aims to address the harm caused, provide support, and collectively determine a fair and proportionate sentence.

Resources for further exploration

To delve deeper into restorative justice and its impact on legal systems, here are some recommended resources:

1. Books: - "The Little Book of Restorative Justice" by Howard Zehr - "Restorative Justice: Healing the Foundations of our Everyday Lives" by Mark Umbreit - "Restorative Justice: Ideas, Values, Debates" by Gerry Johnstone

2. Academic Journals: - "Restorative Justice: An International Journal" published by Routledge - "Contemporary Justice Review" published by Taylor & Francis - "Journal of Social Issues" published by Wiley

3. Organizations: - International Institute for Restorative Practices (IIRP) - Restorative Justice Council (RJC) - European Forum for Restorative Justice (EFRJ)

These resources provide a comprehensive understanding of restorative justice, its principles, and its practical implementation, as well as ongoing research and developments in the field. They are valuable tools for students and researchers interested in exploring this transformative approach to justice within the legal system.

The role of transformative justice in addressing systemic inequalities

Transformative justice is a concept that seeks to address systemic inequalities within the legal system by focusing on the root causes of harm and implementing strategies that aim to transform individuals and communities. It goes beyond traditional punitive measures and instead aims to create sustainable change and promote healing and accountability.

1. Understanding systemic inequalities: Systemic inequalities refer to the structural and institutional biases that perpetuate injustices in society. These inequalities can manifest in various forms, such as racial discrimination, economic disparities, gender-based violence, and marginalization of certain communities. Transformative justice recognizes that addressing these systemic inequalities requires a holistic approach that takes into account historical, social, and economic contexts.

2. Principles of transformative justice: Transformative justice is guided by several principles that help shape its approach in addressing systemic inequalities. These principles include:

2.1. Empowerment: Transformative justice encourages individuals and communities impacted by harm to actively participate in the decision-making process and take ownership of their healing and accountability.

2.2. Healing and restoration: Rather than focusing solely on punishment, transformative justice emphasizes the importance of facilitating healing and restoration for all parties involved in a conflict or harm. This may involve providing support services, counseling, and opportunities for dialogue and reconciliation.

2.3. Accountability: Transformative justice promotes accountability by holding individuals responsible for their actions and helping them understand the impact of their behavior. It seeks to address the underlying causes of harm and prevent its recurrence.

2.4. Community involvement: Recognizing that harm impacts not just individuals but also communities, transformative justice emphasizes the role of the community in addressing systemic inequalities. It encourages collective responses and community-based solutions to promote social cohesion and prevent future harm.

3. Strategies for transformative justice:

3.1. Restorative practices: Restorative justice practices, such as victim-offender dialogues and community conferencing, play a crucial role in transformative justice. These practices provide opportunities for those affected by harm to come together and discuss the impact of the harm, explore solutions, and promote understanding and healing.

3.2. Education and awareness: Transformative justice recognizes the importance of education and raising awareness about systemic inequalities. It aims to challenge societal norms and biases by promoting critical thinking, empathy, and a deeper understanding of the root causes of harm.

3.3. Alternative dispute resolution methods: Transformative justice encourages the use of alternative dispute resolution methods, such as mediation and negotiation, to address conflicts and harm. These methods prioritize communication, problem-solving, and relationship-building over adversarial approaches.

3.4. Community-based support services: In order to foster healing and restoration, transformative justice promotes the development of community-based support services. These services may include counseling, trauma-informed care, and access to resources that address the underlying issues contributing to harm.

4. Case study: The community accountability model:

One example of transformative justice in action is the community accountability model. This model was developed as a response to the failures of the criminal legal system in addressing gender-based violence, particularly against marginalized communities.

The community accountability model centers around the belief that addressing gender-based violence requires a community-wide response. It focuses on prevention, intervention, and accountability. Key components of this model include:

4.1. Prevention: The community accountability model emphasizes the importance of preventing harm before it occurs by challenging harmful behaviors and attitudes. This is done through education and community organizing efforts that promote healthy relationships and challenge gender-based norms.

4.2. Intervention: When harm occurs, the community accountability model prioritizes the safety and needs of survivors. It provides support and resources to survivors and encourages them to participate in decision-making processes regarding their own healing and the accountability of the person responsible for the harm.

4.3. Accountability: Central to the community accountability model is the idea that those who cause harm are held accountable in a way that promotes learning and growth, while also ensuring the safety of the survivor and the community. This may involve a range of interventions, such as counseling, restorative justice processes, and community-based consequences.

5. Resources for further exploration:

To delve deeper into the role of transformative justice in addressing systemic inequalities, the following resources are recommended:

5.1. Angela Davis, "Are Prisons Obsolete?": This book explores the failures of the prison system and offers alternative strategies for addressing harm and achieving justice.

5.2. "The Revolution Starts at Home: Confronting Intimate Violence Within Activist Communities": This anthology examines how transformative justice can be applied within activist communities to address intimate violence.

5.3. Generation Five's "Community Accountability Principles and Definitions": This resource provides a framework for implementing community accountability practices to address harm.

5.4. Project Nia: This organization focuses on promoting transformative justice and ending youth incarceration. Their website offers various resources and toolkits on implementing transformative justice practices in different contexts.

5.5. Restorative Justice Online: This online platform provides a wealth of resources on restorative justice practices, including case studies, research papers, and training materials.

By embracing the principles and strategies of transformative justice, we can work towards creating a legal system that truly addresses systemic inequalities, promotes healing, and fosters a more just and equitable society.

Intersectionality and its relevance to justice movements

Intersectionality is a crucial concept in the field of legal studies, particularly in the context of understanding and addressing systemic inequalities. It recognizes that individuals can experience multiple forms of oppression and discrimination simultaneously, based on their intersecting social identities such as race, gender, class, sexuality, ability, and more. This section explores the concept of intersectionality and its relevance to justice movements, highlighting its significance in promoting inclusive and equitable legal systems.

Understanding Intersectionality

Intersectionality originates from feminist and critical race theories and emphasizes the interconnected nature of different forms of oppression. It challenges the notion of experiencing discrimination solely based on a single identity category and recognizes that the convergence of multiple identities creates unique experiences and challenges.

At its core, intersectionality acknowledges that various social identities intersect to shape an individual's experiences, privilege, and marginalization. For example, a Black woman may experience discrimination differently from a white woman or a Black man due to the intersection of race and gender. This framework enables a more nuanced understanding of power dynamics and systemic inequalities.

Intersectionality and Social Justice Movements

Intersectionality has significantly impacted social justice movements by highlighting the need to address interlocking systems of oppression. It has challenged traditional approaches that tend to focus on single-axis analysis of discrimination and has provided a more holistic lens through which to understand and dismantle systemic injustices.

By considering the intersecting dimensions of individuals' identities, social justice movements can better advocate for the rights and experiences of marginalized communities. For instance, the movement for gender equality has increasingly embraced intersectionality to recognize and address the unique challenges faced by women of color, transgender individuals, and other marginalized groups whose experiences may differ from those of white, cisgender women.

Legal Implications of Intersectionality

Intersectionality has significant implications for the legal system and the pursuit of justice. By recognizing the complex ways in which different forms of oppression intersect, legal scholars and practitioners can develop more inclusive legal frameworks that address the needs of all individuals, especially those at the intersections of multiple marginalized identities.

An intersectional approach to legal studies calls for the examination of how different legal doctrines, policies, and practices impact individuals differently depending on their intersecting identities. It emphasizes the importance of considering the unique experiences and potential barriers faced by marginalized groups when developing and implementing legal remedies.

For example, an intersectional analysis may reveal how certain laws or policies disproportionately affect transgender people of color or individuals with disabilities. By identifying these disparities, legal professionals can work towards developing more equitable legal solutions that address the specific needs and experiences of those facing multiple forms of discrimination.

Challenges and Future Directions

While intersectionality has made significant strides within legal studies and social justice movements, challenges remain. It can be complex to navigate the intersections of various identities and discern the unique impacts of different forms of oppression. Additionally, issues of privilege, power dynamics, and the exclusion of certain perspectives within intersectional analyses can pose challenges to achieving true equality and justice.

Moving forward, it is imperative for legal scholars, practitioners, and activists to continue to engage with intersectionality and develop approaches that recognize and address intersecting systems of oppression. This involves fostering interdisciplinary collaborations, amplifying marginalized voices and perspectives, and continuously reevaluating and evolving legal frameworks to ensure they are responsive to the needs of diverse populations.

By incorporating intersectionality into legal studies, practitioners can work towards dismantling systemic inequalities and promoting justice for all individuals, regardless of their intersecting identities. Doing so not only contributes to the development of more equitable legal systems but also fosters a more inclusive and just society overall.

Resources for Further Exploration

- Kimberlé Crenshaw's seminal work, "Mapping the Margins: Intersectionality, Identity Politics, and Violence against Women of Color," provides a comprehensive introduction to the concept of intersectionality.

- Patricia Hill Collins' book, "Black Feminist Thought: Knowledge, Consciousness, and the Politics of Empowerment," explores intersectionality within the context of Black feminism.

- The Intersectionality Matters! podcast hosted by Kimberlé Crenshaw offers in-depth conversations about intersectionality and its application to various fields, including law and social justice.
- The American Bar Association's Section on Civil Rights and Social Justice provides resources and publications focused on intersectionality and its relevance to the legal profession.

Conclusion

Intersectionality is a fundamental concept in legal studies that recognizes the interconnected nature of oppression and discrimination. By considering how various social identities intersect, legal scholars, practitioners, and activists can work towards developing more inclusive and equitable legal frameworks. Incorporating intersectionality into legal studies is essential for promoting justice movements and building a more just and equitable society.

Chapter 4: The Future of Justice and Equality

5.1.4 The influence of cultural and societal factors on notions of justice

Justice is a complex and multifaceted concept that is deeply influenced by cultural and societal factors. Different cultures and societies have diverse notions of what justice entails, and these varying perspectives shape the development and application of legal systems around the world. In this section, we will explore the ways in which cultural and societal factors influence notions of justice and how these factors can both enhance and challenge our pursuit of a just society.

Cultural perspectives on justice

Cultural perspectives play a vital role in shaping our understanding of justice. Cultural norms, values, beliefs, and traditions all contribute to the development of unique approaches to justice within a society. For example, in some cultures, justice may be centered around collective harmony and the restoration of relationships, while in others, it may focus more on retribution and punishment. These cultural differences significantly impact the laws, legal systems, and social norms within a society.

An essential concept related to cultural perspectives on justice is legal pluralism. Legal pluralism recognizes that there can be multiple sources of law that coexist within a society, including customary law, religious law, and state law. Each of these legal systems is influenced by the cultural context in which they operate and may reflect different notions of justice. Understanding and navigating these cultural differences is crucial for building inclusive and responsive legal systems.

Societal factors and justice inequalities

In addition to cultural factors, societal factors also shape notions of justice. Socioeconomic disparities, power imbalances, institutional discrimination, and historical injustices all influence the understanding and application of justice within a society. For example, marginalized communities often face systemic barriers that prevent them from accessing justice on equal terms. This can lead to an unequal distribution of legal rights, protections, and opportunities.

To ensure a more just society, it is essential to address these societal factors that perpetuate injustice. This requires acknowledging and challenging systems of oppression, promoting social equity, and designing legal systems that are sensitive to the unique needs and experiences of marginalized groups. Intersectionality, which recognizes the interconnected nature of social identities and experiences, can provide a useful framework for understanding and addressing the complex dynamics of societal factors in relation to justice.

Cultural relativism and universal human rights

The influence of cultural and societal factors on notions of justice raises important questions about cultural relativism and universal human rights. Cultural relativism asserts that different cultures have their own distinct values and norms, and judgments should be made within the cultural context. This perspective challenges the notion of universal human rights, suggesting that what is considered just or unjust may vary across cultures.

However, it is crucial to strike a balance between respecting cultural diversity and upholding the fundamental principles of human rights. While cultural considerations are significant, certain rights are universally essential, such as the right to life, freedom from torture, and freedom of expression. Achieving this balance requires engaging in critical dialogue and negotiation that respects cultural differences while promoting human rights.

Cultural and societal challenges to justice

The influence of cultural and societal factors on notions of justice can present challenges in achieving a more just society. Some cultural and societal practices may conflict with principles of equality, fairness, and human rights. For instance, cultural practices that discriminate against certain social groups or perpetuate gender inequality can hinder the pursuit of justice.

Overcoming these challenges requires transformative approaches to justice that integrate cultural sensitivity and social change. It is crucial to engage in dialogue, education, and awareness-building within communities to challenge discriminatory practices and promote more inclusive and egalitarian values. Additionally, legal reform that addresses systemic injustices and ensures equal protection under the law is essential for countering the negative impacts of cultural and societal factors on justice.

Resources for further exploration

To deepen your understanding of the influence of cultural and societal factors on notions of justice, consider exploring the following resources:

1. *Cultural Justice: Cultural Rights in Practice* by Antony J. Lentin

2. *Justice: What's the Right Thing to Do?* by Michael J. Sandel

3. *The New Jim Crow: Mass Incarceration in the Age of Colorblindness* by Michelle Alexander

4. *Law's Empire* by Ronald Dworkin

5. *The Cultural Defense of Nations: A Liberal Theory of Majority Rights* by Liav Orgad

Conclusion

Cultural and societal factors shape our understanding of justice in profound ways. By recognizing and engaging with these influences, we can work towards a more inclusive and equitable legal system. Balancing cultural relativism with universal human rights is a complex task that requires ongoing dialogue and critical reflection. By addressing the challenges posed by cultural and societal factors, we can strive towards a more just and equal society for all.

Challenges and Opportunities in Achieving Justice for All

Achieving justice for all is a noble and essential goal in any society. However, this pursuit is not without its challenges and obstacles. In this section, we will explore the various challenges and opportunities that arise in the quest for justice, as well as strategies and initiatives that can help overcome these barriers.

Challenges in Achieving Justice

1. **Socioeconomic inequalities:** One of the major challenges in achieving justice for all is addressing the deep-rooted socioeconomic disparities that exist within society. These disparities can affect access to legal representation, resources, and opportunities, creating unequal outcomes and perpetuating systemic injustices. Overcoming these disparities requires a multifaceted approach that includes systemic reform, targeted interventions, and inclusive policies.

2. **Bias and discrimination:** Bias and discrimination based on race, gender, ethnicity, religion, sexual orientation, and other factors continue to be significant barriers to achieving justice. These biases can manifest in various aspects of the legal system, including law enforcement, the judiciary, and legal decision-making processes. To address this challenge, it is crucial to promote diversity and inclusivity within the legal profession, implement bias-free practices, and raise awareness about implicit biases.

3. **Lack of legal awareness and education:** Limited legal knowledge and awareness among individuals, particularly marginalized communities, can hinder their ability to navigate the legal system and assert their rights. To overcome this challenge, legal literacy programs and initiatives should be implemented to educate and empower individuals with the information they need to access justice and understand their rights.

4. **Resource constraints:** Limited financial resources and the high cost of legal services can pose significant barriers to accessing justice. Many individuals are unable to afford legal representation or pursue legal action due to financial constraints. Improving access to legal aid, pro bono services, and affordable legal representation can address this challenge and ensure that justice is accessible to all, regardless of their financial status.

Opportunities for Achieving Justice

1. **Technology and innovation:** Advances in technology and innovation present significant opportunities for achieving justice for all. Online dispute resolution platforms, virtual courtrooms, and digital legal services can enhance access to justice, particularly in remote or underserved areas. Harnessing technology can facilitate faster and more efficient legal processes, reduce costs, and increase transparency in the legal system.

2. **Collaborative efforts and partnerships:** Collaboration among various stakeholders, including government agencies, civil society organizations, legal professionals, and community members, can bring about positive change and help overcome the challenges in achieving justice for all. Establishing partnerships and networks to share resources, knowledge, and expertise can lead to more effective solutions and greater impact.

3. **Policy and legislative reforms:** Robust policy and legislative reforms play a crucial role in advancing justice for all. Addressing gaps and loopholes in existing laws, implementing comprehensive anti-discrimination legislation, and enacting progressive policies can help create a more just and equitable legal system. Governments and policymakers should prioritize reform efforts that address systemic injustices and promote equal rights and opportunities.

4. **Public engagement and awareness:** Raising public awareness and engaging communities in discussions and initiatives related to justice issues is vital for achieving meaningful change. Grassroots movements, public campaigns, and community-based organizations can mobilize public support and advocate for justice reforms. Promoting civic education and fostering an understanding of the importance of justice can empower individuals to actively participate in shaping a more just society.

Case Study: The Innocence Project

The Innocence Project is a prime example of an initiative that tackles the challenges and harnesses the opportunities in achieving justice for all. This non-profit organization works to exonerate wrongfully convicted individuals through DNA testing and advocates for criminal justice reform.

The Innocence Project addresses challenges such as bias and discrimination in the criminal justice system by using scientific evidence to reveal wrongful convictions. By leveraging technology and innovations in DNA testing, they provide a means to obtain accurate and reliable evidence that can overturn wrongful convictions.

Moreover, the Innocence Project engages in policy and legislative reforms by working with lawmakers to improve the criminal justice system. Their efforts have led to changes in laws regarding eyewitness identification, interrogation practices, and access to DNA testing, creating a more just and equitable system.

The organization also emphasizes public engagement and awareness by educating the public about wrongful convictions and the flaws in the criminal justice system. Through their advocacy and outreach programs, they mobilize support, raise funds, and facilitate public dialogue on issues of justice. This grassroots approach has been instrumental in generating public interest and support for criminal justice reform.

Resources and Further Exploration

To delve deeper into the challenges and opportunities in achieving justice for all, the following resources can provide valuable insights:

- *Just Mercy* by Bryan Stevenson: This memoir explores the author's experiences as a lawyer advocating for justice reform, highlighting systemic injustices and the need for compassion in the legal system.
- *The New Jim Crow: Mass Incarceration in the Age of Colorblindness* by Michelle Alexander: This book examines the racial disparities and systemic discrimination within the criminal justice system, shedding light on the challenges of achieving true justice.
- *Inequality and American Democracy: What We Know and What We Need to Learn* edited by Lawrence R. Jacobs and Theda Skocpol: This collection of essays explores the relationship between inequality and democracy, examining the impact of socioeconomic disparities on access to justice and political power.
- The official website of The Innocence Project (`www.innocenceproject.org`) provides information on their work, success stories, policy initiatives, and resources for those interested in criminal justice reform and the pursuit of justice for all.

Conclusion

In the pursuit of justice for all, it is essential to acknowledge and address the challenges that hinder equal access to justice. By seizing the opportunities presented by technology, collaborative efforts, policy reforms, and public engagement, we can overcome these challenges and create a more just and equitable society. Through collective action and a commitment to fairness, we can strive for a future in which justice is a fundamental right for all individuals, regardless of their background or circumstances.

Inclusive legal systems and equal access to justice

Legal aid and pro bono services

Legal aid and pro bono services are vital components of the justice system that aim to ensure equal access to justice for individuals who may not have the financial means to afford legal representation. In this section, we will explore the concept of legal aid, the role of pro bono services, and their significance in promoting justice and equality.

Introduction to legal aid

Legal aid refers to the provision of free or low-cost legal assistance to individuals who cannot afford private legal representation. It aims to bridge the justice gap by offering support to vulnerable populations, such as low-income individuals, victims of domestic violence, immigrants, and persons with disabilities.

One of the fundamental principles of legal aid is the belief that everyone should have equal access to justice, regardless of their socioeconomic status. By providing free or subsidized legal services, legal aid programs play a crucial role in ensuring that all individuals, regardless of their financial situation, have the opportunity to assert their rights and seek redress for legal issues.

Types of legal aid

There are various types of legal aid services available to individuals in need. These services can include legal advice, representation in court proceedings, assistance with drafting legal documents, and alternative dispute resolution.

1. **Legal advice:** Legal aid programs often have dedicated helplines or walk-in centers where individuals can seek advice on their legal issues. Lawyers or legal professionals provide guidance on the legal options available and help individuals understand their rights and responsibilities.

2. **Representation in court:** Legal aid organizations may provide representation to individuals who need to navigate the complexities of the legal system but cannot afford a private attorney. This representation can extend to civil matters, such as family law, housing, employment, and consumer issues, as well as criminal defense.

3. **Assistance with legal documents:** Legal aid services can assist individuals in preparing necessary legal documents, such as wills, power of attorney, and immigration forms. This support ensures that individuals can accurately complete these documents and understand their legal implications.

4. **Alternative dispute resolution:** Legal aid programs may offer mediation or negotiation services as an alternative to going to court. These services aim to

resolve conflicts amicably while avoiding the burdensome costs associated with lengthy court proceedings.

Role of pro bono services

Pro bono services, also known as volunteer legal services, involve lawyers providing legal assistance on a voluntary basis, free of charge. While legal aid primarily focuses on serving individuals who meet specific income requirements, pro bono services extend the reach of legal assistance to a broader range of individuals and causes.

1. **Law firm pro bono programs:** Many law firms encourage their attorneys to dedicate a certain number of hours to pro bono work each year. These programs allow lawyers to use their skills and expertise to support individuals or organizations who cannot afford legal representation. Pro bono work not only benefits those in need but also allows lawyers to gain valuable experience and develop their professional skills.

2. **Pro bono clinics and organizations:** Pro bono clinics and organizations connect lawyers willing to donate their time with individuals seeking legal assistance. These clinics may focus on specific areas of law or serve particular populations, such as veterans, immigrants, or refugees. By leveraging the expertise of volunteer lawyers, pro bono clinics can provide legal aid to a greater number of people.

3. **Public interest organizations:** Public interest organizations, such as nonprofit advocacy groups, work on behalf of underserved communities and pursue social justice causes. Lawyers working for these organizations often engage in pro bono work to advocate for systemic change and provide legal representation to marginalized individuals and groups.

Significance of legal aid and pro bono services

Legal aid and pro bono services are crucial for promoting justice and equality within society. Here are some key reasons why these services are significant:

1. **Equal access to justice:** Legal aid and pro bono services ensure that individuals who cannot afford legal representation are not disadvantaged in the justice system. By providing support to those in need, these services help level the playing field and give everyone an opportunity to assert their legal rights.

2. **Protection of rights:** Legal aid helps individuals understand their rights and navigate complex legal processes. It enables them to seek redress for injustices they may have faced, such as domestic violence, discrimination, or unlawful eviction. By

ensuring access to legal representation, legal aid safeguards crucial rights and liberties.

3. **Reducing inequality:** Legal aid and pro bono services play a vital role in combating social inequalities. They ensure that disadvantaged individuals and marginalized communities have access to the legal resources needed to challenge systemic injustices. By addressing the power imbalance between different socioeconomic groups, these services contribute to a more equitable society.

4. **Supporting the rule of law:** Legal aid is essential for maintaining the integrity of the justice system. It ensures that all individuals, regardless of their financial means, can participate in legal processes. By strengthening access to justice, legal aid programs reinforce the principles of fairness and due process upon which the rule of law relies.

Challenges and future directions

Despite the significant contributions of legal aid and pro bono services, there are several challenges that need to be addressed for further advancement:

1. **Funding:** Legal aid organizations often struggle with limited resources, making it challenging to meet the high demand for services. Governments, nonprofits, and philanthropic organizations need to allocate adequate funding to ensure the sustainability and expansion of legal aid programs.

2. **Awareness and accessibility:** Many individuals in need of legal aid are unaware of the services available to them or face barriers in accessing them. Efforts should be made to raise awareness about legal aid programs and improve their accessibility, particularly for underserved populations.

3. **Coordination and collaboration:** Collaboration between legal aid organizations, pro bono service providers, and other stakeholders is crucial for maximizing the impact of these services. Effective coordination can help address gaps in service delivery and ensure that resources are allocated efficiently.

4. **Technology and innovation:** Embracing technology and innovative approaches can enhance the reach and effectiveness of legal aid and pro bono services. Online platforms, virtual legal clinics, and mobile applications can facilitate remote access to legal assistance and streamline service delivery.

In conclusion, legal aid and pro bono services are essential components of the justice system, aiming to provide equal access to justice for all individuals, regardless of their financial means. These services play a critical role in protecting rights, reducing inequality, and promoting social justice. As legal systems continue to evolve, it is imperative to address the challenges and invest in these services to ensure a more just and equitable future.

The role of technology in enhancing access to justice

In recent years, technology has played a transformative role in various aspects of our lives, and the legal field is no exception. The advancements in technology have opened up new opportunities to enhance access to justice, making legal services more accessible, efficient, and affordable. In this section, we will explore the role of technology in empowering individuals and communities to navigate the legal system and seek justice.

Digital platforms for legal information and resources

One of the key ways technology has improved access to justice is through the development of digital platforms that provide legal information and resources. These platforms serve as valuable tools for individuals who may not have easy access to legal advice or representation.

For example, online legal research databases and websites such as LexisNexis and Westlaw have made it easier for legal professionals and individuals to access a vast collection of legal materials, including case law, statutes, regulations, and secondary sources. These platforms offer search functionalities that allow users to quickly find relevant legal information, saving time and effort compared to traditional library research.

Furthermore, there are websites and apps that provide legal self-help information and resources, addressing common legal issues and guiding individuals through legal processes. These platforms often offer plain language explanations, step-by-step guides, and templates for legal documents such as wills, contracts, and forms for various legal proceedings. By providing these resources online, individuals can educate themselves about their rights and responsibilities, empowering them to advocate for themselves effectively.

Online dispute resolution

Another significant technological advancement in enhancing access to justice is the emergence of online dispute resolution (ODR) platforms. ODR refers to the use of technology to facilitate the resolution of disputes outside of the traditional court system.

ODR platforms offer a range of dispute resolution mechanisms, including negotiation, mediation, and arbitration, conducted entirely online. These platforms provide a convenient and cost-effective alternative to traditional dispute resolution methods, reducing the barriers of time, cost, and geographical distance.

For example, platforms like Modria and eBay's Resolution Center enable parties to resolve consumer disputes through online negotiation and mediation. Participants can engage in discussions, exchange documents, and reach mutually agreeable solutions without the need for physical meetings or court appearances. ODR has proven particularly useful in resolving cross-border disputes, where international parties may face significant challenges in accessing legal systems of different jurisdictions.

Legal aid and pro bono services online

Technology has also revolutionized the availability and accessibility of legal aid and pro bono services. Legal aid organizations and law firms now have online platforms to connect individuals in need of legal assistance with qualified attorneys willing to provide pro bono services.

For instance, platforms like Pro Bono Net and Legal Services Corporation's Legal Aid and Defender Association enable individuals with limited financial resources to access free legal services. These platforms match individuals with volunteer attorneys based on their specific legal needs and geographical location. Users can communicate with attorneys through secure online messaging systems, eliminating the need for in-person meetings.

Furthermore, technology has enabled the expansion of virtual legal clinics, where individuals can receive legal advice from attorneys remotely. Virtual clinics leverage video conferencing and secure messaging platforms to connect attorneys with clients who may be unable to travel to a physical legal clinic due to location or mobility limitations. This innovative approach to legal aid has significantly expanded the reach of pro bono services, providing legal assistance to underserved populations.

Challenges and considerations

While technology has great potential in enhancing access to justice, there are several challenges and considerations that must be addressed.

Firstly, the digital divide remains a significant hurdle in ensuring equal access to technology-driven legal services. Not everyone has access to reliable internet connections or the necessary devices to utilize online platforms effectively. Efforts must be made to bridge this gap and ensure that technology is accessible to all, particularly disadvantaged communities.

Secondly, privacy and security concerns must be carefully addressed when it comes to online legal services. Confidentiality and data protection are of utmost importance, especially when sensitive legal matters are involved. Online platforms must employ robust security measures and adhere to strict privacy regulations to protect the integrity of the legal process and maintain trust in the system.

Lastly, there is a need for ongoing monitoring and evaluation of technology-driven solutions for access to justice. As new technologies emerge, it is crucial to assess their effectiveness, efficiency, and impact on individuals and communities. Regular evaluations should identify areas for improvement and ensure that technology is truly enhancing access to justice rather than exacerbating existing inequalities.

Conclusion

Technology has revolutionized the legal field, offering innovative solutions to enhance access to justice. Digital platforms for legal information, online dispute resolution, and virtual legal clinics are just some of the ways technology has empowered individuals and communities to navigate the legal system more easily and affordably. However, the challenges of the digital divide, privacy and security, and ongoing evaluation must be addressed to ensure that technology truly serves as a tool for justice and equality.

Further Reading

- Susskind, Richard. *Online Courts and the Future of Justice.* Oxford University Press, 2019. - Benessia, Alice, et al. "Digital Technologies and Access to Justice: The Way Forward." *UCL Journal of Law and Jurisprudence,* vol. 8, no. 1, 2019, pp. 98-130. - Kulkarni, Shreya. "Harnessing Technology for Access to Justice." *Fordham Law Review Online,* vol. 87, no. 2, 2018, pp. 95-100. - Herrera, Monica and David Oppenheimer. "Closing the Justice Gap: Providing Civil Legal Assistance to Low-Income Americans." *Annual Review of Law and Social Science,* vol. 13, no. 1, 2017, pp. 333-362.

Addressing systemic barriers in legal systems

Addressing systemic barriers in legal systems is a crucial step towards achieving equal access to justice for all individuals. Systemic barriers refer to the structural and institutional factors that contribute to unequal treatment and hinder marginalized groups from fully participating in the legal system. In this section, we will explore some of the common systemic barriers and examine strategies to overcome them.

One major systemic barrier is the lack of legal representation for marginalized communities, particularly those who are economically disadvantaged. Many individuals do not have the financial resources to hire a lawyer, leaving them at a significant disadvantage when navigating the legal system. This imbalance of power can result in unfair outcomes and perpetuate social inequalities.

To address this issue, various initiatives have been implemented to increase access to legal representation. One example is the provision of legal aid services, which offer free or low-cost legal assistance to individuals who cannot afford a lawyer. These services help level the playing field by ensuring that everyone, regardless of their financial means, has access to legal advice and representation.

Another strategy is the promotion of pro bono services, where lawyers volunteer their time and expertise to provide legal assistance to those in need. Pro bono work not only helps bridge the gap between individuals and legal services but also encourages lawyers to contribute to the betterment of society. Bar associations and legal organizations often organize pro bono programs to match lawyers with clients who require legal representation but cannot afford it.

Additionally, technology can play a significant role in addressing systemic barriers in legal systems. Online platforms and resources can provide self-help tools, legal information, and guidance, empowering individuals to navigate the legal process independently. Websites offering legal forms, templates, and educational materials can be particularly helpful for those who cannot access or afford legal representation.

It is important to recognize that systemic barriers extend beyond the issue of legal representation. Discrimination based on gender, race, ethnicity, and other factors can also hinder equal access to justice. For example, individuals from marginalized communities may face prejudiced treatment from law enforcement, bias in judicial decision-making, or limited access to legal information in languages other than English.

To address these barriers, legal systems must adopt inclusive policies and practices. This includes promoting diversity and representation within the legal profession, ensuring that judges, lawyers, and other legal professionals reflect the population they serve. Increasing representation can help foster trust in the legal system and alleviate biases that may exist.

Furthermore, legal systems must actively work to eliminate implicit biases and prejudices that can influence decision-making. Training programs and workshops on cultural competency, unconscious bias, and anti-discrimination can help legal professionals become more aware of their own biases and take steps to mitigate their impact.

Education and awareness campaigns can also play a pivotal role in addressing systemic barriers. Society at large needs to understand the importance of equal access to justice and the impact that systemic barriers have on marginalized communities. Such campaigns can help dispel myths and misconceptions, promote empathy and understanding, and encourage individuals to advocate for a fair and inclusive legal system.

Innovative approaches, such as restorative justice and alternative dispute resolution methods, can also contribute to overcoming systemic barriers. These approaches prioritize dialogue, collaboration, and problem-solving, rather than traditional adversarial processes. By focusing on addressing the underlying causes of conflicts and finding mutually beneficial solutions, they can help reduce the negative impact of systemic barriers in legal systems.

To ensure sustained progress in addressing systemic barriers, it is essential to monitor and evaluate the effectiveness of the implemented strategies. This includes collecting data on outcomes, conducting surveys and interviews to gather feedback from individuals who have utilized legal services, and incorporating their insights into ongoing improvements.

In conclusion, addressing systemic barriers in legal systems is crucial for achieving equal access to justice for all individuals. By providing legal representation, promoting diversity and representation, addressing biases, and adopting innovative approaches, we can work towards creating a legal system that truly serves the needs of all members of society. It is an ongoing process that requires collaboration, adaptability, and a commitment to the principles of justice and equality.

Key Takeaways

- Systemic barriers in legal systems refer to structural and institutional factors that hinder marginalized groups from accessing justice.

- Lack of legal representation is a significant systemic barrier. Legal aid and pro bono services can help increase access to legal assistance for economically disadvantaged individuals.

- Technology, such as online platforms and resources, can provide self-help tools and legal information to empower individuals navigating the legal process.

- Discrimination based on gender, race, ethnicity, and other factors can also create systemic barriers. Inclusive policies, diversity, and cultural competency training within the legal profession are essential to address these barriers.

- Education and awareness campaigns can promote understanding and empathy, while innovative approaches like restorative justice can offer alternatives to traditional adversarial processes.
- Ongoing monitoring and evaluation are necessary to ensure the effectiveness of strategies aimed at addressing systemic barriers.

Resources for Further Exploration

- American Bar Association, Standing Committee on Pro Bono and Public Service: `https://www.americanbar.org/groups/probono_public_service/`
- The National Center for Access to Justice: `https://www.ncforaj.org/`
- Legal Services Corporation: `https://www.lsc.gov/`
- Restorative Justice International: `https://restorativejusticeinternational.com/`

Global Perspectives on Equal Access to Justice

In the pursuit of justice, it is crucial to consider global perspectives and the challenges faced by different societies in achieving equal access to justice. This section explores the diverse approaches and initiatives that seek to ensure justice is accessible to all, regardless of their socioeconomic background or geographical location.

The Global Justice Gap

Across the world, there exists a substantial justice gap, where marginalized communities and individuals lack the necessary resources and support to access the legal system. This gap is especially pronounced in developing countries and regions affected by conflict or political instability. Factors such as poverty, discrimination, and limited legal infrastructure contribute to this unequal access to justice.

Legal Aid and Pro Bono Services

One way of addressing the global justice gap is through the provision of legal aid and pro bono services. Legal aid programs aim to provide free or low-cost legal assistance to disadvantaged individuals who cannot afford legal representation. Pro bono services, on the other hand, involve professionals volunteering their expertise and services to those in need.

Efforts to promote legal aid and pro bono services have gained significant traction globally. Organizations like the International Legal Foundation and the Global Pro Bono Network have played a pivotal role in connecting legal professionals with NGOs and individuals requiring legal assistance. Moreover, governments and bar associations have implemented policies that encourage pro bono work and provide funding for legal aid initiatives.

Technology and Access to Justice

Technology has emerged as a powerful tool in enhancing access to justice on a global scale. The use of digital platforms and mobile applications has allowed individuals to access legal information, resources, and services remotely, reducing geographical barriers. For instance, in many African countries, legal startups have developed mobile platforms to provide legal information, advice, and dispute resolution services to underserved communities.

Online dispute resolution (ODR) systems have also gained prominence, offering an efficient and cost-effective method for individuals to resolve legal disputes without the need for physical court appearances. These systems, sometimes integrated with artificial intelligence, allow disputing parties to reach a resolution through virtual negotiation, mediation, or arbitration.

However, it is essential to address the digital divide, ensuring that technology-driven initiatives do not inadvertently exacerbate existing inequalities. Efforts must be made to provide digital literacy education and ensure internet access for all, particularly in rural or marginalized areas.

Addressing Systemic Barriers

Achieving equal access to justice requires addressing systemic barriers within legal systems. This involves challenging discriminatory laws, addressing biases in legal processes, and promoting inclusivity in legal institutions. It entails recognizing and rectifying the ways in which laws and policies disproportionately affect marginalized communities, including women, ethnic and religious minorities, indigenous peoples, and persons with disabilities.

An effective step towards addressing systemic barriers is through legal reform. Nations worldwide have undertaken legal and judicial reforms to ensure fair and impartial legal systems. This includes revising legislation, improving court processes, increasing legal representation for marginalized individuals, and ensuring the independence and integrity of the judiciary. International organizations like the United Nations and the World Bank provide support and guidance for legal reform projects globally.

Global Collaborations and Partnerships

Collaboration and partnerships between countries, organizations, and legal professionals play a crucial role in advancing equal access to justice globally. Sharing best practices, expertise, and resources can lead to innovative approaches and sustainable solutions.

International legal organizations, such as the International Bar Association and the International Legal Assistance Consortium, facilitate collaboration among legal professionals across borders. These organizations support initiatives that promote legal education, training, and the strengthening of legal institutions in developing countries.

Furthermore, regional human rights courts and tribunals, such as the Inter-American Court of Human Rights and the African Court on Human and Peoples' Rights, contribute significantly to promoting and protecting human rights globally. Their decisions and judgments have often influenced national legal systems and prompted legal reforms.

Diversity and Representation in the Legal Profession

Ensuring equal access to justice requires a diverse and inclusive legal profession that reflects the communities it serves. Diversity encompasses gender, ethnicity, race, religion, disability, and socioeconomic background. A diverse legal profession brings different perspectives, experiences, and expertise to the table and enhances the overall quality of legal representation.

Efforts to promote diversity and inclusion in the legal profession include implementing affirmative action policies, providing scholarships and mentorship programs for underrepresented groups, and fostering inclusive workplace cultures. Bar associations, law firms, and legal organizations worldwide have recognized the importance of diversity and are actively working towards creating equal opportunities for all aspiring legal professionals.

Conclusion

Equal access to justice is a fundamental human right that transcends borders. A global perspective on this issue highlights the need for collaboration, innovative approaches, and legal reform to bridge the justice gap. By promoting legal aid, leveraging technology, addressing systemic barriers, fostering global collaborations, and promoting diversity in the legal profession, we can work towards a more equitable and just world.

The Importance of Diversity and Representation in the Legal Profession

Diversity and representation are crucial aspects of any profession, but they are particularly significant in the legal field. In this section, we will explore why diversity and representation matter in the legal profession and discuss their impact on justice and equality.

Understanding Diversity and Representation

Before delving into the importance of diversity and representation, it is essential to define these terms. Diversity refers to the presence of a wide range of individuals with different backgrounds, experiences, and perspectives. This can include racial and ethnic diversity, gender diversity, socioeconomic diversity, and diversity in terms of sexual orientation, religious beliefs, and disability status, among others.

Representation, on the other hand, means having individuals from diverse communities and backgrounds adequately reflected and included in a particular profession or field. It goes beyond mere diversity by ensuring that different groups have a seat at the table and their voices are heard and valued.

The Link between Diversity, Representation, and Justice

1. **Enhancing Access to Justice:** One of the primary reasons why diversity and representation are crucial in the legal profession is their potential to enhance access to justice. When legal professionals come from a variety of backgrounds, they can better understand the diverse needs and experiences of their clients. This understanding can enable them to provide more effective legal representation and ensure that marginalized and underrepresented groups have equal access to justice.

2. **Challenging Bias and Stereotypes:** The legal system is not immune to bias and stereotypes. Having a diverse and representative legal profession can challenge these biases and stereotypes by bringing different perspectives and experiences to the table. By doing so, legal professionals can work towards a more equitable and fair justice system that takes into account the unique challenges faced by different communities.

3. **Building Trust in the Legal System:** Trust in the legal system is crucial for its effective functioning. When individuals from diverse backgrounds see themselves represented in the legal profession, it can foster trust and confidence in the fairness

of the system. This, in turn, encourages more people to seek legal assistance and engage with the legal process, leading to a more inclusive and participatory justice system.

4. **Promoting Innovation and Creativity:** Diversity and representation can also fuel innovation and creativity within the legal profession. When professionals with different perspectives and experiences collaborate, they bring fresh ideas and alternative solutions to legal challenges. This diversity of thought can lead to more innovative legal strategies and approaches that address the complex needs of a diverse society.

Challenges and Barriers

While diversity and representation are vital, it is essential to acknowledge the challenges and barriers that exist in achieving true inclusion in the legal profession.

1. **Underrepresentation of Certain Groups:** Historically, certain groups, such as racial and ethnic minorities, women, individuals with disabilities, and those from lower socioeconomic backgrounds, have been underrepresented in the legal profession. Addressing this underrepresentation requires proactive measures, including outreach programs, mentorship initiatives, and the removal of systemic barriers to entry.

2. **Implicit Bias and Discrimination:** Implicit bias and discrimination continue to pose significant challenges to achieving diversity and representation in the legal profession. Overcoming these challenges requires ongoing efforts to raise awareness, provide implicit bias training, and create inclusive and equitable workplaces where everyone feels valued and respected.

Promoting Diversity and Representation

To promote diversity and representation in the legal profession, various strategies and initiatives can be implemented:

1. **Recruitment and Retention Programs:** Law firms, legal organizations, and educational institutions should implement targeted recruitment programs to attract diverse talent. Additionally, efforts should be made to create inclusive work environments and provide opportunities for advancement to retain diverse legal professionals.

2. **Promoting Diversity within Leadership Positions:** Increasing diversity within leadership roles is essential to effect meaningful change. Encouraging diverse individuals to pursue leadership positions and providing support and

mentorship to help them navigate their careers can lead to increased representation and influence within the legal profession.

3. **Engaging in Outreach and Community Partnership:** Legal organizations should actively engage in outreach initiatives to underrepresented communities. By fostering partnerships with community organizations, legal professionals can provide mentorship, support, and educational opportunities to aspiring legal professionals from diverse backgrounds.

4. **Creating Inclusive Legal Education:** Law schools and legal education programs should incorporate diverse perspectives and promote inclusive legal education. This can include diverse faculty representation, diverse course offerings, and incorporating case studies that emphasize the intersectionality of race, gender, and social justice issues.

Resources and Further Exploration

For further exploration on the importance of diversity and representation in the legal profession, the following resources are recommended:

1. *The Diversity and Inclusion Handbook for Law Firms* by Jill L. Fieldstein and Barbara L. Safran: This handbook provides practical guidance and strategies for promoting diversity and inclusion within law firms.

2. *Building an Inclusive Legal Profession: A Toolkit for Legal Employers* by the American Bar Association: This toolkit offers comprehensive resources, tools, and best practices for law firms and legal employers to promote diversity and create inclusive workplaces.

3. *Representation Matters: The Case for Diversity in the Legal Profession* by the Law Society of England and Wales: This report explores the business case for diversity in the legal profession and provides insights into the challenges and opportunities for promoting diversity and inclusion.

4. *The Color of Justice: Race, Ethnicity, and Crime in America* by Samuel Walker, Cassia C. Spohn, and Miriam DeLone: This book examines the intersection of race, ethnicity, and justice within the U.S. criminal justice system, providing a critical understanding of the significance of diversity and representation in legal decision-making.

By prioritizing diversity and representation in the legal profession, we can advocate for a more inclusive, equitable, and just society. It is a collective responsibility to ensure that the legal system reflects and serves the diverse needs and experiences of all individuals.

Law and social change

The impact of legal activism on social change

Legal activism refers to the use of legal strategies and advocacy to promote social change and address systemic injustices. It involves applying legal principles and challenging existing laws and policies to bring about positive societal transformations. Legal activists play a crucial role in shaping social norms, challenging power structures, and promoting justice and equality.

Understanding legal activism

Legal activism is rooted in the belief that the law can be a powerful tool for achieving social change. By strategically using legal frameworks, activists aim to challenge discriminatory practices, protect marginalized communities, and advocate for the rights of disadvantaged individuals.

Legal activists employ various methods to advance their cause. They may engage in litigation, filing lawsuits to challenge unjust laws or to seek redress for social injustices. They may also engage in political advocacy, lobbying for legislative changes or supporting policies that prioritize social justice. Additionally, legal activists often leverage public awareness campaigns, media engagement, and community organizing to mobilize support and influence public opinion.

Examples of legal activism

Many transformative social movements throughout history have been driven by legal activism. Here are some notable examples:

- **Civil Rights Movement:** Legal activism played a pivotal role in the fight for civil rights in the United States. Activists like Rosa Parks and Martin Luther King Jr. used litigation and civil disobedience to challenge racial segregation and inequality. Landmark Supreme Court cases such as Brown v. Board of Education and Loving v. Virginia helped dismantle legal barriers to racial equality.

- **Women's Rights Movement:** Legal activism has been instrumental in advancing gender equality. Activists lobbied for and achieved legal reforms, such as the right to vote (19th Amendment), reproductive rights (Roe v. Wade), and protection against gender-based discrimination (Title IX). They also challenged discriminatory laws and fought for workplace equality through litigation and advocacy.

- **Marriage Equality:** Legal activism played a vital role in the struggle for marriage equality for same-sex couples. Activists fought against discriminatory marriage laws, culminating in landmark Supreme Court decisions such as United States v. Windsor and Obergefell v. Hodges, which recognized marriage as a fundamental right for all individuals.

- **Environmental Justice:** Legal activists advocating for environmental justice have successfully challenged harmful industrial practices, pushed for stricter regulations, and protected communities disproportionately affected by pollution and environmental degradation. They have employed legal tools, such as citizen suits, to hold polluters accountable and safeguard the right to a healthy environment.

Challenges and criticisms

While legal activism has made significant contributions to social change, it also faces challenges and criticisms. Some common critiques include:

- **Constitutional limitations:** Legal activism often operates within the boundaries set by existing laws and constitutional frameworks. Some argue that these limitations can restrict the ability of legal activists to effect broad-scale social change.

- **Political resistance:** Activists may face resistance from entrenched political and legal institutions that are resistant to change. This can hinder progress and lead to a slow pace of reform.

- **Lack of resources:** Legal activism requires substantial resources, including funding, expertise, and time. Limited access to these resources can pose challenges for activists, particularly those from marginalized communities.

- **Backlash and opposition:** Legal activism can generate backlash and opposition from those who benefit from existing social inequalities or who hold different ideological perspectives.

The future of legal activism

Legal activism continues to play a crucial role in advancing social justice and shaping the future of our society. As ongoing social issues emerge and new challenges arise, legal activism will remain an indispensable tool for promoting equality, inclusivity, and justice.

To ensure the continued effectiveness of legal activism, it is essential to:

- **Embrace intersectionality:** Legal activism should recognize and address the intersectional nature of social inequalities, acknowledging that individuals face multiple forms of discrimination and oppression. This approach can lead to more comprehensive and inclusive strategies for change.

- **Promote diversity and inclusion:** Legal activism should strive for diversity and inclusion within its ranks. By amplifying underrepresented voices and perspectives, activists can ensure that the strategies they employ truly serve the communities they aim to benefit.

- **Leverage technology:** As technology continues to evolve, legal activists can utilize digital platforms, data analysis, and online organizing to enhance their impact and reach a wider audience.

- **Collaborate with other movements:** Legal activism can be more powerful when it collaborates with other social justice movements. Building alliances and connecting struggles can lead to greater collective impact and meaningful societal change.

Conclusion

Legal activism has a profound impact on social change by challenging unjust laws, promoting equality, and advocating for marginalized communities. By employing strategic legal tactics, activists can transform society and contribute to building a more just and equitable future. As we continue to face new social challenges, legal activism will remain a critical force for driving positive change and ensuring equal rights and opportunities for all.

Grassroots Movements and Their Legal Strategies

Grassroots movements play a significant role in driving social and political change. These movements are often driven by passionate individuals and communities who are directly affected by a particular issue or injustice. They aim to bring about change by mobilizing people, raising awareness, and advocating for their rights. In this section, we will explore the legal strategies employed by grassroots movements to achieve their goals.

Understanding Grassroots Movements

Before delving into the legal strategies of grassroots movements, it is important to understand the essence of these movements. Grassroots movements are characterized by their bottom-up approach, with power and decision-making originating from ordinary people rather than established institutions or organizations. These movements are often fueled by a deep sense of injustice, inequality, or oppression.

Grassroots movements can emerge in response to a wide range of social, political, and environmental issues. Some examples include movements advocating for racial justice, workers' rights, gender equality, LGBTQ+ rights, environmental protection, and access to healthcare. These movements often start at the local level, relying on community organizing and grassroots activism to create change.

Legal Strategies of Grassroots Movements

Grassroots movements employ various legal strategies to challenge existing laws, policies, and practices that perpetuate inequality and injustice. These strategies aim to create legal and social transformation by leveraging the power of the law and the courts. Here are some common legal strategies utilized by grassroots movements:

1. **Litigation:** Grassroots movements often utilize litigation as a means to challenge unjust laws or seek legal remedies for affected individuals or communities. By filing lawsuits, these movements can bring attention to their cause, create legal precedence, and push for systemic change. For example, the Civil Rights Movement in the United States utilized litigation to challenge racial segregation and secure equal rights for African Americans.

2. **Advocacy and lobbying:** Grassroots movements engage in advocacy and lobbying efforts to influence policymakers and bring about legislative changes. Through direct engagement with lawmakers, public demonstrations, and the use of social media, these movements can amplify their voices and push for policy reforms. For example, the movement for gun control in the United States mobilizes grassroots activists to lobby for stricter gun control measures.

3. **Public education and awareness:** Grassroots movements place great emphasis on public education and raising awareness about the issues they are fighting for. By informing the public about the injustices and inequalities

they face, these movements can rally support, build alliances, and generate momentum for their cause. Public education can include organizing workshops, public forums, and awareness campaigns to inform and mobilize communities.

4. **Direct action and civil disobedience:** Grassroots movements sometimes resort to direct action and civil disobedience as a means of nonviolent protest. These actions can include sit-ins, blockades, boycotts, or mass demonstrations. By disrupting the normal functioning of society and drawing media attention, these movements can exert pressure on authorities and force them to address their demands. The Civil Rights Movement's Freedom Rides and the Occupy Wall Street movement are examples of grassroots movements employing direct action.

5. **Coalition building and community organizing:** Grassroots movements recognize the power of collaboration and often form coalitions with like-minded individuals and organizations. By uniting diverse groups and communities, these movements can pool resources, share expertise, and achieve greater influence. Community organizing techniques are employed to mobilize people at the local level, build grassroots power, and create lasting change.

These legal strategies, when combined and tailored to the specific context of a grassroots movement, can be powerful tools for effecting change and challenging systemic injustices. It is important to note that the success of these strategies depends on a multitude of factors, including the political climate, public support, and the resilience and determination of the movement.

Challenges and Considerations

While grassroots movements employ various legal strategies, they also face unique challenges and considerations. Some of these challenges include:

- **Limited resources:** Grassroots movements often operate with limited financial resources, making it challenging to sustain long-term legal battles. Lack of funding can restrict access to legal expertise and resources, requiring creative solutions and reliance on pro bono support.

- **Legal expertise:** Grassroots activists may lack legal expertise, which can hinder their ability to navigate complex legal systems. Seeking collaboration with legal professionals or organizations specializing in social justice can help bridge this gap.

- **Repression and backlash:** Grassroots movements challenging the status quo may face repression, backlash, and even legal persecution. Governments and powerful interests may try to intimidate, suppress, or criminalize these movements. Legal strategies must take into account potential risks and develop strategies to protect activists.

- **Intersecting struggles and inclusion:** Grassroots movements need to address the intersecting struggles faced by marginalized communities. This requires recognizing and addressing the complex social, economic, and cultural factors that contribute to systemic injustice.

- **Sustainability:** Maintaining momentum and sustaining the energy of grassroots movements over extended periods can be a substantial challenge. Effective organizational structures, communication networks, and strategic planning are crucial to long-term success.

Navigating these challenges requires resilience, adaptability, and a deep understanding of the legal and social systems in which grassroots movements operate.

Resources for Further Exploration

If you are interested in learning more about grassroots movements and their legal strategies, consider exploring the following resources:

- Books:
  - "This Changes Everything: Capitalism vs. The Climate" by Naomi Klein
  - "When We Fight, We Win!: Twenty-First Century Social Movements and the Activists That Are Transforming Our World" by Greg Jobin-Leeds and AgitArte
  - "Rules for Revolutionaries: How Big Organizing Can Change Everything" by Becky Bond and Zack Exley
  - "The Activist's Handbook: Winning Social Change in the 21st Century" by Randy Shaw

- Documentaries:
  - "13th" (Ava DuVernay, 2016) - Explores the intersection of race, justice, and mass incarceration in the United States.
  - "How to Change the World" (Jerry Rothwell, 2015) - Chronicles the birth of the environmental movement through the story of Greenpeace.
  - "The Square" (Jehane Noujaim, 2013) - Documents the Egyptian Revolution and the power of grassroots movements in demanding political change.
- Online Resources:
  - Amnesty International - Website: `https://www.amnesty.org/`
  - Grassroots Global Justice Alliance - Website: `https://ggjalliance.org/`
  - Global Nonviolent Action Database - Website: `https://nvdatabase.swarthmore.edu/`

Exploring these resources will provide you with a deeper understanding of grassroots movements, their legal strategies, and the transformative potential of collective action.

Conclusion

Grassroots movements are powerful catalysts for social change, driven by the determination and passion of individuals and communities that seek justice and equality. By employing legal strategies such as litigation, advocacy, public education, direct action, and coalition building, these movements challenge the status quo and create pathways for societal transformation. However, they also face unique challenges that require resilience, strategic planning, and collaboration.

Understanding the legal strategies of grassroots movements allows us to appreciate the role of law in social change and inspires us to actively engage in shaping a more just and equitable society. Whether by advocating for policy reform, supporting grassroots organizations, or participating in collective action, each of us has a role to play in fostering a more inclusive and compassionate world.

Legal challenges to systemic injustices

In the fight for justice and equality, one of the most critical aspects is addressing systemic injustices through legal means. Systemic injustices refer to the underlying structures, policies, and practices that result in discrimination, oppression, and inequality in our society. This section will explore the various legal challenges that arise when attempting to dismantle these systemic injustices, as well as strategies and approaches for addressing them.

Understanding Systemic Injustices

To effectively challenge systemic injustices, it is essential to have a clear understanding of their nature and manifestations. Systemic injustices can occur in various forms, such as racial discrimination, gender inequality, socioeconomic disparities, or unequal access to opportunities. These injustices are deeply embedded in our institutions, policies, laws, and social norms, making them pervasive and difficult to eradicate.

For example, consider the issue of racial discrimination. Despite legal protections against racial discrimination, many communities still face unequal treatment in areas such as education, employment, criminal justice, and housing. These disparities are not simply the result of individual prejudices; they are instead embedded in systemic structures, perpetuating ongoing inequities.

Legal Strategies for Challenging Systemic Injustices

Challenging systemic injustices requires a multi-faceted approach that combines legal strategies with advocacy efforts. Here are some key legal strategies employed to tackle systemic injustices:

1. **Impact Litigation:** Impact litigation involves bringing lawsuits that seek to effect systemic change. These cases target discriminatory laws, policies, or practices to set legal precedents that can dismantle systemic injustices. For example, the landmark case of *Brown v. Board of Education* challenged racial segregation in schools, leading to desegregation efforts across the United States.

2. **Policy and Legislative Reform:** Challenging systemic injustices often requires advocating for policy and legislative reforms. This involves working with lawmakers to enact laws that promote equality and address discriminatory practices. For instance, the passage of the Civil Rights Act of 1964 helped combat racial discrimination in various areas, including public accommodations and employment.

3. **Community Empowerment:** Engaging communities affected by systemic injustices is vital for effective legal challenges. Empowering these

communities through education, organizing, and providing resources allows for collective action in seeking justice. Grassroots movements can play a significant role in driving change and challenging systemic injustices.

4. **Public Interest Lawyering:** Public interest lawyers work with marginalized communities and advocacy organizations to provide legal representation and support. These lawyers often take on pro bono cases and engage in impact litigation, using their legal expertise to challenge systemic injustices. They also contribute to policy advocacy and community empowerment efforts.

Intersectionality and Systemic Injustices

Intersectionality, a vital concept in legal studies, acknowledges that individuals can experience multiple forms of oppression based on various intersecting identities such as race, gender, class, sexuality, and disability. Recognizing intersectionality is crucial when addressing systemic injustices because it allows for a more nuanced understanding of the complexities individuals face.

For example, a low-income woman of color may face discrimination and oppression not only based on her race and gender but also due to socioeconomic disadvantages. By considering the intersectionality of her experiences, legal strategies can be developed to challenge multiple forms of oppression simultaneously.

Current Challenges and Future Outlook

While progress has been made in challenging systemic injustices, numerous challenges persist. Changing deeply ingrained systemic structures requires long-term commitment and sustained efforts. Some of the current challenges include:

- **Resistance and Backlash:** Initiatives aimed at dismantling systemic injustices often face resistance from those benefiting from the status quo. This resistance may take the form of legal challenges, lobbying against reforms, or perpetuating harmful narratives that undermine the need for change.

- **Intersectional Complexity:** Addressing the complexities of intersectionality requires nuanced and tailored approaches. It can be challenging to develop legal strategies that effectively tackle multiple forms of oppression simultaneously.

- **Institutional Inertia:** Systemic injustices are deeply rooted in existing institutions and entrenched practices. Overcoming institutional inertia and implementing transformative changes within these systems can be a significant challenge.

Looking ahead, it is crucial to continue exploring innovative approaches and combining legal strategies with grassroots movements and interdisciplinary collaborations. By amplifying marginalized voices, challenging discriminatory laws, and working towards inclusive legal systems, we can make progress in dismantling systemic injustices and building a more just and equitable society.

Conclusion

Challenging systemic injustices through legal means is a critical aspect of the fight for justice and equality. By understanding the nature of systemic injustices, employing legal strategies, and recognizing intersectionality, we can address these injustices more effectively. Despite the challenges that persist, ongoing efforts to dismantle systemic injustices offer hope for a future where justice and equality are truly accessible to all members of society. Continued advocacy, community empowerment, and evolving legal strategies are key to achieving this vision. Let us join together in this pursuit of a more just and equitable world.

The role of courts in shaping social and political transformation

The role of courts in shaping social and political transformation is crucial in a democratic society. Courts serve as the arbiters of justice, interpreting and applying the law to resolve disputes and uphold individual rights. They play a significant role in upholding the principles of justice and equality, ensuring that all members of society are treated fairly and their rights are protected. In this section, we will explore the various ways in which courts influence social and political transformation.

Courts as agents of change

Courts have the power to bring about social and political change through their interpretations of the law. When courts interpret constitutional provisions or statutory laws, they can breathe new life into existing legal principles, adapt them to the changing needs of society, and provide guidance to lawmakers. Landmark judicial decisions have played a critical role in transforming societal norms, challenging discriminatory practices, and advancing social justice causes. For example, in the case of Brown v. Board of Education, the United States Supreme Court's ruling that racial segregation in public schools was unconstitutional paved the way for the desegregation of schools and marked a significant milestone in the civil rights movement.

Courts also shape social and political transformation by addressing systemic injustices and inequalities. They have the power to strike down laws that violate fundamental rights or perpetuate discrimination. Through class action lawsuits and public interest litigation, courts can address societal issues such as environmental degradation, healthcare disparities, and access to education. By holding governments and powerful institutions accountable, courts can pave the way for social change and influence policy-making.

Judicial activism vs. judicial restraint

In their pursuit of social and political transformation, courts often find themselves at the center of a debate between judicial activism and judicial restraint. Judicial activism refers to an interpretive approach where courts take an active role in shaping laws and policies. Activist judges are more willing to invalidate legislation and expand constitutional rights to address perceived injustices. On the other hand, judicial restraint advocates for a more limited role for the courts, emphasizing deference to the legislative branch and prioritizing strict interpretation of the law.

The tension between these two approaches reflects differing views on the proper role of the judiciary in a democratic society. Proponents of judicial activism argue that courts have a duty to protect minority rights, promote social progress, and act as a check on governmental abuses. They assert that societal transformation often requires judicial intervention, particularly in cases where legislative or executive branches fail to act.

Those who advocate for judicial restraint, however, contend that courts should exercise caution in using their power to shape social and political transformation. They argue that unelected judges should defer to the will of the elected representatives and follow the original intent of the framers of the Constitution. They believe that engaging in social engineering through the courts may overstep the constitutional boundaries, undermine the democratic process, and encroach on the prerogatives of the other branches of government.

Public perception and legitimacy

The role of courts in shaping social and political transformation is not without its challenges. Courts heavily rely on public perception and legitimacy to enforce their decisions effectively. When court decisions are seen as fair, impartial, and reflecting societal values, they have a greater impact on social and political transformation. However, if courts are perceived as biased or out of touch with public sentiment, their decisions may face resistance or be ignored, limiting their ability to effect change.

Public perception and legitimacy are influenced by a variety of factors, including the diversity and representativeness of the judiciary, transparency in decision-making, and public understanding of the judicial process. Judicial independence is another critical factor that determines how courts are perceived. Courts must be free from undue influence, ensuring fairness and impartiality in their decision-making.

To enhance public trust and legitimacy, courts should actively engage in outreach and education programs to enhance understanding of their role and the impact of their decisions on society. Judicial conferences, community forums, and public lectures can bridge the gap between courts and the public, promoting transparency and fostering a sense of trust.

The role of international and regional courts

While much of the focus has been on domestic courts, it is important to acknowledge the role of international and regional courts in shaping social and political transformation globally. International human rights courts and tribunals, such as the European Court of Human Rights and the International Criminal Court, play a critical role in holding states accountable for human rights violations and addressing global issues.

These courts contribute to the development of international human rights norms, influence domestic legal systems, and provide a platform for individuals and groups to seek justice beyond national borders. By adjudicating cases involving war crimes, genocide, and crimes against humanity, international and regional courts contribute to transitional justice efforts, reconciliation, and the promotion of global peace and security.

Conclusion

In conclusion, the role of courts in shaping social and political transformation is significant. Through their interpretations of the law, courts can bring about societal change, challenge systemic injustices, and protect individual rights. However, the exercise of judicial power comes with challenges, including the tension between judicial activism and judicial restraint, the need for public perception and legitimacy, and the role of international and regional courts. It is through thoughtful and principled decision-making, public outreach, and adherence to ethical and legal standards that courts can effectively shape social and political transformation for a more just and equitable society.

Further Reading

- Ackerman, B. (1997). Constitutional moments: Lessons from the American founding. Yale Law Journal, 108(8), 1091-1128.

- Sunstein, C. R. (2006). Radicals in robes: Why extreme right-wingers will run the Supreme Court. Basic Books.

- Hirschl, R. (2008). Towards juristocracy: The origins and consequences of the new constitutionalism. Harvard University Press.

- Slaughter, A. M. (1995). Judicial globalization. Virginia Journal of International Law, 36(3), 805-872.

- Posner, E. a. (1990). Law and social norms: The case of gender. University of Michigan Law School Scholarship Repository, 98(5), 1885-1935.

- de Figueiredo, R. J. P., & Hidalgo, F. D. (2014). The power of the purse: State and local fiscal capacities and policy outcomes. Cambridge University Press.

Building a more just and equitable society through legal reform

In a world where justice and equality are still far from being fully realized, legal reform plays a crucial role in shaping a more just and equitable society. This section explores how legal reforms can address systemic injustices and contribute to the progress of social change.

Understanding the need for legal reform

To lay the groundwork for legal reform, it is essential to recognize the areas of society where systemic inequalities persist. Legal systems can perpetuate bias and discrimination, leaving marginalized communities without adequate representation or protection. It is the responsibility of legal scholars, practitioners, and activists to identify these injustices and advocate for necessary legal reforms.

Recognizing the power of legal activism

A key driver of legal reform is legal activism, which harnesses the power of the law to challenge and change societal norms and institutions. Legal activists strategically engage in litigation, advocacy, and organizing to fight against systemic injustices. Through their work, they expose and challenge discriminatory laws, policies, and practices, paving the way for transformative legal reform.

For instance, the civil rights movement in the United States exemplifies the influence of legal activism in fostering social change. Activists, such as Rosa Parks and Martin Luther King Jr., used legal strategies to challenge racial segregation and discrimination. Landmark cases like Brown v. Board of Education overturned the "separate but equal" doctrine, leading to the desegregation of schools and transforming the legal landscape regarding racial equality.

Utilizing grassroots movements and legal strategies

Effective legal reform often relies on grassroots movements that amplify the voices of marginalized communities and drive change from the ground up. Working hand in hand with legal activists, grassroots organizations mobilize communities, raise awareness, and push for policy reform.

Legal strategies employed by grassroots movements include public interest litigation, community organizing, and legislative advocacy. These approaches bring attention to systemic issues and apply pressure on policymakers to enact meaningful legal reforms. By mobilizing communities and building coalitions, grassroots movements can effect lasting change in the legal system.

An example of the power of grassroots movements can be seen in the fight for marriage equality. LGBTQ+ activists and organizations tirelessly campaigned for equal rights and challenged discriminatory laws through strategic litigation. These efforts culminated in landmark cases such as Obergefell v. Hodges in the United States, where the Supreme Court recognized same-sex marriage as a fundamental right, reshaping the legal landscape regarding LGBTQ+ rights.

Addressing systemic injustices through legal challenges

Legal challenges are a critical tool for bringing about systemic change and dismantling entrenched injustices. By leveraging the courts and legal frameworks, social justice advocates can challenge discriminatory laws, policies, and practices that perpetuate inequality. This requires comprehensive legal strategies, thorough research, and strategic litigation.

For example, in the area of criminal justice reform, legal challenges have played a significant role in addressing racial disparities and excessive sentencing. Organizations like the American Civil Liberties Union (ACLU) have filed lawsuits to challenge discriminatory policing practices and advocate for fair sentencing guidelines. These legal challenges shed light on the need for reform and lead to changes in policies and practices that promote justice and equality.

The role of courts in shaping social and political transformation

Courts have the power to shape social and political transformation by interpreting laws, settling disputes, and upholding constitutional principles. Judicial decisions can redefine legal interpretations, declare laws unconstitutional, and set precedents that influence future cases and legislation.

However, transformative legal reform is not solely the responsibility of the judiciary. The legal profession as a whole, including lawyers, judges, and legal scholars, plays a crucial role in enlightening the courts about systemic issues. By presenting well-reasoned arguments and supporting empirical evidence, legal practitioners can effectively advocate for change and challenge existing legal paradigms.

Furthermore, it is essential to recognize the limitations of the court system in driving social transformation. While courts offer a crucial avenue for legal reform, addressing systemic injustices requires a multifaceted approach that combines legislative action, community organizing, and grassroots movements.

Conclusion

Building a more just and equitable society through legal reform requires a comprehensive understanding of the systemic issues that perpetuate inequality. By recognizing the need for legal reform, harnessing the power of legal activism, utilizing grassroots movements and legal strategies, addressing systemic injustices, and recognizing the role of courts, we can lay the foundation for transformative change.

Through collective efforts, legal scholars, practitioners, and activists can challenge discriminatory laws and policies, redefine legal interpretations, and bring about lasting social change. It is through the pursuit of justice and equality that we can create a more inclusive and equitable society for all.

Index

Printed by Libri Plureos GmbH in Hamburg,
Germany

9 781779 619662